# OUT OF TIME

# OUT OF TIME

## 1966 AND THE END OF OLD-FASHIONED BRITAIN

Peter Chapman

BLOOMSBURY
LONDON · OXFORD · NEW YORK · NEW DELHI · SYDNEY

John Wisden & Co Ltd
An imprint of Bloomsbury Publishing Plc

50 Bedford Square      1385 Broadway
London      New York
WC1B 3DP      NY 10018
UK      USA

www.bloomsbury.com

WISDEN and the wood-engraving device are trademarks of
John Wisden & Company Ltd, a subsidiary of
Bloomsbury Publishing Plc

First published 2016

www.wisden.com
www.wisdenrecords.com
Follow Wisden on Twitter @WisdenAlmanack
and on Facebook at Wisden Sports

British Library Cataloguing-in-Publication Data
A catalogue record for this book is available from the British Library.

Library of Congress Cataloguing-in-Publication data has been applied for.

ISBN: HB: 978-1-4729-1715-7
ePub: 978-1-4729-1716-4

2 4 6 8 10 9 7 5 3 1

Typeset in Minion by Deanta Global Publishing Services, Chennai, India
Printed and bound in Great Britain by CPI Group (UK) Ltd, Croydon CR0 4YY

To find out more about our authors and books visit www.bloomsbury.com.
Here you will find extracts, author interviews, details of forthcoming
events and the option to sign up for our newsletters.

*To Alexandra, my daughter, and Pepito,*
*my stepson, and to all the family.*

*And in memory of Doreen (1950–2015).*

# Contents

Prologue: Stuck in Dunkirk                                    ix

**Before**

1    Another Year                                              3

2    Out of Islington                                         21

3    'Can Yer Sign, Please, Alf?'                             37

4    Blind Beggar                                             53

5    Should Old Acquaintance . . .                            74

6    Last Run of the Mods                                     90

7    No Mugs                                                 108

8    Strike                                                  126

**During**

9    Work                                                    143

10   Crash                                                   160

11   Pundits                                                 175

12   Out of Time                                             191

13   No Dream                                                207

CONTENTS

## After

14  Empire's End                              225

15  Aftermath                                 242


Acknowledgments                              260

Index                                        261

# Prologue

# STUCK IN DUNKIRK

For much of the long afternoon we drove along the north coast of France and Belgium looking for a boat home. In Calais, where we had landed three weeks earlier, we were told we would be lucky to leave before the following day. When we reached Ostend we heard the same story except that we might do better to turn around and head back towards France.

In either direction we passed other vehicles engaged on the same mission. Some drivers had pulled over and parked haphazardly on the grass verges, possibly indicating panic. People stood at the roadside looking at a loss what to do, or studying their maps to review their chances of getting away. Several waved and gave us the thumbs-up in determined solidarity.

In the early evening a line of cranes came into view to our right a mile or so off the road, signalling hope with the approach of another port. It surprised me that this one was here at all. I had heard of it, of course, though had it more in mind as a place from ancient mythology than as somewhere that actually existed. 'This should be interesting,' said my father, pointing at the sign into town. 'I wonder if anyone will rescue us from Dunkirk.'

The date was Sunday 10 July 1966, my 18th birthday and the day before the World Cup started. We all had to be back in London the next day. My parents had their jobs to go to and my sister needed to attend the last few days of the summer term. She had been given the previous three weeks off school on the grounds that a continental holiday would be good for her education. I had to be back for my first day at work.

In Dunkirk harbour, no boats were at hand and none were on the horizon. A little distant from the quay were the masts, sticking out from the water, of some of the many craft that had come to evacuate the British army from Europe in the summer of 1940. Of that heroic fleet – the 'little ships' as we had heard them called – that had carried out the rescue a quarter of a century or so before, they were among the many that had been sunk by the Germans and which had been left as a memorial to this formative moment of our island history.

Two lines of cars had formed near the ferry terminal, with about a hundred people gathered around. Most of them were silent or talking quietly among themselves. Some appeared weary and a few were shaking their heads. The most cheerful was a group of about 20 Germans, laughing and chatting, and oblivious to any historic reverence their location might have had. Before long, some German-speaking Swiss joined them. They were all coming over to England for the World Cup. Of the 16 national teams that had qualified for the final stages of the 1966 tournament, West Germany and Switzerland had been pulled out of the hat to play each other in one of the initial qualifying groups of four. They were to meet at Hillsborough, in Sheffield, in a couple of days' time.

How we were all to make it across the Channel was uncertain. The seamen's strike in Britain had begun in late May and raged for weeks. Nearly 900 ships and 27,000 merchant seamen had stopped work in the biggest strike the country had seen since the Second World War. Many boats had made their way from distant parts of the world: Aden, Hong Kong, and other points 'east of Suez'. As they docked in their home ports, their crews had joined the dispute. Harold Wilson's Labour government had decreed a 'state of emergency'. The army and the Royal Navy would be called on to maintain supplies of food to the outlying Scottish islands. The Royal Air Force would deliver the post to Northern Ireland; the province had troubles enough brewing without having to deal with a strike around its principal ports. Quite unrelated to the seamen's protest, unrest had blown up again between the Protestant and Catholic communities, which had last been seen in the late 1950s.

Angry scenes in Liverpool, Britain's second largest port after London and one of the most militant centres of the strike, had led to some of those few seamen who reported for work being thrown in the Mersey. You saw pictures of them having to swim their way out through the river's oil and grime. The prime minister came to speak in the city only to be abused by crowds of strike supporters. He described the experience as 'not pleasant'.

My family's response to the strike was to take no notice of it and carry on. My parents had in the 1950s visited 'the Continent' about once every four years, unusual for people of our background. We would take the ferry from Dover and the international train down from Calais to Milan. We continued on by local train, in blazing heat and on wood-slatted seats, to Siena. This was to see friends my father had made during the war. As a Royal Signalman he had been part of the North Africa campaign and moved on to Sicily from where, over the years of the military advance through Italy, he had gone from the south to the far north of the country.

He had no background in language, and even in English had no formal idea what a verb or a noun was. Yet he had learned good Italian during the war. This was as well, since on our trips we rarely came across other British people. My mother, of north London Italian background two generations back, did not speak a word of the language but was the main instigator of our holidays. While she had no interest in, for example, the food – other than the occasional sizeable lump of parmesan – she was always curious about the ways of people abroad. Overall, she found them strange. I suspected one of the reasons she liked our holidays on the Continent was because they confirmed to her why we lived in England.

Since 1961, when my parents bought a car, we had gone every year. Initially their choice was a blue Ford Consul Classic, the model designed with a quirkily inward-sloping back window. Two years later my dad traded it in for a Ford Zephyr, in 'British racing green', as he pointed out. This had a no-nonsense appearance and looked a better candidate to take the weight of the roof rack and the several large suitcases loaded on to it for our foreign trips. The boot would be full of food, which my dad cooked up during roadside stops as we made our way across Europe. He used billy cans and a primus stove as if he were back in the army. In Italy in particular, where people did seem to stare a lot, car and lorry drivers slowed down to take in these weird goings-on at the roadside, to the great embarrassment of my sister and me. Our parents were oblivious.

On the outbound journey in 1966, we had used one of the foreign ferries that plied the Channel routes. While we were abroad, the seamen's dispute had, in theory, been settled, although no sudden sense of urgency prompted by the imminence of the World Cup had led to agreement between the sides. Rather, Wilson had accused the seamen's union leaders of being in the pocket of Communists manipulated by Moscow and, as an accompanying olive branch, promised an inquiry into the seamen's grievances. The strike had officially been over for a number of days, therefore, by the time we came in search of a boat back to England, but this did not help matters. Some seamen had gone off to do other things during the stoppage and crews were difficult to muster. British ships and ferries remained, as a result, scattered around the coast with too few of them in the right place for normal schedules to resume. Hence, as my father headed in the direction of the Dunkirk port offices to find out what was happening – and regardless of whether England were due to kick off against Uruguay the following evening in the World Cup's opening game – the evidence pointed to our being stuck.

From a national perspective, this was something we were rather familiar with. People of my parents' age were used to long-running conflicts that left us isolated from our continental neighbours and the world beyond. In the period following Dunkirk in 1940, and until the US joined in the war 18 months later, Britain had 'stood alone'. With this, it had developed an attitude that was thought to stand us in good stead for dealing with the world and its ways.

That world, in its wider reaches, had proved a confusing place in which many countries of the empire no longer wanted the British around. It seemed that against all good sense a string of nations, from India in 1947, had gone their own way. The first that I knew about was Ghana in 1957, which had changed its name – a perfectly good one it had seemed to me – from the 'Gold Coast'. The latest was British Guiana, which had gained independence a couple of months ago in May and renamed itself Guyana. Bechuanaland, Basutoland and Barbados were due to leave us over the remainder of the year, the upshot being that we had very few colonies left.

As for nearer by, Europe remained a territory that spoke in tongues, put garlic in its food and twiddled what it ate around a fork. According to common belief it had caused two world wars and dragged us into them. When, in 1963, Charles de Gaulle, the French president, rejected Britain's application to enter the European Common Market – on the grounds, he said, of our being pro-American – the general feeling was to wonder why the Conservative party, then in power, had applied to 'join Europe' in the first place. The Labour party had long and staunchly opposed the idea.

The circumstances were such that not only my family found itself at this moment stuck in Dunkirk, but the country did, too. We appeared to have been enduring an endless sense of crisis since Harold Wilson and Labour had come to power in 1964.

At the Dunkirk harbourside, meanwhile, matters were taking on a more positive appearance. My father returned to say he had heard that a boat was on the way. Soon, the harbourmaster appeared before the crowd and, through a loud hailer, announced that the ship would be with us shortly. He was apologetic: it was only a 'little ship', he said, not one of the usual Channel ferries. But there would be room for all.

The Germans were first to clamber on board and make themselves comfortable. With the Swiss, they began playing cards at a collection of baize tables set up on the open deck at the stern. A French merchant vessel hastily equipped for the emergency, the boat had an inside area which housed some easy chairs, with red leatherette banquettes around the walls. Members of the crew served a few sandwiches, baguettes and bottled drinks from a counter in front of a galley kitchen.

The boat had come in from Dover, bringing with it a collection of English Sunday papers. These included the *News of the World*, which my family still religiously bought each week. My grandfather had worked in the paper's print room for much of his working life. There was the *Sunday Mirror*, which we also took at home, and *The Observer*, a paper I had not looked at before. Its articles looked dense and needed a few more pictures. Of the seven items on its letters page, not one was about the World Cup. Far from it; its main letter spoke of an ancient manuscript recently found in Istanbul that may have shed some light on the origins of Christianity.

As we passed the masts sticking out of the water, I looked around and was surprised that I seemed to be the only person on board who noticed them. My mother sat with her back to a window leafing through the *Sunday Mirror* while my dad looked out towards the Channel. The Germans carried on with their cards. One English family who had driven in haste across France, successfully avoiding the food along the way, had relented when they reached port and, from a local baker, bought what they thought were flaky rolls. Aghast, they complained of how they found pieces of chocolate inside.

The work I had lined up for the following morning was a temporary job at the head office of the Tote, the state bookmaker, tucked away behind St Bride's Church at the bottom of Fleet Street. A boy in my class who took a studious interest in the horses worked there on Saturdays, the big day for racing. The job appealed to me, since at school I had studied form far more closely than the books for my A-levels. This, plus a great deal of time playing football and a total inability to do exams had contrived to have me fail them. I knew this even though the results had not yet come through, although it was a point I had kept from my parents.

They, however, were content that I was about to make my family's first real jump from blue to white collar. After my stint at the Tote, I would in six weeks' time be taking up a position as an accounts clerk at Islington borough council in the town hall on Upper Street. The thought of being swallowed up by the town hall for a working lifetime promised as much as an early death.

As such, my own prospects were stuck as well. In pursuit of a football career, I had for the last three seasons been on the books of Leyton Orient, the small professional football club in London's East End. I had played goalkeeper initially as a junior and on occasions in the more senior Colts' team of 17- and 18-year-olds. Scrambled victories over Chelsea, in the South East Counties League division two, on our home pitch of the London Transport Ground in Walthamstow, and against West Ham on their training grounds at Chadwell Heath in the

Winchester Cup had raised hopes. Nasty defeats at the hands of Tottenham Hotspur in both competitions, out at their lavish training base in Cheshunt, had done them no good at all.

There was also the small matter to confront of relations with the opposite sex. Through football and general shyness I had reached my 18th birthday without yet having a girlfriend. Let alone that – a first kiss would have been nice.

No matter, there was much to look forward to. Three weeks of football of the highest international order lay before us. Normally, in summer we were left only with cricket but – at the going down of the sun of empire – we were losing at that, too. The sports pages I read on the boat back from Dunkirk reported that we had already slumped to 2–0 down in the Test Series against Gary Sobers and the West Indies.

Not that the England football team was expected to compensate for that by winning the World Cup. As in imperial affairs, we had experienced a consistent history of failure through most of my lifetime, and manager Alf Ramsey's forecast that England would win the trophy prompted the kind of derision often reserved for Harold Wilson. Ramsey had been saying it ever since he took the job in 1963. The view among everyone I knew was that we did not have a hope. A grabbed victory or two might get us through the first qualifying group, in which, beyond Uruguay, we had games against Mexico and France. Thereafter, the balance would swing towards those countries who had established their dominance in the modern game of tactics and guile. With principally brute strength to drive us forward, we would slip further behind the rest.

The minimum we could expect was a good show. For an extended period, there would be something different to watch each night on the television, where live football rarely featured. This might take some negotiation with my mother and sister who, in common with nearly all women, had no interest in football. The ITV schedulers had helped the male cause by bringing forward the start time of *Coronation Street* by half an hour on any of its two nights a week that might clash with a 7.30 kick-off.

One imponderable was the extent to which better-off people might warm to the event. The World Cup was already a 'resounding flop', said an article on the tournament that was hidden well inside my birthday issue of *The Observer*. There were 'no flags' flying, a visitor to London complained. A World Cup information centre had been set up in Piccadilly, but to find it you had to know it was there.

The provincial cities had prepared in their own fashion. Sunderland, in the North-East, was putting on coal-mining tours. I had been up there when my aunt Joan and my dad's youngest brother, my uncle Bim, were married in 1957. She came from the pit village of Silksworth, where a large slag heap dominated surroundings. In Birmingham, folk dancing and jazz events were to take place in the city centre at the newly rebuilt Bull Ring. The city was playing host to Spain, whose fans might have been surprised to find there was no bullfighting going on. As visitors from an authoritarian society run by General Franco, however, they may have been reassured by word that the local police band was to perform at the venue.

Sheffield had scheduled sightseeing trips to its steelworks and the council announced recitals of gramophone records at the municipal library. A public house in the city said it would stage special matches of billiards, giving no indication whether it had researched how many countries in the world outside Britain played the game. Across in Liverpool, the fare was bleak by comparison. Hit hard by the seamen's strike, the city had scrapped its hefty World Cup entertainment budget of £20,000.

On a balmy late evening, only minutes seemed to have passed from when our boat picked up speed beyond Dunkirk's harbour wall until the white cliffs of Dover came into sight. Even the Germans halted their chatter to take in the view. With the World Cup upon us, things – indeed we all – were looking up.

We had felt it coming all year.

# Before

# Chapter 1

# ANOTHER YEAR

We went three doors up the street on New Year's Eve to see my grandma and granddad Mehew, my mother's parents. 'Happy New Year, Jim,' said my granddad quietly to my dad; it was to be just another year. No one kissed. My grandma, who was as warm a person as anyone could meet, had told me a couple of years earlier when my uncle Keith had got married that we were 'not a kissing family'. He had surprised her with a peck on the cheek in the morning. To see in the year, my mum and grandma had a small glass of sherry. The same bottle had been in my grandparents' front-room cabinet for years.

New Year's Day was a normal working Saturday. Banks up at the Angel or on the Islington High Pavement – Barclays, the Midland, Martins – opened in the mornings, like shops in the West End, until 1 p.m. Whether through trade union influence, by general acceptance or both, it was agreed that for most people work took place within the confines of Monday to Friday and the '40-hour week'. My father, a clerk of works, had not worked a Saturday morning on the building sites of London or the South-East since the late 1950s.

My parents were to drive in the afternoon to Sandy, about 50 miles away from where we lived in Islington, north London, along the A1 in Bedfordshire. They did this most weekends and would not be back until one or two on Sunday morning. Sandy was where my father had been born and brought up. My mother also had distant relatives there. During the Blitz in 1940 my granddad had spent weeks driving out of London looking for a place that he could get the family out to, until finally he was reminded of some second cousins. My grandma moved out there with my mum, who was 18, my aunt Olive, a year younger, and my uncle Keith, who had only been born a little before the war started in 1939. My granddad would visit when he could at the weekends. My mother eventually met my dad and they married in 1942, just as he was to leave for Africa.

My father had had seven brothers and two sisters. Those who were most around in the town were my uncles Reg, Cecil (the 'e' pronounced as if it were an 'i') and Bim. Their wives were, respectively, my aunts Hilda, Joyce and Joan. My uncles were warm and friendly to me, as were my aunts. Rural people also said hello to each other on the streets, even if they did not know them too well. My dad had carried on this habit in London, again embarrassing my sister and me in the process. Of my aunts, Hilda was the quietest, Joan the most smiley and chatty (she was the one from near Sunderland) and Joyce the most loud. She was good fun and looked straight at you: 'Wotcha, mate!' We also said that in London but she had a broad Beds accent.

She was a Fage, a prolific Sandy family often whispered to be 'barely more than gypsies'. Chapman was also a common gypsy name. It meant peddler: of pegs, door-to-door remedies of one ailment or another and good omens. My grandma Chapman was originally a Smith, and there was hardly a more Romany name than that. According to the family, she was brought up by her own grandmother, Granny Smith, who had one eye, originated from Ireland and lived in a painted horse-drawn caravan.

Grandma Chapman was a faith healer – a white witch – one of two in the town. She knew about grasses and herbs and, when I stayed with her during summer holidays, would send me to pick a weed called groundsel, which she pronounced 'gruntzel' and fed to the canary. She did things like charm away warts, although told me that this did not work within the family. I'd had a cluster on my knee when I was about nine, which I made bleed playing football. I was taken to the other healer, an elderly man who lived near my uncle Reg, a few minutes from Sandy station. We looked at the warts for a while and began to count them but gave up because there were too many. He said if I forgot about them, they would go away. I confirmed to my dad that I had forgotten about them as we walked home up Pentonville Hill from King's Cross that night. They went in a month.

My dad loved to chat with his brothers, which was the only time Reg and Cecil talked of the war. Reg had been in Burma, Cecil a paratrooper at Arnhem. Their experiences, some of which my dad would report back to me, had been horrific. Uncle Reg had fought behind the Japanese lines and, on occasions, in hand-to-hand combat. He was under siege at the battle of Kohima, spending weeks separated from the enemy by the width of the high commissioner's tennis court, the Japanese troops screaming at the British troops through the nights. Uncle Cecil was involved in the second drop at Arnhem, which I heard my parents refer to as 'not as bad as the first'. Crouched under fire in a doorway, he heard a gurgling sound next to him and turned to see his mate had had his throat cut by flying shrapnel.

Uncle Bim had been too young for the Second World War but spent the Korean War in the early 1950s as a National Serviceman in Hong Kong. He was in the medical corps. Hong Kong itself was quiet but lived in fear of the Chinese coming over the hills. Mao Tse-tung's Communist government supported the North Koreans. Depression was a serious problem among the British troops, said my uncle, and some committed suicide. He brought me back a plastic rifle, which was a thrill but soon broke. We did not see very much plastic and I may have just bashed it about too much. Many people said at the time anything from Hong Kong (later Japan for a while, then Singapore) was of inferior make.

You would not have guessed my uncles' wartime experiences from looking at them. They went about doing what they did without any obvious need for counselling, not that there was any available, or thought necessary. My uncles had all been 'put to a trade' and served their respective apprenticeships as painters and decorators, plumbers and signwriters. The oldest, uncle Sam, was by trade a bricklayer, like my dad. That was what my dad wanted to be and, having left school when he was still 13, went on to complete a seven-year apprenticeship.

My mum got along reasonably well with the country side of the family, though had more London-oriented ambitions. I came home once at dinner time from my primary school – Hanover, at the bottom of Noel Road (we lived near its top end) – and said I had told my teacher I wanted to be a bricklayer. We had been asked that morning what job we wanted when we grew up and I – five at the time – knew of nothing else. This did not go down especially well with my mother, my dad being out at work, and by an hour or so later when I went back for the school's afternoon session I was aware that a bricklayer was not what I was intended to be.

I still used to practise with my dad, in the backyard as he reinforced its walls to keep out seepage from the great pool of muddy water and slime on the bomb site at the back of us. An area the size of six houses in neighbouring Gerrard Road had been destroyed in the war. Regardless of my mother's view, bricklaying enjoyed some high status. Winston Churchill did it to relax in his spare time. My dad laughed at what he called the 'serpentine' nature of his walls. Whatever the old boy's talents as a war leader, he couldn't use a plumb line.

My mother had not fully enjoyed her time during the war in Sandy, where displaced Londoners were thought to be making a fuss. This was regardless of the red glow over London being visible from the town. They were called 'evacuees'; my mum would imitate the accent: 'e-var-coo-eze'. The suggestion infuriated my grandma Mehew, who I never otherwise saw angry. 'We got ourselves out,' she told me later, her point being that in the evacuation of London, they were not part of some state-organised plan. My mother and aunt, 18 and 17 respectively, also arrived owning high heels. A lot of local women, said my mum, walked around in wellington boots.

There had been three Sandy war incidents that I'd heard of. My grandma, with Keith in his pram, had been caught on the

High Street when it was strafed by a German fighter, and had to bundle into a nearby shop. It may have been the same plane that fired off a few rounds at the Little Barford cooling towers nearby, which my dad was helping to build. Before his call-up into the army, he had been employed on what were classified as essential war works. He and those with him on the high scaffold were exposed, and just had to hope the bullets missed them. Before dawn one morning my aunt Laura, my dad's eldest sister, was cycling to work near Bedford when a Messerschmitt attacked the road. She threw herself in a ditch and a male cyclist threw himself on top of her. Once the fighter had gone, they brushed off with few words between them and peddled on their different ways. She was three minutes late for work, she told me, '... and stopped a quarter of an hour's pay'.

The fighting had ended in Europe with my dad still abroad in Italy and my mum making straight back to London. He returned home after another couple of years. He had been in Trieste, on the border with Yugoslavia, where the British army's role was to stop Tito's partisans seizing the city from the Italians. Churchill had made his speech from Fulton, Missouri about an 'Iron Curtain' descending across Europe from Stettin in the north to 'Trieste in the south'. Once back in England, my dad might have insisted, as many men did, that war brides followed their husbands. But he was easy going on the subject, as on many things – and, besides, there was plenty of work for a bricklayer in the ruins of the capital. My mother, anyway, was determined to continue life in London and in Noel Road, where she had been born.

My parents' main mission on New Year's Day 1966 was to visit my grandma Chapman. She lived alone in the three-bedroom council house on St Neots Road in Sandy where my dad had been brought up. She and granddad Chapman had married on Christmas Day 1907. Named Zachariah, he was a farm labourer and expert gardener. He grew much of the family food in the long plot at the back of the house, which stretched towards the King's Cross-to-Edinburgh line. At nights in bed you heard the *Mallard* come past. Equally, it might have been the *Royal Scot* or *Dwight D. Eisenhower*.

My granddad Chapman had died in 1953, with a wound in his side which he had incurred either at Ypres or the Somme and that still needed treating each day. At the turn of the century, he had also been captured in the Orange Free State in South Africa during the Boer War and force-marched across the high veldt before being put over the border into Swaziland. He was lucky: British commandos were shooting their Boer prisoners at the time. For generations, my family, like many others, had been on a war footing. Fortunately, the end of National Service in 1960 had gone some way towards stopping that miserable state of affairs.

My grandma Chapman's condition was very serious but we did not know what it was. No healing powers that she had had for others could help her. Her mind had gone, which was described as being 'senile'. On one of my parents' visits, she had pots of water boiling on the stove. She was preparing dinner 'for the boys'. My dad told her that he was one of the boys: 'Are you?' she said, looking at him. Although during several summers into my early teens I had stayed for weeks of my school holidays with her, visiting her now scared me and I could not wait to leave the house.

From Sandy my parents would move on to Bedford to see my aunt Laura and uncle Geoff, her husband. He had played cricket into his fifties and, as a swing bowler and mid-order bat, would have played for the county had it not been for the war. He was a toolmaker at the Igranic works near Bedford and, when he played for his firm at village grounds from Northolt to Southill, people would come up to us to chat and shake his hand. He was a member of the working men's club in Goldington Road near Bedford rugby ground where he, my aunt and parents would go for a few drinks. I had never seen my dad drunk but, soon, he would have to be careful on the drive home. The AA and RAC denounced the breathalyser test the Labour government was to bring in as an assault on civil liberties.

My aunt Laura had been in service for much of her early working life and for a year before the war was chief cook to David Lloyd George, Britain's prime minister during the First World War. He was charming, she said, and still maintained his reputation for having affairs with high-born ladies. At the outbreak of the Second World War, he told the staff at his London townhouse that he would have to let them go. He was removing himself to the countryside to escape the anticipated bombs.

Uncle Geoff came from near Cardington aerodrome, just outside Bedford, and in his youth had lost the toss with another local kid to be the cabin boy on the *R101*, the airship which in 1930 was about to make its inaugural flight. It crashed into a French hillside killing all but six of the 54 people on board. Uncle Geoff was very good company and laughed at my London accent: 'Faw'ee farsand fevvers on a frush's froat,' he would say (for 'forty thousand feathers on a thrush's throat'). I had not heard the phrase before but he thought it to be typically Cockney. He kidded me, too, about supporting Arsenal and took me to see his team, Luton Town, then of the first division, for the first big game I had been to. This was against Blackpool in 1958. I made a point of supporting the opposition.

I had stopped coming regularly with my parents on these Saturday trips. For much of the year, football took up the day. In the mornings, I played for my school, Highbury, a north London grammar close to Arsenal's stadium. Our 'home' ground of Wadham Lodge was near the Crooked Billet in distant and eastern Walthamstow because Islington had little in the way of grass to play on. Highbury Fields was around the corner from our school but had no facilities for football and was a bit of a tip. Away from home, we played schools at grounds located anywhere from Southfields in the far west of London to Buckhurst Hill in the east.

In the afternoon, there was generally a big game to watch at Arsenal or one of the other stadiums. I might even go to Spurs, as I did on the occasion when I was given a free ticket. This enabled me at least to see the 'Double Team' – Dave Mackay, John White, Cliff Jones among them – on their own turf. They were good, and even as an Arsenal fan you could not get away from that. Their feat of the 1960–61 Double of the league and FA Cup in the same season was a first in the 20th century and spoken about as if it could never be repeated. Arsenal did it a decade later.

Before I was taken on to Leyton Orient's books, I had been to Brisbane Road, Orient's home ground, a couple of times. The East End seemed light years away from north London. A single-decker bus went from the side door of our school to Leyton, while spending an age winding through places like Ridley Road market, where Oswald Mosley, the fascist leader had done his campaigning in the 1930s. A kid at school who collected autographs had persuaded me to see Orient in their promotion season of 1961–62. A couple of years later they also had a pre-season friendly against Morton from Scotland, who had the old Scots and Celtic captain Bobby Evans playing for them in his late career. I had pictures of him I wanted signing.

I had scrapbooks and football annuals full of pictures, either signed or to get signed, and as a hobby it got you around. No one of my acquaintance, for example, had been to see Queens Park Rangers play in west London. In 1962 they shifted from their old ground of Loftus Road to see if they were better suited to the nearby White City, the country's main athletics arena. I went to one of their games there but QPR soon abandoned the idea. They were in the third division and their fans barely filled a quarter of the echoing stadium. The playing surface was also none too even. For 1966, White City had been chosen to be one of London's World Cup venues, and England would make sure not to play there.

South London was yet stranger territory and weird things went on there. My mother and grandparents referred to it as 'over the water'. When I was little a bus was caught on Tower Bridge as it started to go up and accelerated to jump the gap. My grandparents' newspaper – it may have been the *News Chronicle* – had an artist's sketch of the incident and we thought the driver very brave. He broke his leg and several of the passengers were injured. The mum of one of the girls I went to Hanover primary school with was on board.

My Hanover headmaster, Mr Wakeman, was said to live somewhere very south on the Northern Line. One day he took our class in the rare absence of our normal teacher,

Miss Cottle, who seemed very elderly but had many years to go yet. He set us the test of finding out by the following morning which composer had lived in an area of south London called Denmark Hill. The significant sum of half a crown would go to the winner. I arrived at Essex Road library after tea expecting to find a load of other kids, but none were there and I claimed the prize next day.

Mendelssohn was the answer, but Millwall were what first took me to south London on my own. They were playing Notts County, the oldest football club in the world, and possibly for that reason so many pictures of their players – Bert Loxley, Jeff Astle, Tony Hateley – appeared in *Soccer Star* and other magazines that I bought for the photos. The buildings changed as you crossed the Thames and I had the sense of needing my passport. Cold Blow Lane was friendly before the game, as players came out in their normal clothes to walk the pitch, and fans were allowed to wander with them. But afterwards, when Millwall lost to a late goal, grown men beat their fists on the corrugated iron players' entrance demanding words with their goalkeeper, Reg Davies. Not too long after, when I was at Leyton Orient, Davies came, doubtless relieved to join us over there.

I first had the idea of joining Orient in 1960, during my first year at Highbury school. Pat Welton, who had played in goal for Orient more than 200 times, had gone into coaching and took us for our Friday afternoon sessions at Wadham Lodge. 'That's a good save, son,' he said to me one day when I had dived to push a shot around my left-hand post. As I lay on the ground for a few moments, I knew it was, but affirmation from grown-ups was not the most common thing, and this had come from an ex-professional.

The game I went to see in Orient's promotion year was against a very average Bristol Rovers side and, in front of an expectant capacity crowd, Orient lost, and I was aware that they could use some goalkeeping help. Their pre-season friendly against Morton, straight after Orient had come back down again from the first division a year later, was in the second week of August 1963. On the bus trip to the ground the newspaper placards said the Great Train Robbers' haul had risen to over £2 million, a sum that surely otherwise could only be found in the Bank of England. Rather than have me hanging around outside the players' entrance waiting for autographs after the match, the man at the door let me come in and wander around, virtually as far as the dressing rooms. It seemed a friendly place, so I wrote away for a trial. A letter offering me one arrived by return – about as quickly as Ronnie Biggs and most of the other train robbers were being hauled into Aylesbury assizes for theirs.

My first game, on the weekend before JFK died, was against West Ham. We were comfortably beaten but my performance was assessed to have spared us humiliation against our East End rivals. When I arrived in the Brisbane Road dressing room for training the following week, Eddie Heath, the man in charge of the youth squad, interrupted the talking to he was giving the team. 'It went well, then,' he nodded to me. The captain and several of the others said, 'Well done,' and I had stayed ever since.

My agenda for New Year's Day 1966 included revision for my O-level re-sits, maths and French, which I was due to take in a week or so. I had failed both subjects when I had done my GCEs in 1964. I would pass them this time, but at secondary school I had never been any good with exams. What we learned in class and took notes on bore little relation, as far as I could tell, to the questions on any exam paper. To some extent I felt this was teachers trying to catch you out with tricky turns of phrase; certainly that had happened in last year's A-level history. It had the more or less obligatory question on Count Klemens von Metternich, the Austrian chancellor who took it upon himself after the Napoleonic wars to restructure Europe back to what it had been before. 'Metternich's policies after Napoleon were antediluvian,' read the question. 'Discuss.' Kids had mugged up for weeks on the subject but few could answer the question without taking a wild guess at what it was on about. From Archway in the north to the Old Street roundabout in the south, antediluvian just wasn't an Islington word.

Only one teacher taught exam method. A junior Religious Instruction teacher, 'Porky' Harris – he was on the chubby side and nicknamed for a popular brand of sausages – shipped in old exam papers for us to study and see how questions were formulated; often they might look different from one year to the next but amounted to the same thing. He timed us as we practised answering them so we could finish an exam on time and put us down early for the RI O-level. We did fine, but the older teachers didn't learn by example. To them, it seemed, such methods were not in the educational spirit of things and were a bit like cheating. Years later, I discovered that kids in posher schools up the hill in Highgate and Hampstead were being taught this kind of thing as a matter of course. As a result, they were taking up most of the places in all the newer universities that had been springing up of late, even though they were intended more for the likes of us than them.

Exam method probably wouldn't have done me much good anyway. In the sixth form there were too many open spaces in the day when we were meant to 'read around' our subject. This meant too many opportunities for me to skive off down to the bookies in St Paul's Road. Meanwhile, I was struggling with my A-levels. I had chosen history because our former headmaster, Reginald 'Reggie' King, taught me the subject in my first year and was a good teacher. For geography I imagined my travels with my parents would assist me. German seemed an interestingly risqué option given that it was the language of the enemy.

Things, however, had gone wrong. Reggie had resigned after civilisation as we understood it ended with Labour's plans to turn the school comprehensive. We were to be the government's chief inner city experiment with its controversial education policy. My mother disapproved. 'What about discipline?' she said. In confirmation, we learned that Highbury was to be merged with Barnsbury Secondary Modern, a school in a rough part of our poshifying borough (no one had heard of 'gentrification'). Reggie gave a tearful farewell to the upper sixth, who felt he should have kept a British grip on his emotions. I missed his teaching. In the sixth form, he had convened liberal studies classes during which we discussed subjects like the Sino-Soviet split. What were we to do now that the Chinese and the Russians had ended their former alliance and the Chinese had developed their own atomic bomb? I had offered the opinion that the US and USSR had to get together quickly to bomb China first. The grave fashion in which Reggie received my view, I took to be agreement. In another class with us one day, he insisted that our goal after school was to find an interesting job. That thought had never occurred to me. A job was a job.

In his wake, old teachers retired. E. G. Taylor – 'Eggy' – our senior RI master was an aged vicar from Devon, who drove up on Sunday night and back again on Fridays, living in the school's basement boiler room in between. His long-johns and other washing strung out on a line between the pipes, he held after hours' philosophy discussions on such questions as whether we dreamed in black and white or colour. Len Davies, a Welshman and our geography teacher, had lived much of his career in the empire. The 'natives' in Egypt, he told us, spent their time 'dossing around under trees'. He always wore his black gown and, in tones that Richard Burton might have impersonated, when he entered the room ordered us to 'Stand!'. Such traditions now passed with him.

Younger teachers left for posts in the remaining grammar schools, and replacements to guide us to A-level had to be hastily rustled together. A young New Zealand woman came to take us for geography, speaking knowledgably of the Peruvian cordillera and giving the impression that in London N5 she was passing through. After an on-and-off period of German lessons, a middle-aged, softly spoken man arrived to take our class. He said what a relief it was not to be working on building sites any more (I didn't think to tell him what my dad, who had never complained, did for a living). Our affable history teacher conveyed the argument that England was no better off for winning the battle of Waterloo, given that such a bunch of reactionaries as the Duke of Wellington had taken over running the country. He had landed the job straight out of training college.

A full New Year programme of winter sport was competing with my studies. I checked through the cards of the horse-racing meetings of the day – the jumps and hurdles – at Aintree, Newbury and Catterick. Most of the top riders were there: Terry Biddlecombe, Stan Mellor, but no Josh Gifford. The champion jockey had recently appeared in court for killing a man by dangerous driving and was fined £5. The array of race cards meant plenty of material for visits to the bookies, two of which were in the vicinity. The nearest was in Danbury Street, next to the Polish newsagents, but the most likely was Droy's, a hundred yards further away down among the scrap-metal dealers and ex-boxers of St Peter's Street. Here there was less chance of running into anyone who knew my parents.

It was as well to be discreet since the family had 'previous' in this department. My granddad Mehew's father was a compulsive gambler. Around the end of the First World War he had inherited a handsome £100, taken it to Aintree for the Grand National and lost it. He took his time returning from Liverpool – and in some versions of the story had walked, to delay facing the family wrath. 'Think of what I could have won,' he had said. My granddad had lost his brother Ernie at about the same time, killed by a Charringtons coal lorry outside the Mansion House while 'running to put on a bet', my grandma told me quietly. He left a one-year-old daughter. My granddad dismissed gambling as a 'mug's game'.

On New Year's Day football matches were due to kick off at the normal three o'clock. Orient, away to Wolves, were at the bottom of the second division. Their brief rise to the first in 1961–62 had been along with Liverpool, only for the history of the two clubs to proceed in sharply different directions. Many

Orient fans were now choosing to do other things with their Saturday afternoons, such as shopping with their wives, or going off to watch West Ham, where Bobby Moore had led the club to victory in the FA Cup in 1964 and in the European Cup Winners' Cup a year later.

This was a stark contrast from what might have been. In the middle of my time at Brisbane Road, Dave Sexton, chief coach at Chelsea had come to manage the club. Sexton – like me from Islington originally – had been the inspiration behind a very good Chelsea team containing the likes of George Graham, Peter Bonetti and Bobby Tambling. His arrival had been an exciting moment. Under the dim floodlights of the cinder pitch across the road from the stadium, we were called together during training by Tommy Coleman, the Colts' team coach, to hear the news: someone of real weight in the game was taking over.

Quiet and philosophical, Sexton and his methods had sent Orient rising up the table. For the youth squad there was a new verve to Tuesday and Thursday night training. Well rehearsed free-kicks became a feature. The most subtle previously had been someone running up to the ball, jumping over it and leaving it for another player coming from behind. The number of laps we did increased dramatically, to be followed by 12 hard sprints called 'doggies' – at Chelsea the players had done them by the side of the Stamford Bridge dog track. You dashed to a point 40 yards away and back at full pelt, turned and did it again. Following a five-second pause, you repeated the exercise; and again, after another five seconds' scant relief.

Kids threw up their tea. Some did so over the bridge and on to the railway line leading to the marshalling yards at Lea

Bridge Road on the evenings when we trained on Hackney Marshes over by Eton Manor sports club. I had my mum cut back on the pasta she fed me, which was a welcome departure, anyway. Not a meat eater, she poured a can of mince over a plate of 20-minute cooked spaghetti, saying the only difference between that and the dish I had eaten in Italy was the garlic. She would not have that in the house.

Orient had been tipped for promotion again but the moment did not last. Lew Grade and Bernard Delfont were on the board of directors and the men behind *Sunday Night at the London Palladium*. They booked stars from Shirley Bassey to the Beatles. Orient, starved of funds, however, enjoyed no such top billing.

Sexton had resigned just before Christmas.

# Chapter 2

# OUT OF ISLINGTON

Under normal circumstances, I would have been born in Islington. Instead, I was born in a stately home. This was Brocket Hall, near Welwyn Garden City in Hertfordshire. In the approach to the Second World War, the views of the Lord Brocket of the day had been too close to those of Oswald Mosley, the British fascist leader. Brocket was required therefore to make post-war penance by offering his house to be used as a maternity hospital by boroughs such as Islington whose hospitals had been badly bombed. Several thousand babies were born there in the few years that it was used. I was born on the fifth day of the National Health Service in 1948 and for a good while thereafter fed on NHS products such as thick cod liver oil and, equally as thick, a grainy form of orange juice. My instinct has been not to reach for a glass of orange juice since. Between the ages of 13 and 14, however, I sprang up to six feet and a half inch, the tallest person in the family and a good height for goalkeepers. England's first-choice keeper, Gordon Banks, who was born before the days of free cod liver oil, was five feet 11 and a bit.

Back in December 1965, prospects for the England team had surprisingly picked up. A fortnight before Christmas they had beaten Spain 2–0 on a freezing cold night in Madrid. This was a shock: few British people knew there was such a thing as a freezing night in Madrid. The Spanish climate was thought to be unremittingly hot and unsuited to England's style of play. As it was, Alf Ramsey's strange ideas had paid dividends. RAMSEY'S WINGLESS WONDERS headlined *The Mirror*'s football correspondent Ken Jones. Ramsey had picked a team without conventional wingers. Defenders had licence to attack, not least George Cohen at right-back, who would suddenly thrust upfield. Jones foresaw a 'new era' of excitement in football, where defenders would attack like forwards and forwards 'destroy with the skill and resolution of defenders'.

To me the result was a pleasant surprise, but the method not entirely new. Dave Sexton had done something similar at Orient. He had promoted David Webb from evening training with the youth squad straight into the first team, where he often successfully surged from defence and down the right flank. Webby would later join forces again with Sexton, who went on to manage Chelsea. Dashing from the back, Webby scored the winning goal in the 1970 Cup final against Leeds.

Ramsey himself as a player had been a right-back. Born in Dagenham, in the outer reaches of the East End, he had had a quietly distinguished career, most prominently for Tottenham and England. His last international as a player was in 1953, when England were humbled 6–3 by Hungary at Wembley, England's first defeat at home to a foreign side.

Our home record had been under threat for some while before that. The Republic of Ireland had beaten us at Goodison Park in Liverpool in 1948, but that was discounted as the Irish were not deemed to be properly foreign. Only a month before the Hungary match, England had been losing 4–3 to a Rest of the World side at Wembley when, with barely a minute to go, the referee awarded England a dubious penalty. Ramsey, a man for such moments, calmly strode up to net the equaliser.

The Hungarians put on such a display that the capacity crowd stayed on the terraces for several minutes after the match to applaud. In the chill of a smoggy November afternoon, my uncle Bim was there and said it was a thrill to be part of the occasion. My dad, on the other hand, was on a restoration job at the South Kensington museums and did not know the outcome until he heard it being shouted by the newspaper man at the tube. He told me later that he had to walk up and down reading the report of the match and composing himself before his journey home. It was not that he was a football obsessive. With the war so alive in the collective memory, few people would have allowed themselves – or been allowed – to be laid low by a football score. He just knew something big had happened. It was a sense of the citadel having been stormed.

With no adjustment to their approach, England went to Budapest for a return match the following year and lost 7–1. What went for football went for wider aspects of national life. The western European nations in the 1950s were banding together into a community to rebuild themselves after the war. The UK kept out. We had the empire, after all. Or did we? Three years after the Hungary game, Britain launched its disastrous invasion of the Suez Canal. Sir Anthony Eden's

Conservative government of the day was not comprised of types who would have known about football and the Hungary game and, hence, were deprived of this valuable insight into how much the world had changed.

Ramsey was a rare case of one who adapted. The Hungarians had employed 'tactics', a characteristically continental thing to do. English teams went out on the field and 'played the game'; foreigners came with a devious plan. The Hungary players buzzed around in unconventional positions: wingers who wandered, centre-forwards who sprang out of defence. Ramsey resolved to borrow from the dark heart of Europe and to play the tactical game. He went into management and cleverly pulled a fast one. Lowly Ipswich Town rose quickly under his guidance from the third division to the first division and in 1961–62, they won the league title in their first season there.

What Ramsey banked on was that with so little sport on TV few people could fathom what he was up to. On Saturday afternoons, David Coleman introduced *Grandstand*, which was dominated by the main race meeting of the day and the commentaries of Peter O'Sullevan. The programme's climax came at twenty to five, with Coleman and his mic perched over a telex machine as it chattered out the football results. From all divisions, these were as likely to feature Crook Town as Manchester United, though for the really big ones the cameras would home in so that we could appreciate the full excitement of the telex's moving parts. In midweek, Peter Dimmock presented *Sportsview*, but only had a half-hour or so in which to feature far more than football. Ipswich's title triumph came three years prior to *Match of the Day*, and even then the BBC showed highlights of only one game a week. No panel of analysts assessed what each team was doing as a season progressed, and slow motion replays did not exist until the 1970s.

By Ipswich's second season in the top division, their modest squad of players was under pressure. Others now had their measure. I went to see them play at Highbury stadium with Ernie, my mate from the Michael family three doors down Noel Road, who I'd been to primary school with. Crippled from birth, Ernie was not a footballer, but no one intimidated him in the playground lest he kick them with his plaster cast. When he was out of it, he was the borough's breaststroke champion. He and everyone else saw what poor title holders Ipswich suddenly looked, and we laughed along with the crowd as – a rarity in the sixties – Arsenal won comfortably. But for Ramsey it didn't matter. While we had cottoned on to him, he moved on to the England job.

The appointment was a sign of how desperate we had become. His first game, a 5–2 defeat by the French in Paris, was just one more humbling reverse among the many suffered by England in recent years: 5–0 away to Yugoslavia in 1958; 4–1 to Peru in 1959. That had been the first time the two countries had played each other, and I had to look up where Lima was. Ramsey was undeterred as, after the loss to France, he made his forecast that England would win the World Cup in 1966. He was apparently not joking, but as the year itself approached the laugh was on no one but us. An average Austrian team had turned up at Wembley in October 1965 and won 3–2.

In this light, therefore, the result in Madrid was quite something. Spain chose the bulk of their side from Real Madrid and Barcelona. Real had won the European Cup five times and Barcelona once.

No British team had reached a semi-final. Ramsey had a series of other matches scheduled for England's build-up to the summer. Next in line, on 5 January, was Poland from the Communist east of Europe. No doubt a dour Iron Curtain team, they had not qualified for the World Cup and looked useful fodder for another morale-boosting win – the ideal beginning for England to the tournament year.

Away from the sport pages, Britain's politics were in a state of inertia. With a majority of only four in the House of Commons from the election in 1964, Harold Wilson had to have sick and disabled MPs carried in on stretchers for parliamentary votes. Important economic steps could not be taken and it was uncertain whether the government would have the backing to usher through planned social reforms, such as relaxing the laws against abortion and homosexuality.

Although my parents took *The Mirror* – a Labour paper – we were not a Labour family. My grandparents had often referred in semi-whispers when I was little to a 'Mr Attlee'. I didn't know it, but he had usurped the cloak of leadership that was Churchill's after the war. This was so well obscured by the family that I only discovered years later, when I read up on the period, that Clement Attlee and the Labour party had overwhelmingly won the 1945 election.

My dad did *The Mirror* crossword, which he completed with the help of a large dictionary by people called Funk and Wagnall. This he kept on a shelf with a kukri, a curved Gurkha knife in its original leather sheath with tassels. It may have come from Uncle Reg and his time in Burma but my dad also talked as if he had served with the Gurkhas in Europe. At night they went crawling between the lines. Only a narrow distance existed between those of the British and the Germans. A British sentry on patrol, therefore, was at pains to keep his gaiters on. The Germans neglected to wear theirs and the Gurkhas went by feel. A swift check round a sentry's ankles, no gaiters and the kukri came into play. I had no idea whether this was an old soldier's tale or not. (After my dad died in 2004, my mum handed the kukri into Upper Street police station during an amnesty on dangerous knives.)

On a good day, when he was especially pleased at having completed the crossword, my dad would talk it through with us in the evening at the kitchen table. His inspiration was my granddad Chapman, who had once won a large sum of money on a newspaper crossword. This went on doctors' bills for my grandma following an illness she had had after the birth of one of the children. Both my father and Aunt Laura said the prize was a near incredible £1,000.

My father also liked the *Garth* cartoon, which featured a character cast like a bodybuilder. It seemed to borrow from the Charles Atlas advertisements for 'you too can have a body like mine'. These pictured muscular types kicking sand into the faces of seven-stone weaklings. My dad had nearly died from infantile paralysis in his early years and, before he took up his bricklaying apprenticeship, spent months building his frame by humping sacks for Jordan's, the Sandy flour and cereal merchants (much later they ventured into muesli). He was a good boxer in the army – a boxer not a fighter, as he said – and critical of the likes of Freddie Mills, Britain's light heavyweight champion, who took as many punches as he slung. On beaches in Italy, my dad would point at my legs: 'Good legs, boy.' Whether at Jordan's or after, he felt he had not worked on his legs enough and was embarrassed about them. They were a bit spindly, but little different from those of Stanley Matthews and other old footballers I had signed pictures of in my scrapbooks.

*The Mirror*'s Peter Wilson wrote his opinion columns on sport billed as the 'man they can't gag'. I never knew what he had said that might have offended people, though he did err towards the tearfully sentimental: 'I love them,' he had written after a particularly exciting finish to one international marathon: 'I love them all!' Ken Jones covered the main stories on football that I was interested in, and Newsboy and Bouverie gave the racing tips, the former more successfully than the latter and both of them, in my opinion, bordering on useless.

With its huge readership, *The Mirror* promoted itself as the world's largest selling newspaper. Governments, not least Labour, had to listen to what it said. My parents may have taken it because it came in a handy size, later styled 'tabloid'. The other papers opened to the width of your body and stretched arm. A lot of its coverage now concerned the Queen's New Year honours list. The paper's main columnist, William Connor, had been made a 'Sir'. I never read him but he wrote under the name of Cassandra, which seemed a funny thing to call an elderly male journalist. (Cassandra had been the name of the waif of a girl who was the first refugee to arrive at our primary school from the civil war in Cyprus in the 1950s.) Graham Greene, the novelist, had become a Companion of Honour. The one work of his that I had read was a short story in a first-year English class at Highbury called 'The Destructors'. A band of boys had taken against an old man, broken into his house while he was out and systematically destroyed it. One of their last acts was to remove its beams and supports and by some means attach it by rope to the back end of a lorry parked nearby. When the lorry pulled away, the house collapsed.

I had imagined the fate of the old man's house happening to several of those in our street: the ones next to gaps in the terrace caused by bombing. Those surviving houses generally had huge creosoted wooden struts placed up against them, from ground to roof level, to make sure they did not fall down. Number 5, next to my grandparents', nearly had in the 1950s and the council demolished it.

By the sixties the struts had been removed and new houses or flats had filled the gaps, only for other destructors to move in – ones with skips outside their houses, which they were pulling apart. In converting lofts, installing showers and expanding the size of rooms, Islington's increasing number of new residents was apt to rip out the wrong things. The house opposite ours, recently bought by a television broadcaster, had had a structural wall removed which made it sag – near disastrously – in the middle. My dad was called over for his advice and returned shaking his head. These people, he said, mindful of children and my grandparents being within listening distance, wouldn't have known their backsides from an RSJ.

The economic rise of Islington I dated from the turn of the decade. A big black car had appeared outside the print factory, where my mum worked, at the top of the street. Few other cars apart from that of my granddad were ever parked in Noel Road or any of the surrounding streets, and it looked like we had been touched by a dash of Hollywood. When I approached, it turned out that we had. Sitting on the backseat, big-lipped and blonde, was Jayne Mansfield, the American film actress. Mr Lowe, the factory owner, had served in the Czechoslovakian army in the war and retained his central European contacts. Jayne's husband, Mickey Hargitay, was Hungarian, a Mr Universe and Garth of his time. He was in the factory arranging for a series of glossy brochures to show off his muscles and Jayne's bust. She never appeared in Noel Road again but over the next few months Mickey visited to check the progress of the order, brought the Hargitay–Mansfield kids with him and, among the bubbling glue pots and clanking machinery, left them to my mum to babysit.

The area took off. Wasteland was cleared and Camden Passage antiques market, two streets from us, opened on a couple of dingy lanes. Princess Margaret was rumoured to be coming. Instead, Michael Medwin, who played a Cockney corporal in *The Army Game* cut the ribbon and gave a short speech. People were surprised how posh he sounded in real life. The street began to attract a varied bunch: choreographers, dancers, apparently; film producers, none of whom we had heard of; and television stars like William Roache, Ken Barlow from *Coronation Street*. My mum saw him and his wife, also an actor, load up their car one day, whereupon he disappeared down the road to Mrs Snow's at 51, who ran a florist's out of her front parlour. He returned with a bunch of flowers to hand to his wife, who drove off. It turned out she had left him.

I came home from school on one occasion to find a drinks party taking place outside a new double block of 'luxury flats', which for my early life had been the bomb site opposite my bedroom window. Pre-war, the property had comprised two houses, one of which had belonged to a member of the Manze family, the jellied eel people from Chapel Market. Party guests now stood chinking their glasses and smiling in a bemused way at any local who walked past. The confusion was mutual. No one among the original residents, not even the Brays down the street, who frequented the York, the Duke of Cambridge and any other pub in the locality, drank out in the street. The property's owner was someone called Anthony Blond, an 'avant-garde publisher', whatever that meant. A diary item appeared in the *Evening News*: 'I went today to the once seedy backwater of Islington,' it began. The meaning of that, I deduced, was that we had 'arrived'.

Some distance along our developmental path remained to be covered, however. Sir Anthony Wedgwood Benn, the postmaster general, flew off in the first few days of 1966 to Japan to study its phone system. Since its precision handling of the 1964 Tokyo Olympics, Japan was a technological success story. Wedgwood Benn led the way in introducing the all-number telephone number. Previously, phone numbers approximated to the area lived in. Ours was Canonbury 4603 and you dialled the first three letters of the name, as well as the number itself. It gave the impression that we resided in the one select part of Islington near Canonbury Square, which actually was a good mile away. We said the number politely into the receiver on the two or three times a week we received a call. Now it was to become the featureless 226 4603.

I had seen Peregrine Worsthorne, a posh newspaper columnist, take this up with Wedgwood Benn in a television debate. People liked the old numbers, he said, with their areas like Putney included in them. From his voice, and with a name like Peregrine, it was probably the sort of place he lived in. The postmaster general, he continued, claimed that the new numbers meant people could call Los Angeles without going through an operator. Didn't he realize they did not want to phone places like Los Angeles?

*The Mirror* launched a New Year campaign to mobilise the youth of Britain into clearing up bomb sites and the abandoned banks of canals. Voluntary organisations like the Boy Scouts were to help. Our bomb sites were now mainly built over again: the two top corners of our neighbouring street, Gerrard Road, had been the site of November the 5th bonfires in the 1950s and were now council flats, as was the space that once held six houses beyond our backyard wall. The double space opposite us had been filled by the avant-garde publisher. Six doors down on our side, the first gap in the terrace had been filled around the turn of the decade. The new house was divided into flats, and two men moved into the top one. It was not necessarily unusual that men shared accommodation. In this case one was older than the other. The older one looked purse-lipped and bustled along. The younger one wore a leather cap slightly askew. Both carried satchels over their shoulders, of the type you might carry books to and from school in. They were regularly seen in each other's company and, rarely for men in the street, they were around at most hours of the day. Little comment was made that I heard, in keeping with the prevailing principle of the area that people 'kept themselves to themselves'.

As for canals and scout troops, our nearest were a few yards away. The Regent's Canal ran past the bottom of the gardens of the houses on the other side of the street, and beyond that was

Vincent Terrace, where the scouts met in the mission hall at the corner of Sudeley Street. I had been a member until 1960, when I lost any fascination I might have had for khaki, campfires and singing 'Ging Gang Goolie'. The last of the horses employed to pull canal boats on the towpath had wended their way back up our street and to their stables in the 1950s, and since then the canal had become a murky place. From the windows of my primary school at the bottom end of Noel Road, we had seen police frogmen drag the canal for a child from Gerrard Road who had fallen in and drowned. It was improving now. One of the film producers was organising collections for repairs to the tunnel roof where the waterway went underground at Colebrooke Row. It emerged again a good two miles away at the Caledonian Road.

The new Islingtonians had the wacky idea that pleasure craft might one day run through the canal. This was not one shared by my granddad, who on 4 January 1966 celebrated his 72nd birthday. As my grandmother noted, he was two years beyond his 'three score years and ten', the age of mortality as stipulated by the Bible. The average male life expectancy of the time he had beaten by four years. Unusually, for someone who had worked a good deal of his life in the print, he did not drink much beyond a soft drink; if ever he was dragged into a pub, he ordered a bitter lemon. He did not smoke and only gambled on the football pools. From a poor start, he and my grandma had done quite well in life. They were both from Finsbury, the smaller and poorer borough next to Islington. He was born in Exmouth Market and had lost an eye at the age of 11, caused by a firework on Guy Fawkes Night. She lived in more places than she could remember, as her family moved from one rented room to another in the environs of Goswell Road. Drink, gambling or both had been the downfall of three of their parents. The fourth, my grandma's father, a sheet music printer, had gone blind working by candlelight in a basement factory. This was, as she often recalled, under the Adelphi in the Strand.

When my grandparents married in 1920, they escaped across the City Road from Finsbury to Islington, where my granddad put money away out of his earnings. He had trained as a carpenter and was a mechanic for the Royal Flying Corps (the RAF's forerunner) in the First World War, when planes were made of wood. Afterwards, he was a bill poster, often in competition, sometimes uneasy alliance, with the Roberts' branch of the family, who lived in Sudeley Street and nearby City Garden Row. Old Harry Roberts, the master of the family, would have gangs go round to pull my granddad's posters down, and once to even beat him up. Generally working alone, my granddad added to his portfolio of activities by going into the print. Here the chief prize was Saturday nights, when the earnings from the Sunday newspaper production shift could double those of the week.

Each time my granddad saved £250, he had bought an Islington house. At one stage he owned nine. Three were in Noel Road, though none on the cheaper canal side because, he said, of the rats. The houses were intended to be his pension but the Blitz removed five of them in one night, killing my mum's cousin Teddy Clark in the process. This was in Carnegie Street, in Barnsbury. Two more of his houses, in Elia Street off Colebrooke Row, were bought after the war by Islington borough council as compulsory purchases, for which he received a little more than his original £250. These were replaced by municipal housing.

My grandparents lived in number 7 Noel Road, and the remaining one, number 13, they had given to my parents as a tenth-anniversary present in 1953. Two very elderly ladies – Mrs Goldsworthy and Miss Shelford – lived in the house, on controlled rents and in a room each. Against their wishes, my dad had insisted that he convert their gas mantels to electric light. When we moved in, and for some years after, my parents, sister and I slept in the front parlour, the bucket within easy reach. This meant that we didn't have to use the toilet one flight of stairs away and encounter Miss Shelford who, in an old black gown, wandered the house at night. We were separated from Mrs Goldsworthy's room at the back by partition doors. On the night she died we heard her collapse, and so my dad was able to call an ambulance quickly.

Islington house prices had started to climb a little after Jayne Mansfield's appearance and the opening of Camden Passage. We heard a figure of £4,000 in 1960 had reached £10,000 by 1964; two years later now, someone was saying the going rate was £20,000. My granddad watched, quietly amused at the contemporary folly of man and his marketplace, but never once bemoaned his fate – particularly in the case of his lost Barnsbury houses – at being very much a man before his time.

The day after his birthday I imagined I would be watching England's match against Poland with him. My dad usually contrived to miss these moments altogether, having been nervous about watching England ever since the Hungary result 13 years earlier. He invariably found a repair that needed doing in the loft or on the roof. But when I checked, television was not showing it live. ITV had some recorded highlights at 10.30 p.m. The lack of coverage was disappointing, since we had read that morning how important television had become. The memorial service had taken place in Westminster Abbey of Richard Dimbleby, the broadcaster who had died aged 52. His commentaries on the Coronation in 1953 and Churchill's funeral less than a year before his own death had done a great deal to develop the popularity of television itself. 'And I saw a new heaven and a new earth,' a speaker told the congregation, quoting from the book of Revelation. The service, in contrast to the football, was shown both as it happened and with recorded highlights in the evening.

As we had heard, Dimbleby had fought a brave and quite long battle against illness, but the reports were reluctant to say what his illness was. Eventually we learned it was cancer, a word that people hardly allowed themselves to utter. Only some good few years later did it emerge that this had been testicular cancer, an even greater taboo. Dimbleby had seen his problem and could have lived longer had he sought medical attention.

My granddad and I duly got together in the front room at number 7 to watch the late showing of Bobby Moore leading the team out for the match against the Poles. England's skipper looked fit and well after the injury that had kept him out of action over much of the previous season. Most of us thought nothing of it, reported as it was as a routine groin strain. Just as well he was in such good shape. The Poles went ahead on the half-hour. England battered their opponents for much of the rest of the game but failed to get through. It was only Moore surging up from the back who secured a late equaliser.

Fortunate, as it was, that we had not lost, the game was a poor omen for the World Cup itself. All those turn-of-the-year hopes of a path to summer success had been dashed virtually as soon as we had first held them.

# Chapter 3

# 'CAN YER SIGN, PLEASE, ALF?'

In early January, Brazil handed the World Cup back to Sir Stanley Rous, the British head of Fifa, for safe keeping in London. The Brazilians no doubt fully expected – as we did of them – to earn the right to keep it themselves in the summer. A triumph in the final in England and the trophy would be theirs for ever.

This was because they had won it twice already. Their first victory was in Sweden in 1958, which also happened to be the first World Cup with extensive live television coverage. The BBC seemed to have been warming up for the occasion over a number of years. You might hear word on a Sunday that the BBC was planning an outside broadcast and turn on the television to find that it was transmitting from the bridge of a ferry crossing the Channel. It was not very interesting but the Sweden World Cup was possibly a by-product of that exercise.

It was in 1958 for Brazil and at the age of 17, that Pelé scored his first international goal. This was a lucky scuff past Arsenal's Jack Kelsey, in goal for Wales, who otherwise kept the Brazilians at bay in a tightly fought 1–0 game. England had managed a goalless draw against Brazil in the group stage. Possibly the Brazilians were still psychologically smarting from the occasion two years earlier at Wembley when, in the first international between the two countries, England had won 4–2. Stanley Matthews, 41 years old, had an excellent game on the right wing. Matthews, though still playing for Blackpool, did not come to the World Cup in Sweden, preferring to spend his summers coaching in South Africa.

In England's 2–2 draw in Gothenburg against the USSR, Lev Yashin, the Russian keeper, had a tantrum and threw his cap at the referee. The ref had awarded England a penalty with the Russians 2–1 up. Tom Finney, the veteran of both the left and right wings for Preston North End, equalised from the penalty spot. At 36, Finney was the world's most famous plumber, his job when he was not playing football. On match days, he travelled on the same bus as Preston fans, chatting to them on their way to the game, according to what I read in magazines like *Charles Buchan's Football Monthly*. On the rare occasions we saw any footballer talking on TV, Finney always seemed to me a very quiet person.

This was obviously not the case with Yashin. The ref did not take his name, let alone send him off for his antics, perhaps out of fear of antagonising the Soviet Union. They had invaded Hungary two years earlier. When England had played them for the first time, in a friendly in Moscow shortly before the Sweden World Cup, I had been scared stiff on the England players' behalf. Amazingly we came out of that game with a 1–1 draw.

As for Yashin, throwing his cap at the height of the Cold War was a quite Soviet thing to do. Two years later, the USSR leader Nikita Khrushchev was banging his shoe on the table at the UN. Yet just a little further into the early sixties, and from what I heard from almost everyone in Britain sounding off about football, Yashin had transformed into a 'character' and the 'greatest goalkeeper in the world'. After the Cuban missile crisis in 1962, and the relaxing of tension between east and west, we just needed a Russian to love. Personally, I did not rate his keeping. Apart from bits on TV and a few minutes he played in an exhibition match in London, I had not seen him in action. Most people who said how wonderful he was had not seen him either.

From the World Cup in Chile in 1962, which the Brazilians won again, we could not really see anything. The Andes were in the way. What we did witness on TV only arrived 24 hours after a match as film in a can. In total, what we saw was bad. Brazil's Garrincha somehow out-jumped the England defence to score with his head. He had had rickets as a child, was bow-legged and barely five feet tall. He still climbed above Ron Springett in goal and lanky Maurice Norman of Tottenham at centre-half.

In the absence of cars in Noel Road at the time, I went and practised in the street to see how this could have been possible. But the simple reason was that we did not travel well. Peter Swan, Sheffield Wednesday's centre-half, nearly died in the Chilean mining camp where England were based, whether from the food or exotic illness. We were eventually eliminated by the Hungarians, despite their having lost some of their best players, to retirement or exile, after the Soviet tanks rolled into their country in 1956.

What happened in Chile was far enough away to be quickly forgotten. But in 1966 the action would be all too close. With Sir Stanley in the chair at Fifa, England had won the right to stage the tournament and, in the event of humiliation, no range of fiery Andean volcanoes would obscure the view. Wembley was a short drive around the North Circular on the skirts of Dollis Hill.

Until the middle of January, the Beatles were still at the top of the record charts – they had been there since well before Christmas – with their ninth number one. This was their double-sided hit 'Day Tripper' and 'We Can Work It Out'. The lyrics of the latter – 'Try to see it my way' – might have spoken for England manager Alf Ramsey's relationship with the football public. Not that Ramsey was the sort of person to have the remotest interest in 'popular' music. An ultra-serious character, at 45 he was only six months older than my father but came across as more of my grandparents' vintage. If anything was likely to have made him smile it would have been an old joke or routine from the days of music hall: a song perhaps by Flanagan and Allen, ex- of the Crazy Gang. My grandparents used to go and see them with my mum, when she was little, at the Collins' Music Hall on Islington Green. 'Strolling' would have been his kind of number and Bud Flanagan still appeared on television in his shaggy fur overcoat singing it. In their armchairs, my grandma and granddad joined in.

Whether in tracksuit or his England blazer, little visibly ruffled Ramsey. Whenever he made his statements that

England were going to win the World Cup, he gave no hint that he was joking. His face was rigidly set, like that of Anthony Quayle playing a gunship commander as the *Graf Spee* emerged from Montevideo harbour in *The Battle of the River Plate*. This was one of the many films – *The Dambusters*, *Reach for the Sky*, *Bridge Over the River Kwai* – that had told us of the glories of the war and that it was action, not words that counted. Ramsey was a throwback to those taciturn times, although he may not always have been. As a player, he had had a tendency to adopt an 'I'm in charge here' attitude, even when he was not the captain. His fellow Spurs players complained that he could be pompous and nicknamed him 'the General'.

These days there was something, too, about his mumbled monotone: Ramsey's words sounded distinctly posh. Dave Blumson, a schoolmate who supported Leyton Orient, found the answer. Dave's father, an East Ender, concluded that Ramsey, from the industrial east London suburb of Dagenham, could not, by any natural circumstance, possibly sound like that. England's manager had taken elocution lessons.

Ramsey and I were on first-name terms. At least, I was with him. I had met him when he was manager of Ipswich Town. This was in the 1962–63 season, when Ipswich were the reigning league champions. They had risen up from obscurity so quickly that few football fans in the country could believe it. Neither could the Ipswich players. On their days in London, the team left Liverpool Street station for home at about 6.30 and signed autographs so easily that you could get a whole team photo completed in one night. Not for them the diffidence and distance of star players of the game.

The Ipswich squad – Ray Crawford, Jimmy Leadbetter, goal-keeper Roy Bailey and all – chatted to you, enjoying their success while it lasted.

Their manager you did not exactly chat with. I had spotted Ramsey in the cafeteria by the long platform 13 having his pre-journey cup of tea and a ham and tomato roll. I approached him as he made for the train. He was dressed precisely the same as in the picture I had of him in my *Topical Times* album for that season: wide-lapelled blazer with a large Ipswich Town FC crest on the left breast pocket, sensible light brown cardigan, white shirt and closely knotted club tie. His hair was Brylcreemed into his usual just left-of-centre parting. 'Can yer sign please, Alf?' I held out the *Topical Times* opened at his picture and offered him my biro. Ramsey looked at me askance. Actually, he had to look up a bit, since by now I was already taller than him. He must have understood what I had said; he would have recognised my accent as similar to the one he had left behind some while ago. But was he being his normal Ramsey impassive, or was there the hint of a glare? I wondered if I should correct my request to a 'Mr Ramsey' but dismissed that as a formality not called for in the world of football. After a moment's further hesitation he signed, neatly enough, across the width of his blazer's lapels: 'Thank you!' he said in clipped fashion, handing me back my pen.

As school re-started again, the news from Birmingham was that mothers of white children at Grove Lane primary school in Smethwick had called off a strike after assurances from the headmistress that more classrooms would be hastily constructed to allow smaller class numbers. The white mothers said 80% of the children in the school were 'coloured'.

With the new measures, said a Mrs Joan Williams, 'it might be possible to admit more white children and lower the percentage of coloureds'. From Essex, a mother wrote to the *Daily Mirror* to say her seven-year-old daughter's school had banned her from wearing tights. These were once something worn by my sister when she went to ballet classes but had lately become popular daily wear among teenage girls and young women because of the fast rising hemline of the miniskirt. The school in Essex said tights were 'unhealthy'. As the angry mum noted, her little girl would now have to go back to wearing stockings and garters.

In the condemned building of our school – soon to be demolished to make way for the comprehensive – the upper-sixth arts occupied a small top-floor room overlooking the road to Highbury Barn. On the first day of term, the acting headmaster, Raymond Wood, made his way up to check that the ten of us were present. A bulbous brow gave his head the shape of an inverted triangle. Some kids, who had read the *Eagle* comic in their earlier years, styled him the 'Mekon', after the aliens in the Dan Dare cartoon. A senior English master, he had the job of maintaining morale through the grammar school's final days. He was only in the top role while the governors and ministry of education took their time choosing a future leader for the school and for the important role intended for it in government strategy.

He took me aside, first to look critically at my hair. A half-hearted Beatle effort, it was combed forward to cover the acne on my forehead, which as a result made the spots worse. Had the hair been over my ears or long around the neck, he would have ordered me to get it cut. He turned his attention to my newspaper, stuffed in my blazer pocket and opened at the racing page. I would need to read something other than *The Mirror*, he said, when it came to getting a job. I mentioned that I was not influenced by its politics but he countered that that was not the point. It was a question of breadth of learning, for which he recommended *The Times* and *The Telegraph*, neither of which I was especially familiar with. The school library had copies of *The Times* so I went and took a look.

Its sport was tucked away on some inside pages, and you had to search for it. Looking back to see how it had covered the Poland game, I found its report: 'From Our Association Football Correspondent.' It did not give a name, possibly to avoid heaping further shame on someone writing about football.

Ramsey had claimed that Bobby Moore's late equaliser had all been planned. The Poles had refused to make a game of it and Moore had licence to head upfield leaving Nobby Stiles to guard the rear. The team fell short, however, said *The Times*, and 'lacked the flexibility and flair of R. Charlton', a reference to Bobby Charlton, who had gashed his leg in training and could not play. England had taken to the field thinking they would be 'required to pay little more than some peppercorn rent'. There was something in what the Mekon had said. That was not the kind of phrase I would have read in *The Mirror*. Another one I was more prepared for. England, had been 'all smiles after Madrid', said the paper, but not following their game against the Poles when the 'euphoria evaporated'.

I had looked up euphoria two years ago. Harold Wilson had announced Britain was going to withdraw its presence 'east of Suez', whereupon Lee Kuan Yew, Singapore's prime minister, came to London to find out what that meant. Most of us knew vaguely of Singapore; the father of a primary school friend of mine from St Peter's Street had been captured there by the Japanese and eventually arrived home from a prisoner-of-war camp minus a leg. But we had not heard of Lee Kuan Yew. After talks with Wilson, he appeared on the steps of number 10 Downing Street and, asked how he felt about Britain leaving Singapore, smiled broadly and said he was neither 'manic depressive nor euphoric'. Singapore was already doing very nicely, thank you. Opinion from commentators and public alike expressed surprise at a 'Chinaman' having such linguistic command. People called into the BBC wondering if we couldn't have a prime minister like him.

*The Times* gave a lot of praise to Poland's team. Anticipating Ramsey would play without wingers, they concentrated on tying England up in the middle of the muddy Goodison pitch. They were an all-round spirited bunch, a point I should have known. Their Polish church around the corner from us in Devonia Road was full every Sunday, even though the only Pole I knew in the area was the newsagent in Danbury Street. They came from all over, spilling out and chatting on the pavement afterwards, as if they were on the Continent. My sister weaved through them, making her way back from 'our church', St Peter's – C of E – at the other end of Devonia Road, which had been emptying since the late 1950s. She went to keep her voice in practice in the choir and, on some Sundays, the choir was the congregation.

The unnamed *Times* man also framed his report in sometimes military language: 'The tough relentless Polish forces might have been defending their capital to the last man.'

I had heard my mum on a similar theme when we had gone past Monte Cassino, the monastery overlooking the Rome-to-Naples *autostrada*, a couple of years ago. Fighting alongside the Poles in the battle for the monastery in 1944, her cousin Arthur Clarke had been missing assumed dead. It was a terrible time for the family, especially my great aunt Ada, who had already lost Teddy in the Barnsbury bombing. The fighting was so awful that my dad had been held up with the advance at Naples. He saw Vesuvius erupt while he was there. Arthur was fortunately found alive. His other brother, Stanley, was also in the area but soon sent off to India, to a sense of relief all round.

Of the England team, credit went to Moore for his late, successful effort to save the game. He was one of a small core of truly world class players that England had to rely on if we were to achieve any success in July. Others were Charlton of Manchester United and Jimmy Greaves of Spurs, both goal-scoring veterans of the national team, except neither had been on top form for some while now. Greaves as well as Charlton had missed the game against Poland through injury, though the Spurs striker had also not played in the victory against Spain. This had prompted questions as to whether Greaves would win his place back in the team. 'It will be there for him,' Ramsey had assured.

Moore I had met about four years before at West Ham's ground at Upton Park. I had gone to hang around outside the Green Street gates during morning training. Teams did most of their training at their main stadiums back then. The bigger ones had expansive grounds on the city outskirts – Arsenal at London Colney, Spurs at Cheshunt, West Ham at Chadwell Heath – but they were not easy for teams to get to every day. Not all the players, the reserves in particular, had cars. I went during the Easter break with our school team captain, Jimmy Dunkley. Jimmy had not shown any previous interest in autographs but asked to come along. I was not expecting any trouble, but being the toughest kid in the year, Jimmy was good to have around. He came from around the run-down streets and post-war prefabs near Highbury stadium, on its rougher side by Holloway Road.

From Barking in the far reaches of the East End, Moore had parents with either a sense of humour or social aspirations, who had given him the middle name of 'Chelsea'. Having risen through the West Ham youth ranks, he was on the point of being named team captain and already an impressive figure. Tie perfectly tied, he was endlessly patient as he signed everything put before him by the 20 or so boys hanging around. He often had a few friendly words: 'Very well, thank you, son, and how are you? Yes, you're right, it has been a good season. I hope you're enjoying it. Ah, an Arsenal fan.' His handwriting was flowing and carefully formed and, like us at Highbury, he might have been given special lessons in it at school to improve his chances of getting a job. 'Best wishes,' he added to your bigger pictures. Most players did when asked, though not all. Moore even used his own pen. Jimmy did not stop talking about him on the long bus ride home. Within a year he had left school and was on the books of Fulham as an apprentice pro.

Other players in the England team were in the workaday mould Ramsey had developed at Ipswich: Jack Charlton of Leeds in the centre of defence, Roger Hunt of Liverpool up front, and Ray Wilson the Everton full-back, though recently of Huddersfield Town, had spent many of their seasons in the second division. Right-back George Cohen at Fulham lived under constant threat of being there. 'I don't choose necessarily the best players,' said Ramsey in one of his speech-like moments. 'I choose the best players for the job that I want them to do.'

Gordon Banks, the Leicester City goalkeeper, I had had a liking for since the moment I saw him take off into the air and across half the width of his goal. In the 1962–63 season, when Leicester were visiting Highbury, I was standing behind him at the Clock End, by chance, and witnessed the most spectacular dive I had seen. Stretching to the top far-left corner, he had taken the ball cleanly with his body at four to five feet on the horizontal. Unfortunately, he fell with such force on to his left elbow that it knocked the ball from his grasp and a foot over his goal-line. It took a second or so for this to register with the Arsenal crowd, but within their cheers I heard echoes of my school and club coaches: 'Use your feet, son! Use your feet!' Still, that was OK. His effort, as I could see, showed a lot of promise. All Banks needed was to develop his technique in making ground with a few swift steps across the goalmouth before launching into his dive. Get that right and I reckoned he would save anything.

I had accosted him on the morning of that game outside the Great Northern Hotel behind King's Cross station. Leicester had their pre-match meal there when playing in London and would take a stroll either before or after lunch – not that King's Cross was much of an area for strolling. I had seen a lanky spiv with a rolled Rizla on his lips once snatch an old lady's handbag there and sprint off for York Way. England's goalkeeper signed the picture I had of him in my *Topical Times* with no messing about, which was good. The big kids – spivs all of them – were around and I, too, had to be quick on my feet.

In days before Britain had a motorway system, most clubs travelled to away matches by train. Visiting teams stayed overnight in the capital. Several big clubs – Sheffield Wednesday, Blackpool – used the Hotel Russell in Russell Square. Players might go for a few Friday night drinks in Soho. Having missed the last bus one night, Sheffield Wednesday's players walked back, kicking a few bottles in readiness for the next afternoon's game. Blackburn Rovers, with two or three England players in their number, stayed at a hotel in Half Moon Street, Mayfair, within ambling distance of the red light lanes of Shepherd Market. I wandered with them and saw none go for the goods on offer. Manchester United stayed further west in Lancaster Gate, and Manchester City at Bailey's Hotel near Gloucester Road tube.

You could also run on the pitch and mill around with the players during the five-minute kick-about that passed for their warm-up, just before a game. On an occasion when Glasgow Rangers came to play a friendly at Highbury, I ran on again at half-time to get a player I had forgotten earlier and the referee delayed the re-start of the game. The police were no problem and gave up the chase once you had vaulted the barrier and made it on to the playing surface, for what today is a criminal offence.

Worse of a weekend was confronting the three big kids who 'ran' the stations and hotels. Aged 18, they were three and four years older than the rest of us and apt to steal your signed pictures or your money, or beat you up. Reggie Duke, the nutcase of the troika, might do all three. The head butt his speciality, he crept up on me one Friday afternoon when I had come straight from school for the arrival of Everton. From the shadows of the Euston Arch, a quiet voice behind me enquired what I was doing there and I turned to find Reggie's forehead at the level of the bridge of my nose. The beginnings of rush-hour meant he was constrained. 'Go away,' he said gently. Not many people got a second chance from Reggie.

He and one other of the three, Paul Viollet, were Islington boys from around the Essex Road. Paul carried his books in a builder's bag of the type my dad kept his trowels and spirit level in, though I doubted he was 'on the tools'. Maybe he had made it to hod-carrier. I heard later that he became a Bank of England messenger, one of those you saw on the news as they dashed in a top hat from Threadneedle Street whenever the interest rate changed.

Reggie and Paul may have fancied themselves as adolescent versions of Ron and Reg Kray, the twin gang leaders developing a reputation around Bethnal Green, Whitechapel and other quarters east of the Tower. The third big kid was Tom Smithson, who was from one of the poorer parts of west London and similarly of a pre-sixties age. He styled his hair in a greasy Elvis quiff even after the Beatles came in. He launched himself at me one evening with a flying drop kick outside a hotel behind Selfridges where Glasgow Rangers were staying. I sidestepped, he missed and I made sure to be away before he was back off the ground again.

Between them, they maintained a 'balance of terror', a Friday and Saturday night version, at the London stations and hotels, of the Cold War. The US, USSR and China now, with its recently exploded bomb, were mutually assured of destruction if they moved against each other, which encouraged initiative among those who existed around them. I understood guerrilla warfare long before I had heard either of it, of Vietnam or the advice in Chairman Mao's *Little Red Book* on when to advance or to disappear from view.

I got caught only once. When it finally dawned on Reggie, Paul and Smiffy that their time could be better spent doing things other than chasing footballers around – possibly even pursuing girls – three East End kids filled the vacuum. One was a fat kid with a cleft lip called Jackson, and another was a little one, who had all the lip and was called Scobie. The third kid didn't seem to have a name. From a collective background, they worked and stole systematically as a pack, which was far worse than the individualist ways of the previous three. Someone even called Reggie back one evening to beat up Jackson outside Bailey's Hotel, which was a shock for the Friday night South Kensington crowd.

But they persisted. They nabbed me early one Sunday morning when Sunderland were departing. No train left King's Cross on a Saturday after a game that reached Sunderland at any reasonable hour that night so the team stayed over in London. Scobie and the kid with no name had all my pictures after I lingered too long with Brian Clough, who was happy to sign the many photographs I had of him. I should have cut and run, but it didn't matter. I gained revenge of sorts when Scobie turned up a couple of seasons later for a trial at Brisbane Road and I, already on the Orient books, watched from the stands as he was turned down. It had been time to move on anyway, and to attempt to get into the world of signing autographs rather than collecting them.

The trouble I had walked into at King's Cross was caused by the fact that some players were naturally good with kids. Clough was one of them and, to my knowledge in his playing days, never turned down a request from a young fan. But some were not like that. Outside Upton Park on the day I went with Jimmy, Johnny Dick, West Ham's first-choice striker and Scots' international, strode right through us at the gates.

After I thought all the players had gone in for training, a local kid had sidled over to us. It might have rung warning bells, but he was friendly. He pointed to my West Ham team photo. I had cut it from the *Reynolds News*, the Sunday paper that printed such pictures across half a page in grainy colour and that went out of business long before any other newspaper experimented with colour. 'You wanna get that bloke over there.' He pointed to a tall serious character standing as if to attention by the far side of the gates. I had seen him but not recognised him as a player. 'That's our reserve left-half.' In the team photo he indicated the figure standing next to Moore in West Ham's claret and blue. 'He's Geoff Hurst.'

Hurst had been standing there for a few minutes, staring out at the morning crowd on Green Street. The sun was out and he was squinting a bit as he seemed to be looking into it. He looked like he was concentrating on something. Why was he there? What was he staring at? 'Oh, he always does that,' said the West Ham kid. 'He pretends he's waiting for someone but he's really seeing if anyone will ask him to sign. Any pictures we've got of him have all been done.' As I walked over to him, Hurst gave the impression of not seeing me coming. 'That's OK, son,' he said smartly as I thanked him. He carried on peering at Green Street but within another minute was in the stadium. Within a season, Johnny Dick was out injured and West Ham, on a whim, moved Hurst from playing defence in the reserves to being first-team striker, in the hope he might score a few goals.

On the morning I scored his signature, I felt I had done him a favour.

# Chapter 4

# BLIND BEGGAR

My introduction to the East End had mainly been through football. One afternoon a week, coaches picked us up at the school's side gate by Highbury Grove and bussed us to games in the big-sky country of Walthamstow. Post-war governments encouraged the use of breezy open spaces to build kids up physically and mentally. England's World Cup team was a product of that approach. The school gave us sixpence each to make our way home. No one was molested or went missing but if we messed about or spoke too loudly on the bus older passengers – from the era of when kids were meant to be seen and not heard – might say they had noted from our blazers what school we went to and that they would report us to the headmaster. I took the 38 from the Crooked Billet, one stop past Walthamstow dog track. As far as I knew the Crooked Billet was a local pub, though I don't recall seeing it. Walthamstow Avenue played somewhere down the road. They were among the leading amateur clubs in the country – Dulwich Hamlet,

Barnet, Bishop Auckland – who on Amateur Cup final day drew big crowds to Wembley. Before Walthamstow Avenue disappeared I never did see where their stadium was either.

If I was using the 38 route to get to Brisbane Road, this involved getting off about halfway along the length of Lea Bridge Road and walking nearly a mile to the Orient stadium. This took you past the Caribonum, a large factory behind gates and poplars, as if in Elysian Fields. My schoolmate Peter Francis – the only one of us in the sixth form who argued the Labour party cause – had moved out with his family to that part of Leyton from Islington's Copenhagen Street, a move that rated as a step up from being near the Caledonian Road. Just one problem was that the Caribonum produced things like carbon paper and – of an era when factories proliferated in London – at night belched the smell of plastic across the area.

Eventually I had forsaken that route to the stadium for the Central Line. Early one Saturday morning some months back when I was coming in for a game, I had seen Dave Sexton sitting calmly at the end of the carriage. I wanted to go up and introduce myself to him as his junior-team goalkeeper but, both there and on the walk from the tube through Coronation Gardens, he looked so deep in thought that I couldn't bring myself to do so. Now, since he had gone, no one had really assumed the managerial reins of the club.

At the youth level, life more or less went on. Harry Spinner took charge of the juniors. Harry, in his forties, walked with a heavy limp, which, someone said, he had incurred in the Malayan Emergency. He talked broad east London – 'co' blimey, yus' – and had always been supportive of me, even after games when we had been well beaten. Millwall generally pulled off this feat.

On one occasion, Barry Kitchener outjumped me on a cross to score with his head. This was pretty shameful for a keeper, with the advantage of using his hands, although Kitchener did go on to play more than 400 times for Millwall, who named a stand after him when they moved to the New Den from Cold Blow Lane. As an ex-military man, though, Harry was not without his disciplinary limits. One week I made it to the London Transport ground only ten minutes before a game against Queens Park Rangers. The Saturday earlier we had been hammered 9–2 by Tottenham but Harry had argued for keeping an unchanged team. The result had been a fluke, he said, and riddled with poor refereeing in Spurs' favour. Now he looked exasperated: so was this how I repaid his faith in me? I changed quickly, made it to the pitch just before the whistle for the start of the game and we beat QPR comfortably.

We had had other decent results, too. A 2–2 draw away to Chelsea at their swanky playing fields on Honeypot Lane was one. Peter Osgood had just graduated with a lot of fanfare from youth level to the Chelsea first team but, as we had to pass through their dressing room to get to ours, we noticed kit had been neatly laid out beneath a peg marked with his name. This wouldn't have happened at the London Transport Ground, where Harry tossed shirts, shorts and socks to us across the cramped dressing room. If in Chelsea's case it was an early exercise in mind games, it failed. After a nervous first few minutes when we got it clear to ourselves that Osgood wasn't present we went on to get our draw. Back for the return a couple of weeks later in the long grass and deep mud of our place, a Ronnie Wigg hat-trick won the game. From near Bishop's Stortford, Ronnie to us was a world-class centre-forward. After the O's, he played for Ipswich and went out of the English game via clubs like Grimsby and Scunthorpe, before he ended his career coaching in the US. Very sadly, Ronnie died still in his forties, in 1997.

Tommy Coleman, a short, blond, thirty-something, ran the Colts team and generally had the main say-so on how our training sessions were conducted. He'd scream as we did our doggies, 'You're bloody nigh walking!' Tommy's words would further guide us as we ended the night's session with a mixed Colts and juniors game. 'Spread out!' he'd demand. 'You're on top of that ball like flies round a lump of shit.'

Both he and Harry reported to Eddie Heath, the dark eminence of Orient's youth outfit. Eddie, black-haired, well over six feet tall, sat in the office in the bowels of the stadium where the weekly team-sheets went up. He ultimately decided whose names went on them.

Fortunately, I had got on well with Eddie following my first performance against West Ham. Even the disaster of the big defeat by Spurs over on their training ground had done me no harm, thanks to Harry's special pleading. That, in fact, had turned into an 'if only' game. Spurs were at the top of the South East Counties League and we were by tradition near the bottom. Just walking on the pitch, you could tell they still lived in the glow of the Double team's glory. They had players with accents from the north, and even as far away as Scotland. From Islington, I was the nearest thing we had to a foreigner. We were on top for the first 15 minutes, during which we hit the bar. The shot cannoned back down towards the goal-line – whether it had crossed it or not was obscured by one of the Spurs' full-backs tottering backwards and sitting on the ball.

No linesman's flag waved in favour of our appeals. Within a couple of minutes, I had also saved a penalty. As I dived to my right and took the ball cleanly around the pit of my stomach, I'd for a moment imagined what this would mean once the story got back to Brisbane Road: 'A penalty save against the mighty Spurs,' they'd have said as word circulated rapidly, and it would have almost certainly made my career. Except when I regained my feet, the ref was signalling for the kick to be retaken. 'You moved!' he said. This was true, and I wanted to say to him, 'Yes, ref, as illegal as it is, I moved before the kick was taken. But keepers always do and, by the way, we are the O's and they are the Spurs; they do the Double, while we get promoted then relegated the next season. So why not give us a chance?'

It would have done no good, other than getting me sent off. He had probably been in the army during the Normandy landings, or some such, so wasn't about to listen to a teenager whining. He gave them another penalty a few minutes later for no obvious reason. The crowd along the Cheshunt sidelines – all pro-Tottenham – bayed in disbelief and Eddie Baily, the Spurs coach who had played for both the club and England alongside Alf Ramsey, yelled the foulest obscenities imaginable at the ref, saying he had ruined the game. At that point, the floodgates of the nearby River Lea might as well have opened. Wave after wave of Tottenham attack saw goal after goal go past me. We were 7–0 down at half-time. Back in the dressing room, Harry didn't blame me for any of them. 'They scored seven in the first half,' he said. 'And we'll just go and score seven in the second.' We didn't, of course, but held our own to draw the second half 2–2 – which was the story we took back to Brisbane Road.

The defeat to Spurs in the Winchester Cup quarter-finals a few weeks later, this time 3–1, also left its scars, not least because en route we had easily disposed of West Ham at Chadwell Heath. Back at Cheshunt again, the Spurs centre-forward rendered me near unconscious with a mid-air charge in the first few minutes. Harry would normally have limped on with his aluminium bucket of cold water and magic sponge but Tommy had been drafted in for the game, so important was it considered to be. Equipped with a full medical chest, he cracked an ammonia stick under my nose, which nearly took my head off. I would like to have said that I was still recovering when Spurs scored their third to seal victory near the end, but I wasn't, and the goal went down as my fault.

The only thing to do in the face of such reverses was to shrug them off. Several rivals for my position in the junior team came and went. One let in ten against Portsmouth. Another I had played against in a Colts game a year or so ago on the day of Churchill's funeral. All normal league matches had been postponed to mark the sombre moment, but Eddie fixed some other games to keep us in practice. We played a club team on a pitch called Flanders Fields behind East Ham town hall and won easily, 5–0, but the other keeper had so much to do and played so well that Tommy invited him for a trial. After one game on the Brisbane Road pitch, he told me he really did not fancy this level and wanted to get back to playing with his mates. Another kid walked out when Eddie kept picking me instead of him. Personally, I felt he was better than I was, a thought that I kept to myself. Most of us felt he was a bit dense, which may have had something to do with his high level of confidence between the posts; he just didn't think to worry. But he didn't stick it out, and I last saw him playing Sunday mornings, actually quite brilliantly, over at Hackney Marshes.

One night after training when Eddie intercepted me as I was leaving the stadium began the process of my undoing. I had been chosen, he said, to play at Eton Manor sports club the next Saturday in an annual five-a-side competition. Eton Manor stood behind high walls enclosing full-sized football pitches, boxing and weightlifting gyms and other facilities designed to keep the youth of the area off the streets. On the edge of the marshes, it had the look of a cavalry fort in flat and hostile country. Eddie could have chosen two or three older keepers, so it was an obvious promotion and a chance to establish myself.

The tournament involved nearly all of the many sports clubs of east London, with Leyton Orient the only professional club invited to attend. West Ham, a mile and more further away than us, were shunned. Consequently, we left Eton Manor's teeming dressing rooms as hot favourites. To reflect our self-regard, we wore a natty line in blue and white striped shorts, which had surprised us when we pulled them out of the kit basket delivered from Brisbane Road. (Every other team participating in the day would have brought their own kit with them.) We had never seen striped shorts before and they would have looked very fetching next to Orient's traditional royal blue shirts, had we been anywhere but in the East End. 'Flash bastards,' mumbled the surly crowds as we strolled confidently through them to get to our pitch.

They repeated it loudly and more cheerily as we trailed back having gone out in the first round 3–2 to a club we did not know. The striped shorts disappeared into the skip never to be seen again. Imagining we had won before we started, I was too late in getting down with my hands to a shot for one of the goals. To the side of me and fast along the ground, it went in under my body. Peter Shilton would do the same when Poland stopped England qualifying for the 1974 World Cup, but neither of us had any excuse. The shame of our loss was something that Eddie, brooding in his office, would always remember.

World Cup tickets had gone on sale in the early days of the year and soon all 6,000 grandstand tickets were snapped up for matches at Goodison Park, where Brazil were to play. In the North-East, where Newcastle's St James's Park was not deemed to be of World Cup standard, Sunderland and Middlesbrough sold £7,500 worth of tickets on the first two days of their being on offer. Just about every man and boy over 15 in such places worked in a shipyard, a steel mill or down a mine. The much fancied Italians would be playing there, as would rank outsiders North Korea. The tickets were selling at £4.14s, £4.70 in future money and no mean sum. You could move to Australia for £10. Australia House still placed large adverts in the papers telling you so and kids of my age travelled free. I had no plans in that direction but, what with my 7s 6d (37½p) a week pocket money I doubted I would be getting any match tickets either. My trips to the bookies would make sure of that.

Ramsey decreed that our task was to look to our immediate futures, by which he meant the game against West Germany at the end of February. The Germans would be a 'real test' for England. They had qualified for the summer finals and were the type of European team we were likely to run up against. To a certain extent this was true, but I could not see how the Germans constituted the test he claimed. Our history said we had never lost to the Germans in football or otherwise. England and Germany had first played each other in 1930 – a 3–3 draw in Berlin – and five times since. All those games we had won, the last being a 1–0 victory in Nuremberg only eight months ago.

As my family's wartime experiences testified, the Germans could be relied upon to get off to a quick start but a fatal flaw would be their undoing. Following the evacuation from Dunkirk my uncle Bim, aged 11, was convinced he would see German tanks on Sandy High Street the next morning. Instead they had turned their army towards Russia, imagining the Luftwaffe could bomb us into submission. Hence the upright piano was put against the basement window of number 7 each night for the eight months and more of aerial assault. My mum and my aunt Olive walked to their jobs in Old Street in the morning through the rubble and fire hoses on City Road. My granddad got them out to Sandy in November just as the bombers, heavily laden, flew in low over the sand hills for the raid on Coventry.

In my dad's case, from Tunis to Trieste he had followed the Germans' line of retreat, arriving in towns, sleeping in abandoned royal palaces and meaner bivouacs that had been vacated hours before. The German weak link in football, he told me, would be their goalkeeper. My dad knew this because that was the position he played. During the advance in Italy, he took part in army games on the baked surfaces of the main football arenas left abandoned by the war, from the old Olympic stadium in Rome to the Stadio Comunale in Florence. British goalkeepers were allowed to be spectacular, he said, but principally they were safe and universally accepted as the finest in the world. We had the right mentality, detached and disciplined, not flashy like the continental crowd. One thing that particularly annoyed him was that keepers from the Continent wore a number 1 on their back. I quite liked it. Everyone knew who the goalkeeper was, he told me firmly, and they did not need to advertise themselves other than by doing the job.

My early geography studies at school confirmed the keeper's role. The British stood apart, as the atlas showed. We were of the European team rather than in it. As needed, we came to sort out the problems of the Continent – such as its two 20th-century wars – like goalkeepers advancing from our lines. When, thanks to us, the danger cleared, we went back again. Then there were the vast areas of the empire shaded pink on the map that we were responsible for and which depended on us. We were both Europe's and the world's natural goalkeeper.

Such theory was all very well, but in practice things were not working out that way at Brisbane Road. While detachment was an essential of the goalkeeping make-up, you could do little to impress with your steely nerve under pressure when you were not seeing much action. By now too old for the juniors, my prospects of a regular place in the Colts were slim. Some of my squad mates were going on to apprentice contracts. A wage of £7 a week to scrub the toilets, terraces and senior players' boots, while hoping for the occasional game in the third team or reserves, was not much to hanker after. I would, nonetheless, have been open to the offer.

At the end of our training sessions, Eddie would make sure to get along to the dressing room as we arrived back at the stadium. We would hear his deliberate gait and steel-edged shoes heading towards us along the concrete corridor, perfectly timed as we slipped out of our gear and towards the communal bath. While we wallowed in the soapy scum – showers would only replace this dressing-room feature with the arrival of HIV in the 1980s – he sat on its raised edge, smiling and enjoying the de-briefing, as it were, of how training had gone.

In the course of things, the chat would turn to a series of violent incidents in the East End, with the prevailing view that these were the work of the Kray twins. Ronnie Kray held court in the Grave Maurice, a pub in Whitechapel Road opposite the London Hospital. His name had been linked with Lord Boothby, a Tory peer, who I had heard interviewed on television listing sex as among his main interests, a rare statement for the time. Not that this was publicly discussed, but Boothby, a large character, swung both ways. He had had a lengthy affair with the wife of the former Tory prime minister, Harold Macmillan. When Boothby was in other moods, Ronnie Kray procured East End boys for him.

The Krays' exploits appeared well known to some of the squad. Nearly all among us were East Enders, although several of the players' families had moved out from areas like Plaistow and Manor Park to Romford, Ilford and beyond to the Thames estuary. Johnny Eve, one of the newly signed-up apprentices, who had scored with a spectacular 30-yard drive in one of our otherwise ill-fated games against Tottenham, travelled in each day from Southend. Coming from Islington, I was a rare 'outsider' in the bath and contented myself with listening in. Some newspaper stories suggested that the twins' activities reached as far as Newington Green, more or less around the corner from my school.

In overseas news, an increasing amount of coverage was being given to the Vietnam War. *The Mirror* called it a 'barbarous mess' and said something should be done about it. As I had understood things, the Americans were fighting to maintain our freedom. Then again, the North Vietnamese leader, Ho Chi Minh, had once worked as a pastry chef in a London hotel and sounded less than threatening. Even the US troops, I had read, called him 'Uncle Ho'.

Just in mid-January a US B-52 bomber – the type the Americans used in Vietnam – had lost a hydrogen bomb on a training mission over southern Spain and would not find it again until Valentine's Day. The B-52 had collided with another plane and its bomb, fortunately not ready to detonate, had fallen into the Mediterranean. The US embassy sent some of its staff to swim in the sea, hoping to make the point that there would be no ill-effects on anyone in the area. Spain's beaches were preparing for the holiday season in a few months' time and the new phenomenon of a large influx of British tourists. *The Mirror* had forecast a 'Sunshine Stampede'. Six million Britons planned to book a holiday abroad this year, said the association of British travel agents. What did they mean by 'planned'? Maybe that number of people had just popped into the nation's tourist offices for a brochure. The Costa del Sol was 'so sunny that bananas and sugar grow there'. A fortnight in 'modern bustling' Torremolinos would cost £60. Cosmos advertised 11 days on the Costa Brava for 25½ guineas (a little under £27).

But, on the whole, Britons remained suspicious of 'abroad', with its strange food and policemen in dark glasses. On one of our annual drives through rural France, we had seen a gendarme peeing in the gutter. Although he had the decorum to swivel and aim at some bushes when he saw our car approaching, this was not a scene for the opening credits of *Dixon of Dock Green*. Tour operators felt they had found a way of cocooning travellers from such experiences: the 'package holiday'. Holidaymakers could be conveyed from home airport to foreign hotel, where they ate egg and chips and the beach was just across the road. Mates or friends of friends of mine had bummed around the Costas for the past couple of summers. Some had run out of money and were miserable when all you could do was sit on a beach and stare at the sea. Some had thieved to eke out another week or two. One was thrown out of Spain for indecent exposure – for doing on a beach what a French gendarme might do in the bushes – but tore the incriminating page out of his passport and returned again. Reports suggested that such freelance adventures were near their end and mass tourism was upon us.

In Britain, Vietnam had come to play a part in politics. The Labour party MP for the Yorkshire constituency of Hull North had died, leaving Harold Wilson's government in danger of having its Commons majority cut still further. The deceased MP had only won at the last election by a thousand votes and the loss of the seat in Hull, it was thought, might bring the government down altogether. An anti-Vietnam war candidate, Richard Gott, a *Guardian* journalist, put his name down for the by-election, reasoning that if he took a thousand votes from the Labour candidate then Labour would lose, the government fall and proper attention be drawn to the war in Vietnam. I did not know what *The Guardian* was until John Crowley, a kid in our sixth form who wore an embroidered waistcoat, played the drums and developed the aspiration of going to Cambridge, started to read it. He told me he especially enjoyed the columns of Michael Frayn. I nodded in fake recognition.

What I did know was that Hull's football team played at Boothferry Park, which was useful for rainy day sports quizzes when we couldn't go out in the playground. A similar sort of thing went for Grimsby, Hull's neighbour and fellow fishing port, whose team was the only one in the country without a stadium in its home town. (Grimsby played in Cleethorpes.) All I otherwise knew about such places was that they were a long way away. Hull City possibly went home from London by a train that left from King's Cross, but in my autograph days I had never seen them do so. Bound for a place stuck out by the mouth of the River Humber, its players may as easily have made the trip by Dogger Bank trawler.

This sort of idea engaged the minds of those taking part in the Hull by-election. Travelling up from London to seek votes, *The Guardian*'s man Gott felt he should have another issue in his campaign to add to Vietnam. He focused on Hull's remoteness; he called for a bridge across the Humber. Sensing danger, Wilson sent his transport minister, Barbara Castle, to the city, where she miraculously revealed her own plan for such a bridge. It would only cost £350 million. Labour's candidate won a much increased majority at the polls and Hull's voters – happily bribed – would eventually get their bridge.

Harold Wilson had addressed us just a few months earlier in November at a gathering of London sixth formers in Westminster Central Hall. The building was filled to its upper gallery roof – not only with sixth formers but with the expectation of what the prime minister might say of our futures. He had only uttered a sentence or two into the microphone when word was slipped into his ear of the Smith government's Unilateral Declaration of Independence – UDI – in Rhodesia. He promptly made his excuses, left and, with Parliament across the road, gave the impression that if he got there quickly he could end this problem straightaway. The chairman called for a show of hands condemning the Rhodesian government's illegal act. Negotiation out of empire was meant to be conducted with Westminster, and the white minority had refused to have black Africans in any post-independence government. We all complied with the chairman's request – all but the one arm among the many thousands that was raised in dissent. It belonged to a boy with red hair and glasses in our lower sixth named Farn who, someone said, had family in South Africa. With such tenuous support, the Smith regime in Salisbury (later Harare) lingered on for 15 years.

A lot of British ex-servicemen had gone off to the various bits of the empire after the war. An education at a minor public school and a junior officer's experience on the bridge of a ship in the Royal Navy was considered good background for growing sisal in Tanganyika and rubber in Malaya. In Africa, Kenyan coffee was an option; cattle and tobacco farming in Rhodesia were among the others. I heard that the officer class chose Kenya – or 'Keen-ee-ah!' as the commentator on the newsreel that we saw at the cinema called it before independence. The NCOs – ex-sergeant majors and similar – settled for Rhodesia. The whites insisted the blacks were happy and that the vote was not going to people who decided things, as Smith claimed, by 'the pointing of bones'.

Our regular *News of the World* took the Conservative line that Wilson needed to soften his approach towards the 'tragedy of Rhodesia'. He should not speak to Africa's 'violent black elements'. Among these it included Nigeria's leader, Sir Abubakar Tafawa Balewa, a Muslim teacher knighted by the Queen for his services to education. The syllables of his name we heard on the news frequently enough for the sixth form to learn off by heart. When Tafawa Balewa was killed in a military coup in Nigeria, this was used as an example of how post-independence Africa was such a mess that the white Rhodesians deserved to have their way.

'Smith's got a point,' said Tim Lane, during one school break-time discussion in our upper-floor room. He was the only one of us who had got all eight O-levels and had also passed his driving test first time. Bobby Blake from Jamaica, our single West Indian sixth former, bluntly dismissed the view and said the British had run the empire in the interests of 'exploitation'. This was a shock. The word was exclusively employed in my experience by trade union leaders when calling for higher wages. It was part of the vocabulary of Frank Cousins, the former head of the Transport and General Workers' Union, who Wilson had taken into his cabinet as minister of technology. I had not heard it in a colonial sense, least of all applied to us. The Belgians in the Congo, yes, but we didn't 'exploit', surely? Nonetheless, it usually took a lot to make Bobby angry.

When West Germany came to play at Wembley towards the end of February, the crowd turned their anger on the England team. Ramsey appeared confused in his team selection. He gave Geoff Hurst his international debut as striker but not the number 9 shirt that went with it. He handed that to Nobby Stiles, who played at the back of defence. Things became no clearer during the game. Hurst arrived either too early or too late for balls played through for him, while Stiles scored the only goal, a scrambled effort from about a yard. What with Moore scoring against the Poles and now Stiles in this game, the wrong people were getting on the score-sheet. Unreasonably, the Germans were not. They had what looked like a good equaliser disallowed and the home crowd of 80,000 booed. Ramsey complained that the fans were being very unfair.

Wilson called an election a few days later. Cheered by the Hull result, he sought a 'mandate' from the people, he said. Bobby, the keenest student of British civics among us, knew what this meant. I looked it up in my dad's Funk & Wagnalls: an 'authorisation to act'. Wilson had had enough of slim majorities in the Commons and wanted one he could work with. He fixed the election date for 31 March. The result would be known on April Fools' Day.

Government, regardless, carried on. 'Decimalisation' was to happen in five years' time. How much of the arithmetic we had learned at primary school would become useless we did not know. If 12 pence to the shilling was to be abolished, what of the length of ten cricket pitches making a furlong in horse racing? Colour television was to come in a year – too late for the World Cup; we would still have to watch the yellow and blue finery of Brazil in black, white and shades of grey. Did we need it? For millions of people late-night snooker on TV was as exciting as sex. You imagined your own colour.

Lord Willis, a Labour peer and television screenwriter who had created *Dixon of Dock Green*, said in March he would introduce a bill to 'brighten our Sundays'. Present laws, some going back 500 years, dictated that people should not do anything entertaining or profitable on Sundays, the idea being to steer them towards church. The laws were often ignored but it was always open to someone to ask the courts to enforce them. Sunday sport had been banned since the 1600s. Willis's idea was to get more people enjoying themselves with sport, theatre, cinema and, eventually, even shopping.

Watched over by the Lord's Day Observance Society, sabbaths were drab. In the mornings, I usually came back from the Polish newsagent's with the *News of the World*, *People* and *Sunday Mirror*, which we had on order. If my uncle Keith had been working on the Fleet Street vans, he might have put a spare copy of one of them through the door, which meant cancelling from the newsagent. He would grumble about how he couldn't sell an extra newspaper at this late stage of day (it would be about 9.30 a.m.). After poring over the football results and reports for an hour or so, there was only homework to fill up the time until *Round the Horne* at 2 p.m. This had slipped into the radio schedules at the end of the fifties under the innocent title of *Beyond Our Ken*. Kenneth Horne, who spoke perfectly BBC, was its lead voice, acting as a foil to those of Kenneth Williams, Betty Marsden and Hugh Paddick. Marty Feldman and Barry Took wrote the script. The programme had recently changed its name to *Round the Horne*, which may or may not have been innuendo in keeping with the liberalising times. Williams in particular would 'camp it up' – a term most of us only then learned – for the half-hour, speaking Polari and giving Horne the verbal runaround: 'Oh, ain't 'e bold?' he would say. 'How nice to vada your dolly old eek again.'

Some said Polari borrowed from the ancient language of strolling Romany players and circus workers, others that it was how people in the theatre world spoke. Williams probably made a lot of it up himself. 'Bona' was good, 'lallies' meant legs and 'eek' your face, neither of the latter two for any obvious reason. An 'omi' was a man and a 'polone' a woman. An 'omi-polone' was a homosexual. 'Gay' was not used in this context until the 1970s. Williams was homosexual but few people would say so, least of all him. With homosexuality illegal, no one round my way wanted to talk or know about it. It was frightening wondering if you might be 'that way'. Each week a few sixth-form girls came from Highbury Hill school up the road to use the physics lab and, as they walked through the playground, I was able to decide that I was not. A girl known as Bennie played a leading role in this. I had dropped science in the fourth year and, alas, never spoke to her.

On *Round the Horne*, Williams was the first person to put one particular bit of Islington on the map. The Balls Pond Road, which ran from Essex Road to its rougher extent at Dalston Junction, caught his attention and the lurid way he said it brought a laugh each time. Denis Parsons, who left school at around O-levels, had a Saturday job for much of his Highbury career in a shoe-repair and keys-cut shop at the road's Dalston end.

Years later I read that Williams had been to our street. This was to visit the two men in the house six doors along. One was eventually to have his diaries published and wrote that following Williams' visit, he had walked with him down Pentonville Hill, along Euston Road and as far as Williams' flat near Baker Street. On a Sunday evening, he had time to kill and spent it telling Williams that he himself should be bold and openly admit he was homosexual. All I knew of the two men in the street was that they had been put in jail in 1962 for defacing Islington council library books. Williams, proudly self-educated, attributed much of what he knew and his success as an actor to sessions he had spent as a child in his local public library.

Lord Willis worried that his Sunday idea might be seen as too continental and put people off. Yet even in Ireland, which was still run by the ancient Éamon de Valera and the Church, people had a good time on Sundays. The Republic played its football then. Northern Ireland, as directed by the Protestant church, turned out on Saturday. Some footballers, of ambiguous cross-border heritage, had managed to represent both south and north on the same weekend. Johnny Carey, formerly of Manchester United and Orient's manager when they had won promotion, had during his playing days.

On 8 March, a Tuesday, I went training as usual at Brisbane Road. I wouldn't have known but at the same time there was what the police called 'an affray' at Mr Smith's, a nightclub in Catford, south London. One person was killed and several injured in a territorial clash between rival gangs. One was from south London and the other from the East End. For my part, I was still failing to spot the signs of pending trouble. Standing in the doggies' line imitating Kenneth Williams speaking Polari was never going to be an East End vote winner, certainly not with Harry. He ordered me back to the dressing room for an early bath. By the time I went to Eddie's office to get my expenses, Harry had already reported in. 'OK, Pete, you needn't come back,' said Eddie. 'OK, Ed,' I answered casually. I told my parents later that I was fed up with the place and had decided not to go again.

George Cornell's mistake the following evening was to drop in for a drink at the Blind Beggar on Whitechapel Road. He had visited a friend in the London Hospital who had been shot the night before in the Catford affray. As an old member of the Kray gang who had defected to their rivals, the Richardsons in south London, Cornell's presence was a provocation. Never being one to be scared of the Krays, he had also once referred to Ronnie's penchant for teenage boys by way of calling him a 'fat poof'. Ronnie heard in the Grave Maurice that Cornell was no more than 200 yards away and, needing no one to speak on his behalf for homosexual rights or requiring any mandate but his own, made his way to the Blind Beggar. In the public bar, Cornell nonchalantly lifted his pint glass to his mouth and said, 'Well, look who it ain't.' Ronnie shot him through the head.

Whether along the Whitechapel or Brisbane Road, the message to those who failed to take the ways of the East End seriously was clear. Delivered differently, it came down to the same thing: 'Fuck off. This is our manor.'

# Chapter 5

# SHOULD OLD ACQUAINTANCE . . .

Thieves stole into the Methodist Central Hall in Westminster on 20 March 1966 as deftly as Harold Wilson had slipped off the premises those few months earlier on hearing news of Rhodesia's UDI. The World Cup had gone on show there and disappeared, on a Sunday, with the building open for normal business. 'Raiders strike during hymn service,' said *The Mirror*: HUNT FOR THIN MAN. More than one person was involved and the thieves had 'sneaked into the building among the throngs of worshippers'. The Cup was in a hall on the floor below where the service was held. From their headquarters at Scotland Yard – all of 150 yards away by Westminster Bridge – the police were hunting for a man of thin build and of about five feet ten. This narrowed things down a bit. On the diet of the day, most people were thin; five feet ten, however, was tall for the time. The police revealed another distinguishing feature of the person who they believed could help with their inquiries. He had a scar on his face.

Methodists were known for a number of things: a simple way with religion and no great liking of the established church; an active role in setting up trade unions, hence when my granddad spoke of his time at the *News of the World* he had mentioned the person in charge of the union there being the 'Father of the Chapel'. Football was not a Methodist strong point. In the 18th century John Wesley regularly turned out on a Sunday at Bunhill Fields just down City Road from us, but this was to sing and preach. His mission was across the road.

The World Cup had been on display in the hall not in its own right but as an adjunct to a stamp exhibition. In times when everyone was expected to 'have a hobby' stamp collecting and football enjoyed comparable popular appeal as pastimes pursued almost exclusively by boys and men. Stamp collecting was thought the more mind-enriching. It had royal approval. The late King George V – the Queen's grandfather – found an escape from ruling a global empire by spending several afternoons a week perched over his stamp albums. As long ago as 1904, he had bought a two-penny – or 'tuppenny' – Mauritius for the enormous sum of £1,450. He could have bought half a Barnsbury street for that. Stanley Gibbons, the stamp collection company with offices down the Strand, had organised the exhibition. I was aware of Stanley Gibbons. They were one of the stamp companies that sent out packs of stamps to junior collectors 'on approval'. At the age of eight, you were hardly expected to know what that meant and that a charge might be involved. I certainly 'approved' of receiving the stamps out of the blue and duly stuck them in my album. My mum, hearing from me by chance of this, instructed me to unhinge them and send them straight back, in an unstamped envelope. Thus the postman would make Gibbons pay double on delivery. It was the best penalty she could think of for this bit of dubious selling.

The police said they were 'baffled' by the theft. Some reports estimated the trophy's value at £3,000, but that was incorrect. It was not the solid gold they said it was and was actually silver plated with gold and on a base of something called lapis lazuli. If melted down by the man in the mews at the top of Frome Street, who you could take scrap metal to round our way, it would have fetched less than £2,000. Joey Pattman's dad just along in Allingham Street would have no doubt matched that price; Joey had been at primary school with me and his dad spent the afternoon in Droy's the bookies in St Peter's Street. Why, wondered the police, given such a low value object, would thieves have ignored collections of stamps in the hall that were worth millions and gone for the World Cup instead?

Any of us could have told the police that any man with a scar on his face was unlikely to have been the least bit interested in stamps. They did not attract that kind of person. The kids at our school who collected stamps stood around talking about them in the playground. At home, they combed through catalogues, used tweezers to lift their collection with care, and stared at stamps through magnifying glasses to determine whether an irregular perforation qualified them as rare and of enormous value. None of them played games for the school or went in for anything rough and tumble enough to cause them facial disfigurement.

I had collected stamps for a couple of years or so and filled umpteen pages with the offerings of Hungary and San Marino. It also proved useful in developing a fascination for exotic place names. 'Nicaragua', whose page remained stubbornly empty in my album, I was unable to read or pronounce until I worked there nearly 20 years later. I discovered then that it did not enjoy a well-organised postal system, one – among many – of the reasons why the especially nasty dictator it had at the time was overthrown. I gave up stamp collecting when I was 11.

But then there was the question of the World Cup's symbolic value. Why had the Football Association lent the World Cup to a stamp collecting company? Joe Mears, the present head of the FA, and also the chairman of Chelsea, said he had no idea the trophy was anywhere but under lock and key in FA headquarters in Lancaster Gate. He would not have allowed it to leave the building had he been asked. The culprit was Sir Stanley Rous, ex-chief of the FA and now head of Fifa. A former Watford grammar school teacher, he had given permission for the Cup to go to the exhibition, possibly seeing it as a way of winning respectability for the game. He was out of contact on a trip to the US and apparently had no idea of the weight of international feeling among other football playing countries at the theft. The head of the football association in Italy, holders of the World Cup during the Second World War, had hidden the Jules Rimet trophy from the Nazis in a box under his bed. Uruguay, otherwise known for Fray Bentos tinned steak and kidney pie, had won the World Cup twice to enormous international acclaim. They and others were said to be furious. The Brazilians, of course, had been looking to claim it as their own come the summer.

English football, on the other hand, had never taken the World Cup seriously. Its creator, Jules Rimet, was a French humanist who believed football could unite the world. The British took offence at him thinking so about a game they had created. The World Cup had first kicked off in 1930, with England not entering until 1950, the fourth time it was staged. The Scots, snootier still, did not join in until 1954. The tournament had become more important now that England was to host it, but not so much so as to deter a decision to lend the trophy to people who traded in things you stuck on envelopes. The people in charge of the game in England were behind their time. The thin and scarred characters who sneaked into the Central Methodist Hall were, relatively speaking, men of vision.

Coming into the spring, England and Scotland were lining up for their towards-the-end-of-season grudge match. Not long ago, this was regarded as the game that annually decided who the real world champions of football were. The first international football match staged had taken place between Scotland and England in 1872 in Glasgow and ended 0–0. In matches won, the honours had more or less been evenly shared since. Scots players like Denis Law of Manchester United, Jim Baxter of Glasgow Rangers and Dave Mackay of Spurs were among the finest in Britain and the world. The next encounter was to be at Hampden Park, Glasgow, on 2 April. Given that most members of both teams played alongside each other in the English league, the game would not indicate much about England chances against continental or Latin opposition in the summer. At stake were pride and morale. England had not beaten the Scots in the last four matches: not since a Jimmy

Greaves hat-trick and a 9–3 victory at Wembley in 1961. On that day, injuries had forced the Scots to play with their third-choice keeper, Frank Haffey of Celtic and, as Haffey's defence gaped open in front of him, Greaves strolled through. The Scots had put that behind them. When the teams next met at Wembley, three years ago in 1963, Baxter had scored both goals in a 2–1 victory for Scotland.

Following that match I had been the one kid in London who knew where the Scots' team was going to be. When my parents were not around to query the extravagance, I had called, via the operator, the Scottish FA in Glasgow to ask which hotel the players would be staying at. The friendly voice who answered the phone said he had no word on that but did know they would be having a drink after the game: at the St Ermin's Hotel in Westminster. I was surprised and had the feeling that if I had phoned the FA in Lancaster Gate asking for similar information, I'd have been told to piss off.

The friendliness extended into the hotel itself. After the players' coach arrived on the forecourt, I strolled in with Mackay, Law and the rest anticipating that the doorman was going to hoof me out. They let me join them at the bar as they celebrated and signed everything I put in front of them. Law had me run a message, scrawled on hotel notepaper and stuffed in an envelope, to John White of Tottenham across the other side of the room. I did not see what he wrote but it was probably some friendly insult. White answered with a scribbled note of his own.

A month later, Law opened the scoring for Manchester United in their 3–1 Cup final victory over Leicester City, United's first trophy since the Munich air crash five years earlier. A few weeks into the summer, White, aged 27 and the inspiration of the Spurs' forward line in the Double-winning team, was killed by lightning on an Enfield golf course. One among the Scots players who seemed shyly detached from the fairly typical footballers' fun in the hotel bar had been Baxter, the goalscoring match-winner. He signed but did not answer when I congratulated him on the victory. Baxter still had some way to go in a sometimes brilliant career, and then would have no idea what to do once his football days were over. Eventually, he drank himself to death on the streets of Glasgow.

The imminent World Cup gave the 1966 international an extra edge. The Scots had not qualified and there was a sense of England leaving them behind – albeit as hosts England had not had to qualify themselves. Players like Law and Scottish managers such as Chelsea's Tommy Docherty forecast that England stood no chance of winning the competition. English supporters agreed, while objecting to the Scots saying so. Docherty's views rubbed off on one of his emerging talents, Peter Osgood. Although an apparent England star in the making, Osgood aired opinions on TV about England's chances that were far closer to Docherty's than Ramsey's. Ramsey never forgave him for shouting his mouth off and, in what could have been a rich international career, Osgood only went on to play for England four times.

Ramsey straddled both old and new camps. He was from the days when the England v Scotland game was the international highlight of the season but he was also deadly serious about the World Cup. He worried the football establishment with his seriousness. When he had taken over he demanded that the FA hand him full powers as manager, which principally meant the right to choose his players. Previously teams had chopped and changed in the hands of a board of selectors. A group of elderly men, some of them club chairmen, chose the team with the aim of getting in as many players from their own clubs as possible. Ramsey insisted that the line-up for any match would be his. Now that he turned his mind to immediate business, the Glasgow game was not one he was taking lightly. He had 'the opinion of a dissatisfied, disbelieving public piling up against him,' wrote Ken Jones.

The headlines were promptly stolen again by the World Cup. Early on the Sunday evening a week after the trophy had gone missing, a man and his dog had found it while about to go for their evening walk together. The reports would vary as to whether this was in a hedge, under a tree or by the wheel of a parked car, but the discovery was made in Beulah Hill in Norwood, south-east London, one of those places north Londoners had never heard of. The dog, Pickles, a black and white mongrel, sniffed out the trophy, which was wrapped in brown paper.

His owner, David Corbett, was a Thames lighterman who worked on barges that carried goods from ship to shore in the docks of the port of London. Lightermen read the tides of the river, and West Ham's Martin Peters came from a lighterman family, so I learned. Ramsey would say Peters was one of the best readers of the game ever: 'ten years before his time'. By chance he dropped my pen when I got his autograph once but, lifting his foot, caught it on his instep: 'See that?' he said.

Lightermen were in one of the dying trades of late-imperial London. At primary school in the 1950s, we had still been taught that the Pool of London – the area from London

Bridge to around Limehouse – was the largest port in the world. More lately we heard dismaying word that the title had gone to such minor names on the map as Antwerp, Rotterdam or even Yokohama.

Corbett had hastened in his carpet slippers to hand in the trophy at Gipsy Hill police station and fell under immediate suspicion. He was held until 2 a.m. convincing the police that he had nothing to do with those who had stolen it. The suspicion lingered that the object he handed in was a fake and the real World Cup had been melted down. The FA had a reproduction crafted while the search for the trophy was going on, which did not help alleviate the suspicions that the original had disappeared for ever. For the theft, the police arrested an ex-serviceman, who had fought in North Africa and Italy during the war and since fallen on hard times. I saw no mention of how thin he was or whether he had a scar.

Joe Mears of the FA put in a claim for the reward, having helped the police attempt to set up a meeting with the thief, or thieves, during the hunt for the trophy. But the press ran reports that Mears lived in a £15,000 house in Fulham and so was rich enough. He withdrew his claim, suffering stress and angina. Corbett received a reward of £3,000, to which he added £100 that he had saved himself and bought a house in Lingfield, not far from the racecourse in suburban Surrey. Mears was to die in late June, days before the World Cup began. Pickles had a briefly star-lit career. He won a year's supply of Spillers dog biscuits and a role in the film *The Spy with a Cold Nose* with comedians Eric Sykes and June Whitfield. He died in May 1967, having escaped from his master and chased a cat up a tree. He had his lead on and was found hanging from the branches.

For myself, I was caught by a picture of Pickles in *The Mirror* only a few days after he had found the World Cup. He was at a reception at the Royal Garden Hotel in Kensington where the National Canine Defence League awarded him a silver medal for giving 'prominence to the canine world'. He appeared to be yawning, which was little wonder. Next to the report of his medal was a far more interesting story.

The members of a north London gang known as Little Highbury had been found guilty of stabbing and slashing a 14-year-old boy in Stoke Newington. He was walking home from synagogue. The gang members were aged 15 and a 'contemptible bunch', said the judge. He sent most of them to detention centre for sentences of three to six months and put the others on probation. If you were one of Little Highbury you aspired to graduate to Big Highbury. One night between them, they had run amok, slashing the faces of a group of Streatham kids at the Chez Don club in Kingsland Road. It stood above Burton's the tailors. Having heard the music was good, the victims had had the audacity to come from south London. Several of the Little Highbury bunch still went to Barnsbury. 'What about discipline?' my mum had said and, when you thought about it, she had a point. This was the type who would soon be coming to our school.

Whether on the subject of comprehensive education or other matters of electoral debate, however, the news was progressively dominated by the national polls due at the end of March. Harold Wilson had set off in search of his mandate, conspicuously turning up the collar of his mac as he did so. He was more aware of what he looked like than previous prime ministers and in this election 'image' was the coming thing.

I had noticed that whenever Wilson saw a TV camera he lit his pipe. Pipe smoking spoke of wisdom beyond cigarettes; pipe smokers were likely to be thoughtful and meditative people. They indulged in 'ready rubbed shag' rather than Weights and Woodbines and tapped out their dead tobacco tidily into an ashtray, or from the heel of their shoe into the gutter. Cigarette smokers threw their dog ends in the street.

Postmaster General Wedgwood Benn sucked on his pipe as he spoke of a pending special issue of stamps for the World Cup. In the months before the tournament this was the only sign that the government had noticed the event was coming. Jimmy Greaves was photographed smoking his pipe with a cheeky smile on his face, reinforcing his image as the artful dodger of England's forward line.

Wilson's mac was a Gannex. The prime minister wore his mostly in beige and not quite buttoned to the top. The coat opened at the neck to reveal a darker inner material, often a tartan. Wilson had worn one for a number of years yet now captured the spirit of the times in being seen as a bit of a sixties' trendsetter. Wearers ranged from LBJ in the US to Mao Tse-tung in China. The Queen and Prince Philip were seen in the Gannex, as was Roger Moore of the Sunday night TV series *The Saint* and a future James Bond.

The mac was designed and manufactured by Joseph Kagan, a friend of Wilson's with a factory in Yorkshire. No saint around our street, he was well known as a Friday night visitor who did not leave again until Monday morning. He was, in my mother terms, 'carrying on' with a tabloid journalist far younger than he was and with whom he had a child. She lived further down the street on the canal side. By now the waterway had been tamed and the borough rat catcher called in. Kagan would arrive for the weekend in his Jaguar, carrying bundles of French bread and bottles of wine. He left his wife of longstanding up north minding the factory.

Somewhere between the World Cup in Chile in 1962 and the pending 1966 tournament, Noel Road had become clogged with vehicles day and night. At the same time, while Kagan had encouraged his friend the prime minister to worry about image, it was not something that bothered him. He roughly parked his Jaguar in whatever half spot he could find, charging front and back into the cars of others. My uncle Keith queried this method of winning local friends and influencing people, to which Kagan gave a dismissive wave and snarl as he made off for his mistress's place.

Years later, I discovered he had survived persecution by the Nazis in Lithuania and Romania so was not likely to be fazed by a few local questions about his parking habits. As it turned out, he was also under observation by the British intelligence services. Along with Robert Maxwell, the publisher and Labour MP, Kagan was one of Wilson's friends of east European descent that MI5 and MI6 objected to the prime minister having. We were used to neighbours who attracted the attentions of the police station opposite the old Co-op in Upper Street but would have been alarmed to know that we had perceived enemies of the state among us. Wilson was made aware of the intelligence services' suspicions long before we were and came to believe they were out to get him.

For the general election, Wilson's efforts were paying off. He was up against Edward Heath, the new leader of the Conservative party, which was also turning its mind to image matters but lagging behind. The Tories had said the public persona of their previous leader Sir Alec Douglas Home was 'appalling'. Sir Alec was a shy Scottish earl and the Conservatives emphasised that Heath was not aristocratic. His father had been a carpenter who had gone on to enjoy business success, but this hardly made him a man of the people, noted *The Mirror*. Heath's earnest features, it said, were 'unscarred by the battle of life'. Heath was a bachelor. No public inference was drawn from that on his sexual preferences, other than a vague sense that he was not interested one way or the other. He could have no understanding of the economic struggles of a typical family, some critics said, which was as near as anyone publicly came to the subject. Heath played the church organ and went sailing a lot. From such 'hobbies', it followed that he spoke plummily middle class, yet he could have usefully employed Alf Ramsey's elocution teacher. With Heath, 'now' and 'how' came out as 'neeow' and 'heeow'. But *The Mirror*'s claim that he had never uttered a statement that anyone could remember was nonsense. I recalled that three years or so earlier when the Beatles had hit one of their early peaks, Heath said they did not speak 'the Queen's English'. He would still have time for people to forget that kind of statement given that the voting age would not be lowered from 21 to 18 until the election after this one.

Nonetheless, we were being drawn in. The headmaster of a secondary modern school in Cromer in Norfolk had caned two brothers for putting party political stickers on their bicycles. The boys, aged 15 and 13, supported the Labour party, and their head gave them three strokes of the cane across the hands. Norfolk aimed to 'keep education out of politics', said its education authority. With Little Highbury in mind, you could surely have found more grievous offences at a secondary modern to beat someone for but a place like Norfolk set different norms.

I had been to Cromer with my parents, invited by a couple, Connie and Charlie, who were good friends of theirs and old Islingtonians from near Packington Street. Connie, who worked with my mum at the Noel Road corner print factory, was the only woman any of us knew who liked football and had first taken me to see Arsenal in the late 1950s. Behind the Clock End goal, the crowd around us stayed protective and respectful, on one occasion during a Blackburn Rovers visit calling out to opposition players in the goalmouth to stop swearing because 'can't you see there's women and children here?'. Charlie had been evacuated during the war to Cromer, where adults sat around eating a lot of freshly caught mackerel. I absented myself to play pitch-and-putt in a gale on the seafront, unable to manage the bones.

In Islington, corporal punishment was a living theme. Risinghill school, in the street-fighting areas at the top of Chapel Market, had banned it some years earlier. Against a background of attacks from the papers that the school was collapsing into chaos, Risinghill had shut a few months ago. At Highbury, Reggie King had beaten us with the cane or the gym slipper depending on his mood or the gravity of offence. Others had different ways. One of the games masters leathered me around the face with his hand for bringing in my swimming gear on a gym day. From Reggie, I got three of the cane for not attending choir practice, a crime that hardly qualified me as public enemy number one. The stripes across my backside stayed visible in the Wadham Lodge showers for at least a couple of school games. The more galling was that membership of the choir was voluntary and I was only in it because my mother insisted that I do some school activity unrelated to sport. No one, as far as I knew, reported back on getting the cane to their parents. From stricter times, they would – we suspected – have said 'serves you right'.

Reggie reserved another punishment for younger boys. His heavy five o'clock shadow appeared by midday, and any pre-pubescent youth committing a minor misdemeanour, like yawning in class, was likely to have him grip them by the chin and back of the head and wipe his beard across both sides of their face. It took until five years after leaving school, when discussing Reggie with another of his ex-pupils, before this struck me as weird and, later still, that his career at another time might have ended in court.

As it happened, his undoing had come in his effort to beat back the sixties. He gave eight of the cane to the ringleader of a shoplifting trio, who had gone about their work in Woolworths during a school trip to Portsmouth. Other members of the class had given them their shoplifting lists, when all concerned were meant to be paying a patriotic visit to HMS *Victory*. This was in 1961 and punishment was doled out before an assembly of the whole school, female teachers included, with the Portsmouth Three having to drop their trousers to half mast. The accomplices received the normal six-stroke maximum and their leader his two extra. Reggie – grey-faced now – took a run-up of several steps to deliver each blow.

The next year, he had more or less had to give up. Two fourth years stole a consignment of cigarettes from a factory in Highbury Barn and had been seen selling them in the main playground. With the proceeds, they ran off to Ireland. In tones of total non-comprehension as to what was happening around him, he reported this to us at morning assembly and that the matter was now in the Irish police's hands, not his. Even before his resignation over the comprehensive question, Reggie was a broken man.

By contrast, Wilson strode on and had drawn far ahead in the public opinion polls. This was not intelligence I picked up from the newspapers, radio or TV so much as from Droy's the St Peter's Street bookies. Opposite Cluse Court, it was well placed to attract the custom of a large part of the male and to some extent female population of the large double block of council flats. One of the kids of about my age who spent as much time in Droy's as I did, asked me who I thought should win the election. Out of family allegiance, I said the Conservatives, to which his face twisted: 'Nah, Wilson'll win easy,' he said. ''E's in it for his fucking self, that 'Eaff.'

I assumed he had got this from his family but, when I thought about it, my own opinions were if anything more flimsily based. A decade and more ago, during what may have been the 1955 election, my granddad and uncle Keith had asked me who I thought would win it and when it was clear I had no idea, my uncle said, 'What's your favourite colour?' Blue was apparently Conservative and I had not reviewed the question since.

# Chapter 6

# LAST RUN OF THE MODS

The election fell in Grand National week, as did an unusual amount of snow. At school, Pete Francis kept the political kettle boiling as he argued tirelessly for Labour. Pete was a Tottenham supporter who came from near the Angel, hence was unusual. South of Islington tended to be Arsenal, and north of Seven Sisters Road more Tottenham. I was grateful to him because he had arrived in our first year, from Copenhagen Street primary school, as a very good goalkeeper but quickly decided to play up the field. This had given me an easy run into the school team. As for politics, he said steel nationalisation was a question of 'Clause 4' and taking control of the 'means of production'. I understood each word he used without having any grasp of what he said.

Martin Grossman, the one Jewish kid in the upper sixth, was our sole voice for the Liberals. They had won four seats in 1964, gained several million votes in the process and were pushing to recapture some of the glory of the Lloyd George days. One of their MPs in the West Country, Jeremy Thorpe, had campaigned for the '64 elections using 'cavalcades'. These amounted to two or three cars covered in party posters rolling in line through outposts from Barnstaple to Bodmin, with Thorpe speaking to people by way of a loudhailer. BBC reporters styled this 'Kennedy-like' razzamatazz.

I knew just two of my family voted anything but Tory. They were the only ones who really ever discussed politics: Aunt Laura, who after working in service had voted Liberal or Labour at different times, and Uncle Bim. As the youngest of my dad's brothers, he had sat around with me watching Cup finals on TV and discussing horse-racing results. I had also seen him play for Sandy Albion and, in all, his was an opinion I valued. At the time of the '64 election he had told me public services were not meant to make a profit; that was why they were public services. Having served during the Korean War in Hong Kong, he also felt it was time that we were out of such places.

The election issues were many: prices and incomes was one. Beer and bread had gone up by a penny on the pint and loaf – rises of about 5% and 7% respectively. Wilson aimed to keep wages down, but prices were getting more expensive. There was also the matter of whether we could afford the cost of a battleship any more, now that we did not need so many of them. What was our place in the world now that it was not what it used to be?

'Come off it, Wilson,' scolded *The Mirror*. It was time for him to stop telling the Europeans how hard we were going to bargain if they wanted us to come into Europe. Let's have less of the nonsense, said the paper, about how we would maintain our ancient trading links with the Commonwealth, as nice as it was to get our lamb and butter from New Zealand. Cutely stamped with a fern leaf, it felt like it might have come from fields and farms scarcely beyond London but was actually shipped from a world away.

Otherwise Europe did not feature much as a debating point. The one person who mentioned it was Mosley, the old fascist, and then only to tell us on TV that he was a 'European'. He had been exiled there during the years since the war, so why wouldn't he be? He came back to run in the election for the seat in Shoreditch. This was somewhere east of the Old Street roundabout but I couldn't place it. My dad had worked there when I was little, building a council block opposite the Geffrye Museum. He claimed to have broken the bricklaying world record after a lorry dumped a load of muck – mixed sand and cement – at his feet with only an hour of the working day left. If he had not laid the bricks to clear it, it would have set by the following morning. He liked the site because he could get home quickly in the evening.

A couple of kids, Tom Newby and Alan Foster, came from around there and called it Hoxton, with the aitch always silent. My great grandma on my mum's side, who died just before I was born, had settled there when she migrated from Somerset in the late 19th century. At the time it was said that if the police could throw a rope around Hoxton, they could contain the worst criminals in London. The music hall there they called the 'Sod's Opera'. She had quickly moved on to build her life from Exmouth Market, which was salubrious by comparison.

Tommy had left school at 15, the earliest time allowed. Alan I was friendly with in the first year, and the day off the

Queen gave us for Princess Margaret's wedding in 1960 we spent ambling around Dalston. Briefly a star for both the football and cricket teams, he lapsed into sullen moods and picked fights with the wrong people. Jimmy Dunkley sorted him out early on in the Highbury playground but he never really learned. In our fifth year, Barnsbury turned up in force to beat him up outside the gates for some offence he had caused one of them.

Wilson's major theme for years now had been the 'Balance of Payments'. To my knowledge, until he came along we had never heard of it. The Conservatives, when in office, used terms like 'retail price maintenance' at Budget time just to show that they were the people who knew about money. I suspected my granddad supported them for this reason, though he never disclosed which way he voted to me. But a few days later, they would drop the clever stuff, wary of showing off their education too much in front of ordinary folk. Not so with Wilson. He had 'made it' from a lowly background in Yorkshire to become an Oxford don – in economics, so it was said – and was going to let us know about it. Arcane terms were his stock in trade. 'Redeployment' was another one, which was apparently what we would have to do at some stage in the future to find a job; it meant 'move to other parts of the country'.

The Balance of Payments problem amounted to our not having very many colonies any more. They had provided the markets of old to sell our goods to: buses, cars, aeroplanes. Not long ago, like everything else we made and did, our goods were the 'finest in the world'. Now, suddenly, not enough people abroad wanted them. The problem was made worse by our buying too many things from other countries, like Japanese motorbikes and German cars. Older people said it made you wonder who had 'won the bloody war'. Each month the news reported the disastrous trade figures, only to have us sigh with relief as we were saved by the 'invisibles'. These were things like banking receipts and insurance abroad fixed by the City of London. The sense on the news was of 'thank god for the gents in the bowler hats' but the City, just to the south of Islington, was a ghost town most times I went through it. It was dead before 9.30, after 5, at weekends and during Ascot week, but we weren't to worry about that because these people just did magic you couldn't see.

Wilson's critics in his own party advised him to shut up. Brian Walden, the talkative MP for Birmingham Ladywood, said his leader was making too much of the Balance of Payments. The Conservatives had stayed quiet about it during the 13 years that they had been in power up to 1964 and Walden believed Wilson should speak about the good things. Everyone was in work, for a start, at least all men of employable age were, as the official figures showed.

The prime minister could not be deterred. Labour had come to power with great plans for science, computers and automated factories, but Wilson seemed determined to look back rather than forwards. His message was that we had to dig in. After years of retreat, and through our economic crises, we could yet recapture our glories if we summoned up our 'Dunkirk Spirit'. By this he meant the grit and determination that had seen the older generations through the bleak early years of the war. Those of us who had not been around at that time were assumed to have had this passed on, if not through our mother's milk then that provided by the NHS in powdered form.

My classmates and I guffawed at the thought. Things had been looking up for a while. Once the Cuban missile crisis had eased tension in 1962, we had been able to concentrate on such debates as whether, of the main Liverpool groups on offer, the Beatles or the Searchers would last longest. The Searchers had faded when they ran out of Jackie DeShannon songs to cover. In the West End, Carnaby Street was flourishing. It was pricey but there was the alternative of the army surplus store in Upper Street, by Camden Passage, that did imported Levi's which we shrank and bleached in the bath. Labour wanted us to stop all this and be miserable again.

At Aintree the going was soft in the approach to the National and Sandy Abbot – Johnny Lehane onboard – proved a good each way in the Topham. The horse came third at 100/8 and, at one quarter the odds for a place, returned a decent profit on my five shilling stake. A good numerate education was to be had at the bookies, while the price they exacted could have got you to Eton and Harrow. With my winnings, I made my way to St Pancras for the trip to Bedford and evening training at Bedford Town, the semi-professional football club in the Midland League.

My uncle Geoff and aunt Laura's Saturday nights at their local working men's club brought them into regular touch with one of Bedford's coaches, Joe Campbell, a bluff Scotsman, and they had told him I was a sharp prospect. Since the Midland League was not one of the four main divisions, Bedford were officially a 'non league' club. But they aimed to win admission to the league proper, using their strong tradition of giant-killing in the FA Cup as credentials. As my aunt and uncle reminded me, Bedford Town had nearly beaten Arsenal in the 1955–56 competition, drawing at Highbury and going down unluckily at home. This season they had eliminated two league clubs – Exeter and Brighton – on their way to the fourth round where they met Everton of the first division.

Bedford had been drawn to play at home which, with the match televised, enabled them to show off their stadium. Nicknamed the Eagles, the club played at the Eyrie; it held 18,000 fans, was next to the station and as well appointed as Brisbane Road. But Everton told Bedford to keep the cameras away. TV was not good for the game, said the Liverpool club, which had behind it the Moores' family millions made from running the football pools. One of Bedford's semi-pros had been an apprentice toolmaker to my uncle. Bedford told Everton to stuff it and welcomed the cameras. Everton, 3–0 winners, would progress to the Cup final. With the publicity, Bedford Town had the consolation of feeling themselves a step nearer to joining the league (which unfortunately never happened).

The chance for me at Bedford was a good one. At a semi-professional club you could combine what you did for a living with football and get a fair bit of money for it – either paid directly or 'in your boot' as quiet acknowledgment of your efforts. As soon as I arrived for training, Campbell had me change and get out on the pitch. He fired balls at me from all angles: high, low, crosses from the wings. He tried one of the more difficult shots for a goalkeeper to save: too high to reach when it is straight above you and that you have to arch back for as it threatens to dip late under the bar. Nothing got by me. 'You'll do,' he said and took me to meet the manager,

Ron Burgess, a former captain of Tottenham and Wales. As a Spurs player, he had spent much of his club career with Alf Ramsey. At home I had the match programme of the game in October 1953 when Burgess had captained the Rest of the World XI, the 4–4 draw at Wembley in which Ramsey had stepped forward to score England's last-minute equaliser. Burgess knew his goalkeepers. He had managed Watford, for whom he'd discovered Pat Jennings, now Spurs' keeper. I would be well looked after, he told me kindly, and might get a run-out with the reserves. He gave me his home number; I was to call at any time.

Wilson's time came as I returned home that evening with the first election results coming through. The BBC's innovative swingometer – a cardboard arrow pinned to what might have been the backside of a dartboard – forecast an overwhelming victory for Labour. The prime minister told the cheering crowds in his constituency of Huyton, in Liverpool, the next day that his priority was to bring to heel the renegade Rhodesian regime. Easily misled, they let pass his hints about serious economic measures being needed. With this, he went off with his pipe and mac to play football among boys on nearby waste ground. It was a piece of unprecedented image-making from a British prime minister, but he didn't fool me. His arms and legs were everywhere, and he had no idea how to kick a ball.

With the England and Scotland match due the next afternoon, the mystery remained of who was going to do what. Were England's attackers actually going to score? In place of Jimmy Greaves, injured again, Geoff Hurst was getting a chance to redeem himself after his performance against the Germans. Would Nobby Stiles perhaps get out of his way and stop hanging around on the opponents' goal-line? Surely Ramsey would demand that Stiles show his qualities at the back if the Manchester United man wanted to firm up his place in the World Cup squad. 'Tenacious,' some reports called Stiles, but I was not sure about that. Manchester United players were just difficult. In a club that was too famous, they always had a lot of people hanging around them. On the steps of the stadium, doting dads and their sons got in the way. At the station, the big kids had always been out in force. The team took the 5.55 p.m. from Euston, which meant at the end of a game the players had little over an hour to shower, change and board the team bus for the trip across London. By the time they arrived at the station, the players, Matt Busby and the man with the kit basket were moving at pace for the train. Doling out signatures was not their priority.

The best way of countering this was to take to the pitch during the players' five minute kick-about just before the start of a game. Running the length of the Highbury turf during a downpour in the 1961–62 season, I had been the only kid to leap the barrier. The police, in their capes, stuck to patrolling the cinder track around it, rather than stepping into mud that would have defied any Grand National horse. My target was Harry Gregg, the Manchester United keeper and hero of the Munich air disaster, who had gone back into the burning wreckage to pull people out. Harry was a great character who I knew would sign but, en route, I thought I might as well go for one other United player.

Bobby Charlton – head down, deadly serious and pummelling shots at Gregg in the goalmouth – was out of the question, so I approached this small bloke who had been the last one out of the tunnel. His eyebrows and nostrils were covered in Vaseline and he smelt powerfully of horse liniment. He was staring in awe at the 68,000 crowd, and I guessed it was his first time at Highbury. He failed to see me approach by his right shoulder and when I shoved my pencil under his nose – biro wouldn't have worked in the rain – he jumped: 'Go away!' He said it under his breath, looking round as if fearing Busby or the crowd might see us in conversation. He was not as used to being on this stage as I was and was lucky to have me come after him at all. So I persisted. I then made it to Gregg and, once I had jumped back into the crowd, needed the help of the programme to decipher who else I had on paper. Manchester United coincidentally had two players with the peculiar northern name of Norbert. Nobby Lawton was an established first-team player and famous. The 'N. Stiles' I read before me was not. With disappointment, I realised I had cajoled into signing the one Man United player no one south of Coronation Street had heard of.

Stiles played as England slogged out a 4–3 victory in Glasgow. Geoff Hurst scored his first international goal. Roger Hunt laid the ball gently across the face of goal and, unchallenged, Hurst took an age putting it into a gaping net from a few yards out. Had he missed, it would have been his last England game. With seven goals to reflect on, Kenneth Wolstenholme commented that it was a match people would be 'talking about for years'. In England we quickly forgot about it and – with the world to aim for – the yearly fixture with the Scots would never be very important again.

With Easter cold, a similar situation went for the confrontations that had been a fixture of Bank Holidays in recent years. Clashes between Mods and Rockers were anticipated, and in Brighton about a thousand youths thronged the seafront. Sixteen were arrested. The reports from Great Yarmouth were of six arrests as 'mobs of teenagers' pelted police with eggs. But these were not the riots of recent times.

In Islington, the sides ranged up across the Essex Road. The Rockers congregated in a small café near Packington Street, where they hauled their motorbikes up on to the wide pavement. The Mods, far more in number, populated the amusement arcade opposite Islington Green. With its domed roof, the arcade was next to the Rex, the fleapit of the five cinemas in the area. My uncle Keith had taken me there for Saturday morning pictures in the 1950s and got into fights with the commissionaire who said I was underage. As going to the pictures fell out of favour, the Rex was the only local cinema that the developers and bingo-hall owners felt unworthy of takeover. A lone survivor, it was later done up and called the Screen on the Green.

The respective camps were separated by Anderson's wood yard and the remains of the Collins' Music Hall. The Collins' stood on the eastern flank of Islington Green, which had the war memorial at its centre. A granite horse trough at its western tip, which I had not seen used for its original purpose for about a decade now, marked where Upper Street and Essex Road divided, the former leading north eventually to Edinburgh, the latter east to Southend.

Anderson's was partly responsible for the Collins' closure. A fire in the yard, which backed on to the Collins, had eight years previously caused sufficient damage for the owners of the music hall to reflect that theirs was not the future of public entertainment. On a Saturday night, I was on the way with my parents to the theatre of Islington town hall to see a performance of the Gang Show, staged by local Scout troops, and another theatrical spectacle threatened by the evolving times. Tonight's performance would end with a stirring chorus of Al Jolson's 'Mammy'. We watched the flames streaking up from the Collins' as we waited for a bus at the Angel. Great Aunt Ada, Teddy's mother, had played in the Collins' chorus line to Charlie Chaplin before the First World War. Another of my grandma's sisters, Aunt Alice, had been with her and neither thought Chaplin a nice person. It was no great loss when he left for America. In a future incarnation, the Collins' building would become a Waterstones. For the moment, there was not a market for a large bookshop in the area, although some said the Mods had a penchant for 'existential' literature. I had not heard such reports and, if I had, would not have known what they were talking about.

Ernie, my friend from primary school, who lived just down the street, had a brother, Barry, in his late twenties who was a Rocker. He made good money labouring on building sites, and hung around playing the pinball machine in the Essex Road café. One night the door opened suddenly on to a mob of Mods, their spokesman sneering, 'Right, let's 'ave you lot outside.' The Rockers escaped past the chip fryer, over the back wall and loose on to the Packington estate before the Mods set their Hush Puppies in motion.

The Rockers' turntable needle had stuck on Bill Haley, and their motorbikes meant nothing to me. For that matter, neither did the Mods' Lambrettas. Given the weekly expenditure on luridly coloured clothing that being a Modernist entailed, few at our school could afford it. Archie McGillvray, who played centre-half for the school and was very hard on the field – while being quiet and soft off it – regularly turned up in a different outfit. Terry Bloxham had the budgetary advantage of being a bookie's son from Dalston Junction. Terry told me he had been seduced by an older woman who lived near him. I didn't know if I believed him – I certainly didn't want to – but it was an incentive to see what funds I could rustle together and start shopping in Carnaby Street. If this was the way to get a girlfriend – or even a kiss – so be it. My first purchase, a pair of herringbone tweeds in salmon pink, was an idea borrowed from Archie's wardrobe.

A group of us went down to Soho to the Marquee a couple of times a week. Peter Edmonds had virtually discovered The Who the year before, when they were the club's resident Tuesday night group. John Sharman, the school's best guitar player, appeared to have the most experience with girls. He would talk about it a bit and then stop, commenting sagely that talking about it was not the thing you would do if you were really doing it. John and Peter came from off the Essex Road, by the Packington estate. Others among us included Paul Fuschillo, son of a taxi driver. An inside-forward, Paul had both stayed on into the sixth form and attracted the interest of Arsenal.

John Mayall's Bluesbreakers were one of the groups we went to see, John (Sharman) being a fan of Eric Clapton, their lead guitarist. The audience stood, arms crossed in silence, watching the performance, applauding at the end of a number or a particularly good solo. Gary Farr worked up the crowd more on Friday nights, introducing his set with 'Can I Get a

Witness', the early Marvin Gaye number. With borrowed songs, he never made it big, though my dad was impressed I had seen him. Tommy Farr, his father, the heavyweight boxer, had gone 15 rounds with Joe Louis in 1937.

The club sold coffee and Coca-Cola. We touted for pass-outs to save on the steep 7s 6d it cost to get in. People coming out at half-time, with the tube or bus to catch to faraway places like Hornchurch and Richmond, often handed over the pass-outs they had been given. Getting in late meant you would forsake the support act. When we saw Spencer Davis and Stevie Winwood in the lead spot one April night, 'Somebody Help Me' had just gone to number one. We missed Jimmy Cliff doing the warm-up, but I hadn't heard of him. On Sunday none of us bothered to go. In his regular afternoon set, David Bowie was not a name we went looking for.

When the Moors murder trial began in the same month it was said the whole 'permissive society' was in the dock. Ian Brady, 28, a stock clerk, and Myra Hindley, 23, a shorthand typist, were charged with killing two children, their bodies believed to have been buried on Saddleworth Moor near Manchester. Brady was also accused of having invited home and killed a 17-year-old boy, attacking the victim from behind and hitting him several times in the head with an axe. In one report, *The Mirror* had referred to the couple as 'blonde Myra Hindley and her friend Ian Brady'. Brady's hair colour went unmentioned.

The case provided the first real test of the Murder (Abolition of Death Penalty) Act. Although it had found its way into law some six months earlier, it was still open to being dropped if Parliament did not renew it within five years. For many people, getting rid of hanging was the symbol of how society's discipline had been allowed to falter, and had a public vote been taken it would have overwhelmingly favoured bringing back the rope.

While bunking the price of Marquee ticket was fairly near to the limit of my permissive experience, matters were different across the breadth of the UK. Figures released in April 1966 said illegitimate births in England and Wales had doubled in the past ten years. Students at Regent Street Polytechnic in London chose the moment to draw attention to the 89 recent pregnancies at the college. They demanded that contraceptive slot machines be installed in the men's toilets. The poly's authorities were resisting the idea.

Gambling, the personal trap that I was falling into, was well within society's accepted norms, bookmakers having been legalised since 1960. Ernie and his family were the influence on me, although by no means to blame. Ernie had left Barnsbury when he was 15 to work for one of many of the clock- and watch-making companies around St John Street in Clerkenwell. His dad, a skilled watch repairer on the side, worked in an engineering factory in the alleyway next to the Islington Green amusement arcade. Their family of mum, dad, six children and adopted cousin Melvyn, never went without, in spite of Ernie and his dad losing a fair amount of their wages at the bookies.

With *The Mirror* having pages of race cards each day, the structure of gambling appealed to me, and I studied form with the same resolve I had applied to my football albums. The books I had for autographs were converted into form books, with any spare pages given over to the day's many race meetings. Results were analysed, with the horses that had finished in the frame underlined and colour-coded for first, second and third. Jockeys and their favoured racecourses were noted. What weight was a horse carrying last time out? If it had come second, beaten by half a length and finishing fast over six furlongs, next time out over seven and carrying half a stone less, it would have every chance of nosing in front at the winning post.

Such thinking enabled me to have visions of becoming a professional gambler. If I worked at it, I could be out at dawn on the Newmarket gallops catching sight in the mist of new two-year-olds that lesser punters had not yet seen. A year ago such a colt named Charlottown won its first ever race, this over seven furlongs and as favourite. Who was it knew so much about him already that he was favourite without having appeared on a public racecourse? The idea of joining such a fraternity seemed realistic for a while, as I reserved my money for the horses I had studied over a lengthy period and a string of them came home as winners. But soon, the heart began to rule the head. Instead of waiting out a day when none of my fancied horses were running, I would back others on the grounds that they had won for me before or, worse still, because two might have similar names and I could link them in a fancy double.

The scrap metal dealers of Allingham Street who spent their afternoons in Droy's often seemed to be coining it in. I saw one of them toss a £10 tip to the bookies' clerk who had worked out his £179 winnings on a four-horse Yankee. We gathered round the grille as the money was counted out. One of the clerks later succumbed to fiddling the till and, as we read in the *Islington Gazette*, was sentenced to several months in jail. As for the metal merchants, what they lost they could just take out of the tax they didn't pay.

Emphasising lifestyles more in the West End and Chelsea than on the backstreets of Islington, the US press was now fully on to the idea of 'Swinging London'. An April copy of *Time* magazine appeared in our school library: Mick Jagger and David Bailey, the photographer, were among those who led the way. Harold Wilson was part of the scene, less for his Gannex than his age: at 50, he was the youngest prime minister of the century. Pictures showed King's Road people in their PVC macs of many colours and Twiggy as the new face of the age. She commanded fees of ten guineas a session.

Then again, as London swung and was the place to be, kicking a ball against the factory wall at the top of Noel Road could land you in trouble. This was not the location to find yourself on a lengthening spring evening when a group of Mods wandered by. The two men of library book fame had hastened past as we halted our game for the seconds required, but the Mods sauntered up to us, stopped to light cigarettes and chat with their girlfriends trailing behind. Ernie and his cousin Melvyn were with me. So was Ernie's older brother Barry, of Rocker background and who urged them to 'get a fucking move on'.

When they returned from the amusement arcade with bottles and knives and having trebled their number, Barry had gone for the evening. They circled for a while sizing us up and, when I got a tap on the shoulder, it was obvious what was coming. A kid who had been saying nothing but beaming a menacing smile had his arm pulled back so far that I had time to make my escape in slow motion. Ernie and Melvyn made it through behind me with the bottles raining down about them, all of which missed. Turning from a safe distance down the street to watch them go, we reflected unharmed on the last run of the Islington Mods. Any suggestion that they had an intellectual wing, we would have regarded as probably nonsense.

# Chapter 7

# NO MUGS

I would happily have sat around talking about football most of the time but few of my classmates were interested, including those I talked to most of all. Bobby Blake preferred to go to White City to watch the British athletics team compete against visiting countries such as the Kenyans, in 1963. He would hang around the competitors' entrance and engage the stars of English track and field in intelligent conversation: 'What are your plans for next season?' he would ask the likes of Adrian Metcalfe and Robbie Brightwell. Peter Edmonds, who lived near Essex Road, and who I walked home with some evenings through the leafy streets of Canonbury, also favoured individualist sports like running and rowing. In his case, he also went hiking with the Boy Scouts.

Peter was the only one of our number with divorced parents. His father had been with the British army of occupation in Germany and had married a local woman. They moved to England and, when they separated, his father won custody of

Peter. In the divorce cases that regularly featured in the press, custody of children was often a subject of wrangling. There was little in this case, with the courts making sure that the boy would not be taken to Germany. Peter's mum, though, was doing OK, as Germany increasingly seemed to be doing on our journeys through it. With her help, he was the first among us to buy a car, a second-hand Triumph Herald. He parked it in the small driveway at the front of the school, something which no boy had done before, and right next to the headmaster's.

Most of the football boys had left by the time of the sixth form. The first was Jimmy Dunkley who, before his O-levels, went off to Fulham. Jimmy came one night to Brisbane Road with Fulham Colts to play Orient in a London youth cup competition and we chatted by the dressing rooms afterwards. Henry Tonbridge, who left school following the O-levels, was on the books of West Ham and had played against me in my first Orient game. Neither Jimmy nor Henry was to make it to full professional level. Tom Newby, another member of the school team, left without any exams to become a bingo caller. His family lived near Columbia Road, the market street in Hoxton, where there was little in the way of spare cash but numbers were Tommy's speciality. He later went into the money markets and moved to New York, where he became expert in dealings with the yen. His working life would outlive the Twin Towers.

The City of London was beginning to recruit from the children of working-class families, having expanded to the extent that the public schools could no longer exclusively meet its needs. It was also alive to the idea of hiring 'native talent'. If your dad or an uncle had a street market background then he knew how to shave the price of potatoes and sprouts through the working day such that his stall was clear at the close of business. Such skills, handed on through the blood, would do nicely for the City. A number of teammates who I had played football with at school joined firms of stockbrokers or stockjobbers.

Although it was not what the school was meant for, some kids left content to have stayed blue collar. Fred White became a self-employed painter and decorator: 'I wanted to work for myself,' he told me at an old boys' dinner. He always had money and enough work to employ some former schoolmates if they needed it for a while. Denis Parsons had had his part-time cobbling and keys job at the corner of the Balls Pond and Kingsland Roads and took over the shop as manager virtually as he left school. Paul Gregory from the year below left at 15 to be part of the central-heating boom. So many people were having it installed that he was getting, he told me, £60 a week in his hand. Even if he wasn't, and had doubled the true figure, that was still amazing.

My parents had central heating put in, my dad talking knowledgably with the blokes about pipes and radiators, no doubt to convey the impression that, at a stretch, he could have done the work himself. 'Too big a job for one man,' he told me, ours being a house with a basement, ground, first and second floors. In theory, having central heating put us on a par with the new residents of the area. It had made their bathrooms and the prospect of more than one bath a week bearable. Actually, they showered, which we deemed a cultural frivolity. The lady opposite did it every night, as was apparent through the blinds as she dried herself off. These people continued to live by different standards. She also had a son in his twenties called Jasper, another first for our street.

Alas the central heating had come too late for my O-level re-sits back in January. In a snap of cold, I had trailed upstairs to my room in gloves, school blazer and, on one night, even my smart navy-blue mac bought from Dunn's up at White Lion Street. In revising my lengthy list of French regular verbs, *négliger*, to neglect, was one that stood out: past participle *négligé*. It allowed warming thoughts of the school's visiting French assistant, Mademoiselle Boulet. In practice, my parents hardly turned the central heating on. By their wartime benchmark, it was not necessary, except in the sitting room where my mum would sit on the pouf watching television by the one radiator that they had working.

At Bedford Town, Joe told me I needed to meet the team's main trainer, and so took me along the Eyrie's inner corridors to his office. It amounted to not much more than a chair and a table, at which he was reviewing the racing page of *The Mirror*. His name I didn't catch or recognise and he told me to get along outside. He'd be right out, he said. Several of the reserve and first team were waiting for me, and I knew this was a bit of a trial. They put in shots for twenty minutes or so but I was prepared and things went well. Normally in a kick-about, the key for goalkeepers was to look composed and not go throwing themselves about. One of the saves I made, a reflex catch to my left without losing my feet, drew shouts of approval.

As they were fading, the trainer emerged from the tunnel and said, 'OK, let's get on with it.' My impression was that we had been getting on with it. The others, I told myself, would surely report to him how I'd done. He organised a practice game and I was put on the better side, as a result of which I had little to do. For the last couple of weeks of the season, I checked the team-sheet after Thursday evening training to find I wasn't in the reserves for their weekend game. This was no great surprise. They had a keeper named Derek Bellotti, who was about eighteen months older than I was and had played all season. My uncle Geoff said he was flashy but that was probably on account of his continental-sounding name. Besides, having been out of decent match practice for a while between Orient and Bedford, I didn't feel ready for this rise up in level. I would be next season.

Next in line for England were Yugoslavia on 4 May, and everything I knew about the east Europeans said this would be a tough game. At the time when my dad was in Trieste facing Tito's partisans, Yugoslavia spelt its name not with a Y but a J. They were 'no mugs, the Jugs', my father said, using the common term employed by the British soldiers. In football they were uncompromising. In 1958 in Belgrade, they had hammered England 5–0. Eddie Hopkinson of Bolton Wanderers was in goal. I liked him; he was a good goalkeeper. Subsequently, I had met him with the Bolton team, too, at St Pancras and knew him to be a nice bloke. Hopkinson was five feet eight. He briefly had to vie for the England spot in the pre-Ramsey days with Alan Hodgkinson of Sheffield United, who won his five caps at a height of five feet seven. For a while, the two of them seemed to take it in turns to play because, as it was suggested, the old selectors who chose the team kept getting their names mixed up. Hopkinson found he was holding the short straw for the Belgrade game and, as the ball kept flying past him, not much else besides.

Whenever England players got anywhere near the Yugoslavian penalty area, so I read at that time, the home defenders threw themselves into rugby tackles. At Wembley, this could never have happened, while on foreign soil, predictably, it brought no sanction from the referee. One blessing about the approaching game was that, since it would be played at home, the uniformed man in the middle – even if he was foreign – would have to supervise matters in line with the dictates of British fair play.

In war, as in football, the Yugoslavs had been a hard bunch. As part of the western military effort in Trieste immediately after the war, my dad had been involved in preventing Tito – Josep was his first name but people rarely used that – from taking over the city, ostensibly for communism. In fact, the Yugoslavs pointed out that Trieste had been part of the old Austro-Hungarian Empire and so rightfully belonged to them rather than Italy. The upshot was that while my dad was there Slovenian snatch squads stole down from the Istrian hills to kidnap Italians off the streets. British soldiers who wandered off limits into the mountainous frontier looking for cheap wine were also at risk of never being seen again.

The Yugoslavs were clever as well as ruthless. As a signalman, my father tapped out his Morse code from Miramare, the castle built by Maximilian just outside Trieste, but was based further west along the Venice road around the bay at Sistiana. His unit woke one morning to find its fleet of Land Rovers and trucks standing on bricks. The Yugoslavs had come across the bay in dinghies during the night, removed the army vehicles' wheels and made off with them. No one heard a thing and the raiders had simply paddled away before dawn in the direction of Rijeka and Opatija.

My father's experiences abroad had certainly been formative. In Caserta, north of Naples, he had seen people drop dead of typhus on the streets, with the army forbidden to climb down from their trucks to help, partly in fear of the disease but also because of the likelihood of being mobbed by people in bad need of food and medicine. The troops were billeted in the, admittedly abandoned, royal palace nearby. In Bari on the east coast, he had been thrown across his room in a shower of glass as an Allied ammunition ship blew up in the German air raid on the port in December 1943. The bodies of those close to the blast were found to have turned yellow. The ship, among its other materiel, had been carrying mustard gas, illegal under the rules of war. 'We had it just in case the Germans ever used it on us,' he told me, as he had been told at the time.

The nearest my dad came to dying was in a convoy on the hilly cross-country road between Bari and Caserta. Johnny Botley, the driver of the truck that he and several others were in, and who my dad always referred to as 'Little' Johnny Botley, lost control of it on a steep incline and had his foot on the running board ready to abandon the vehicle before he was hauled back in. He had inadvertently slipped the truck out of gear. In the mid-sixties I remember my father returning from a trip up Chapel Market to say he had heard a bus at the Angel loudly sounding its hooter. When he looked, Little Johnny Botley was waving to him from behind the steering wheel of a number 43. Drivers on that route made the journey up and down Muswell Hill several times a day.

In recent years my parents had diverted from their usual trip to Trieste to take a quick half-day across the Yugoslav border. The first time, the visa took up a whole page in my passport and came with stamps and signatures. The guards had rifles slung over their shoulders and stooped to eye us through the Zephyr windows. The country looked backward and far more rural than Bedfordshire, with wagons drooping large piles of hay. There was a general smell of manure. We drove as far as Ljubljana, which defied pronunciation and looked communistically severe and dull. But lately things had changed; there was no visa and we went for a drink at night-times. Tito had changed, or our views of him had. He didn't like the Russians and was almost one of us. Like Archbishop Makarios and Jomo Kenyatta in the empire, a terrorist one day became a bloke you negotiated with the next.

Nonetheless, it was surprising how well the game went. Moore was rested and Jimmy Armfield, Blackpool's veteran right-back, drafted in as captain. Armfield had walked right by me and the full-page picture I had of him in my *Buchan's* outside the Russell three years earlier. 'Royalty cinema,' he had said to the cab driver and, when I ran and beat the traffic easily to the far end of Kingsway, he walked by me again, angrily this time, and in to see Marlon Brando in *Mutiny on the Bounty*. I was not one to forget these things, but I could forgive. Moore, with no mention of the groin strain, would be back before long anyway.

Only 55,000 people turned up and, with expectations low, England won 2–0. Greaves and Bobby Charlton found themselves for the first time in a long time in the same England team and put in a goal each. At last, the right players were getting on the score-sheet.

Formative experiences abroad had likewise shaped the careers of Charlton and Greaves. Charlton survived the Munich air crash, which killed many of his Manchester United teammates. Among the dead was Duncan Edwards, a commander of play in the middle of the field who unleashed thunderbolt shots on goal. When I had first started playing football in any organised way at the age of eight, every kid wanted to be Duncan Edwards. Quickly realising I was never going to be him, I converted to playing in goal. Edwards likely would have been England's 1966 captain. According to Bobby Charlton's older brother Jack, 'our kid' – as Jack always called Bobby – had not been the same since the disaster. From cheery and outgoing, he had become withdrawn. But then Bobby had always seemed inaccessible. I knew when I had run on to the pitch at Highbury that there was no point in approaching him, whereas Jack – publicly a far more bumptious character – was very receptive to junior fans. Then, Jack played for Leeds and by comparison was little known. Every kid in the land was after Bobby, who had been a star since his teens. Chiefly, his fame came from sympathetic memory of Munich. Even mums adopted him as 'our kid'. A few months after the disaster, he had appeared on *Double Your Money* answering questions about 'pop music'. But for him, the show would not have considered this a suitable topic. Bobby sat tortured in the soundproofed booth reserved for those going for the big money, forcing out his answers, urged on by the national audience. When he won the £1,000, he nearly doubled his income for the year.

Greaves' foreign experience had been unhappy in a more prosaic way. A young star at Chelsea, he was transferred to AC Milan and much appreciated by the home fans. Every time he took to the pitch, he scored, but he could not settle. The food was strange and the Italians did not serve a decent cup of tea, or any tea at all. My parents had always taken theirs with them (loose and never in tea-bags, which were struggling to grip the British imagination). Greaves returned to play for Tottenham, the glamour outfit of the day, where in his first game he scored a hat-trick against Blackpool just before Christmas 1961. His initial strike was a flying scissor-kick. My *Topical Times* annual showed pictures of that and of him leaving the pitch after the game, smiling awkwardly as boys surrounded him. Ever chirpy with reporters, among his junior fans Greaves had always to me seemed inordinately shy.

As reserved as the nation's two favourite footballers were, they were inevitably the duo on whom fans pinned their hopes. A natural left-footer, Charlton passed or struck a ball with equal accuracy and venom with his right. He was from Ashington in the North-East – a so-called pit village that was actually a sizeable coal-mining town – where the tradition was that if you could not kick a ball with both feet, you practised against the wash-house wall until you could. Greaves was primarily a leftie – a *mancino*, as Italians had called him – who could do the spectacular or as easily sneak in behind defenders and steal goals from a yard. Charlton was a superb header of the ball. Heading was the one thing Greaves never did.

They were among the few players pursued by advertisers. Stanley Matthews had advertised cigarettes, Bobby Moore would draw attention to the attractions of a British pub. Half pages in the papers in the build-up to the World Cup showed Greaves and Charlton drinking Robinson's Lemon Barley Water, which was also on tap at the urn under the umpire's chair during Wimbledon. 'Good 'n' refreshing' and 'delicious hot or cold', they were said to find it. When Jimmy was in training, commented Mrs Greaves, 'he practically lives on it'.

Mindful of the nation's well-being, the Office of Health Economics said middle-aged men needed to avoid excessive smoking. Two packets a day – that was to say, 40 cigarettes – more than doubled their risk of contracting heart disease. Advertisers carried on undaunted: the menthol cigarette Consulate was as 'cool as a mountain stream'. Senior Service 'satisfied'. Through its name, it claimed identification with the Royal Navy. Craven A, which was endorsed by Stanley Matthews as 'the cigarette for me; smooth, clean smoking', also claimed to be 'kinder to your throat' than other varieties, and hence sent one of the first signals that cigarettes might not be good for throats at all. Tom Jones, the Welsh singer, was pictured smoking next to a report that he had had his tonsils out. His voice had recovered, said his agent.

In matters of the law, the Moors murderers Brady and Hindley were sent to prison for life: 'The only sentence the law now allows,' said the judge at Chester Assizes. The body of 12-year-old victim Keith Bennett would never be found. Pictures of one of those murdered were discovered in a station left luggage locker, the ticket for which police found in Hindley's communion prayer book.

*The Mirror* reported that 'long haired disc jockey' Jimmy Savile was arrested in London's Haymarket wearing a Royal Marine combat suit and carrying a rifle. He was due to take part in a Royal Marines exercise on Dartmoor during the Whitsun weekend. 'We can see nothing wrong in Mr Savile's behaviour,' said a spokesman for the Royal Marines. He had attended a

Friday luncheon given by the Royal Variety Club where he was guest of honour as 'Britain's top DJ'.

Judicial and police action featured the next day in the story of the FA Cup final between Everton and Sheffield Wednesday. On a hot afternoon, Everton came back from two goals down to win 3–2 in one of the best Cup finals for many years. People called it a showpiece for the game, but behind it all both teams had struggled to recover from a betting and bribery scandal, which had seen three players who should have been on the pitch thrown in jail the year before.

Wednesday had lost Peter Swan, the former England central defender who had nearly died of sickness in Chile during the 1962 World Cup, and David Layne, their up-and-coming striker. Layne was known as 'Bronco', after Bronco Layne in the TV cowboy series of the same name, but appropriately, too, because he was the first player I saw celebrating one of his goals by leaping and punching the air. It was called the 'Layne leap'. Everton had been deprived of the services of Tony Kay, their former captain. All three had been playing with Sheffield Wednesday when the affair happened. They had – unsuspectingly, as they told it – been pulled into a gambling ring that operated and fixed matches across the country.

Jimmy Gauld, an old Scots centre-forward, organised the ring. Gauld had played around the lower leagues of football for teams like Plymouth Argyle. For much of his career, he and all other players in the country earned no more than a maximum of £21 a week. The ceiling had been removed in 1961 after pressure from the footballers' union, but lower division players were still not on a great deal more than the old maximum wage. Many were easily drawn into gambling. A footballers' life was often boring, with a lot of empty afternoons after training with little to do but hang around the local snooker hall or bookies.

Layne in one stage of his early career had played for Swindon Town in the third division, and Gauld knew him from there. I had met Layne at King's Cross station in 1961 when he was a Bradford City player and the team were on their way home after a cup-tie at Arsenal. This was during a typhoid outbreak in Bradford, which was blamed on the city's new population of Pakistani immigrants. At one point, it was suggested that the football team might be forbidden to travel to London. I made sure to be at King's Cross, where the team was leaving from a deserted platform. One of the few Bradford players I had a picture of – and a tiny black and white one at that – was Layne. Wide-eyed, he showed it around to his teammates. He had had no idea that the picture existed and thanked me for showing it to him. He was the professional footballer and I was 13, yet he was the one overawed. He signed it 'Best Wishes' even though such a modest photo did not merit it, and I had not asked him to.

Soon after Layne had been given the big break in his career and transferred to top division Sheffield Wednesday. Gauld told Layne to let him know when he had a game coming up that he thought Wednesday might lose. He would lay a few pounds on the result for him. If Wednesday won, Layne would lose the bet but get his win bonus from his club. If they lost, he would get his winnings from the bookie to compensate. Where was the harm? Layne mentioned it to Swan and Kay, who threw in some cash of their own.

In making his bets, Gauld would link the game with others. Players in clubs from Portsmouth to Hartlepool told him about matches that they thought their teams would lose. Desperate for money, some contrived to make that the case and threw their games. Kay, Layne and Swan were insistent they did not. The matter took on the appearance of a national conspiracy against the bookies, as Gauld combined matches in doubles and trebles to crank up the odds and potential winnings.

The *Sunday People* had been investigating rumours of match-throwing for some while. Its suspicions were guided towards little-known players in the lower divisions from clubs like York City and Mansfield Town. When the paper happened upon the apparent involvement of players in the top rung of the football league, it had had a major scoop on its hands. As a result, Kay, Layne and Swan had been brought to trial on charges of fraud in early 1965, during the same week as the funeral of Winston Churchill. Many British people – judges and juries included – were reflecting on the transition from an old to a permissively new society. 'What chance did we have?' Layne said later. All three went to jail for four months.

Layne had shown a lot of promise, not least when he had starred in a friendly game for Wednesday against visiting Brazilian side Santos, who had Pelé playing for them. Swan was moving towards the end of a career during which he had won a number of international caps. Possibly the worst hit was Kay, a player I liked. Prior to the scandal his football stock had risen so fast that Everton had bought him for inclusion in the team that won the first division in 1962–63. Kay was good with kids. Chased away by the hard nuts from Euston on the night Everton had sealed the first-division title in London, I was idling through St Pancras and came across him heading for a train. Kay had left the Everton party and was off to see his parents in

Sheffield. A player much in demand from young fans, he was friendly and accommodating.

In the game he was alleged to have thrown, Kay was made Sheffield Wednesday's man of the match, according, ironically, to the report of the game in the *Sunday People*. When this was put forward as evidence for the defence, the trial judge said it was irrelevant. If Kay had been playing deliberately below form, then he had certainly shown lots of ability as an actor. The game in question was against Alf Ramsey's Ipswich and, after Ramsey moved on to the England job, he brought Kay into the international team. A red-headed, hard-tackling half-back who also had a lot of skill, Kay's best club match was a cup-tie for Sheffield Wednesday a few seasons earlier against Manchester United. At Manchester's Old Trafford ground, Kay was up against Nobby Stiles in the middle of the field and came out the clear winner; as did Wednesday, sensationally, 7–2. With Kay banned from football after being sent to jail, Ramsey needed a replacement in the England line-up. He chose Stiles.

Three months on now from when Everton had wanted the cameras banned from Bedford Town, I was watching the Cup final on television as Everton scored their late winner. A jubilant fan ran on to the pitch to celebrate. A bobby chased him and grabbed his coat, which came off and left the constable sprawled on the turf. It was funny, with no harm done. Another policeman hared after the fan and had almost caught him up, at which point an easy arrest would have been possible. Instead, the copper's lower lip seemed to curl like that of Alf Tupper, the backstreet athlete in my Saturday morning comics of earlier years, and he launched into a rugby tackle that had the two of them crashing down. The policeman was so overcome by his enthusiasm for the moment that Gordon West, the Everton keeper, came out of his penalty area to appeal to him to calm down.

This was not the kind of police action we were used to of a Saturday evening. PC George Dixon was due on the BBC in the next hour in his regular *Dixon of Dock Green* role. Played by Jack Warner, his opening line was always, 'Good evenin', all,' as he introduced the audience to that week's fictional tales of an ordinary bobby on the beat. Dixon was caring to old people, and no doubt any kid he clipped round the ear-hole would have thoroughly deserved it. He was such a durable British institution as to have been brought back from the dead. Warner had played him in the fifties film *The Blue Lamp*, at the end of which Dixon was shot and killed. In response to the mood of national shock, the BBC resurrected him and created the TV show, which had run for the many years since. In later years, political correspondents would describe Richard Nixon's rise to the presidency in the US as the 'greatest comeback since Lazarus'. That title had already rightfully gone to Dixon not Nixon.

The Cup final policeman made the papers and a TV chat show the following day. As a matter of course, we had learned in our post-war lives that Britain had the best of everything in the world – the finest air force, army, empire, motorbikes, goalkeepers and so on – and the police were up there in the frame of honour, too. Evidence to the contrary, however, had been building for some time.

At our school, we had had the case three years previously of one of the Cypriot kids arrested during a demonstration in the West End against Queen Frederika of Greece, who was visiting London. A thoughtful type, he was well ahead of most of us in political awareness and held views on the Greek regime's human rights record, which was not all it could have been. The police took exception to royalty being shouted at on the streets of the capital, especially since Frederika was the Duke of Edinburgh's sister. They charged the boy with carrying an offensive weapon, a piece of brick, in his pocket. Curiously, this seemed to match other pieces of brick found on other people recently arrested by the central London police. The boy's father, having fled from the Cyprus civil war of the 1950s, was not about to let police corruption stand in the way of his family's development within British society, so took the case further. The brick and its various pieces were found to have been planted by a detective chief inspector named Harold Challenor. The DCI was quietly retired 'on health grounds' amid reflections on his distinguished war record. Apparently, he had been captured by the Germans, escaped from a prison camp and somehow walked home.

Such an exercise was difficult enough through the streets of Canonbury, let alone in formerly occupied Europe. One recent evening walking with my Essex Road mates, I had made the mistake of saying 'Evenin', all' to a copper who crossed the pavement a few feet in front of us. Not appreciating the joke, he dragged me by the collar of my school blazer to pin me against a wall opposite the Canonbury Tavern. What he was 'fucking going to do' to me he could not decide. Take me down the police station in Upper Street and charge me, he spat out as one suggestion. For all I knew, they might have had some spare pieces of masonry lying around looking for a friendly pocket to line. He eventually released me into the custody of my mates, with me spluttering about the language he had used. 'You didn't know they were like that?' John Sharman said, as they fell about laughing.

As a regular school fixture, we played the Metropolitan Police cadets out at their base on the old Hendon aerodrome. With the wind whipping across the Second World War expanse of it, the earache I developed in the second half neatly balanced the one I gained in the first. We had lately won 2–0 against a team of tough but, in their way, sporting kids, all more used to the streets of Glasgow than the Dock Green byways characterised on the BBC. They shook hands and said 'well played' at the end, having spent most of the 90 minutes scything us down.

The Cup final copper was more of that ilk, and showed a new style of doing things. The old ones let me run on the pitch at Highbury and either stayed dry in their dugouts or calmly carried on patrolling the surrounding cinder track. The new breed would have you crashing to earth. Everton had not wanted the cameras at the FA Cup for the 'sake of football', but socially the case for their being there was inarguable. The TV millions had finally witnessed the spirit of George Dixon laid to rest.

# Chapter 8

# STRIKE

For weeks the seamen had been getting angrier and in the last week of May called their strike. Passenger ferries were first to be immobilised. The stoppage stranded 11 transatlantic liners at Southampton, including the *Queen Elizabeth* and *Queen Mary*.

I was easily tempted from my revision into going to Speakers' Corner. Hyde Park was full and debates ranged from abortion to race relations and off into interplanetary communication. No one mentioned the World Cup. No construction deadlines had shamefully been missed as football pottered along in a universe detached from that of the affairs of state. All the stadiums to be used were old and had undergone what small repair or paint jobs were thought necessary, and the England team was preparing to go off on a leisurely pre-tournament summer tour.

Against the backdrop of Marble Arch, a speaker of roughly university student age with a dark beard rose to the top of a short ladder to argue the merchant seamen's case. Their wage was £60 a month before tax and most of their weekends and time off were spent at sea. They had called for a rise of 12s 6d a month (67½p). From the elevated political heights of Parliament a couple of miles away Harold Wilson had projected another view. The stoppage was a 'strike against the state, against the community' and was not as benign as it appeared. Not only was Britain's proud history as a seafaring nation at stake, but also Communists were part of the plot. Activists linked to the Soviet Union had met in the houses of the seamen's union leaders and the strike, therefore, had become part of the ideological battle between east and west. The seamen and the nation, said Wilson, were in the hands of a 'tightly knit group of politically motivated men'. The union's leaders answered back. Wilson was a 'silly little man' who had messed up everything from the seamen's dispute to Rhodesia. The union's members were determined to continue with their protest, even though it meant possibly more suffering for them than anyone else. The National Union of Seamen's 65,000 members stood to receive £3 a week each in strike pay from the union. A whip-round for the strikers in the House of Commons among a hundred or so Labour MPs had raised £40.

There was no great sympathy for unions in our house, where my mum occasionally referred to people intent on 'putting the world to rights'. You worked no matter what. My granddad had worked throughout the Depression in the 1930s. In the building trade, my dad would often find himself laid off in winter during days of freezing weather, so you took work when it was available. In his case, as a skilled tradesman, he could also pick up his toolbox and move if a building site was not to his liking hence he was not one for the complaints of unions. In his role now as clerk of works, he was site supervisor, a management position.

That said, my mum and my granddad had been in the National Union of Printing, Bookbinding and Paper Workers, and my uncle Keith still was. In the print you needed to be in a union to get work. Earlier this year it had merged with NATSOPA, another print union, though with a full name too complicated to remember, to form the Society of Graphical and Allied Trades. The names spoke for a sense of lengthy industrial tradition. Wilson had just set up an inquiry into the seaman's strike and, in an effort to win the workers' trust, had appointed to it the head of the National Union of Blastfurnacemen, Ore Miners, Cokeworkers and Kindred Trades. My granddad's objection to the union was prompted by his wayward cousins around in Sudeley Street and City Garden Row. In truth, not all were cousins. They intermarried so much that some were just relatives of indeterminate kind. They would join anything, he said – a union, the Communist party, the Masons – not through any principles other than it might bring advantage to them. His best advantage, he felt, had been served by operating alone, but he joined in here and there. Each year, the *News of the World* had a day trip to Brighton for union members and their families; when I was little my nan and I went and walked the seafront while the men had lunch in the Corn Exchange. On Saturdays in the fifties, the unions had open nights in the print room on Bouverie Street. Surrounded by the comfortable smell of machine oil and newsprint, one man made the tea, another got in the jellied eels. It was their Saturday night jobs to do that.

Derby day was the final Wednesday in May and, in heavy rain, Charlottown spread a plate at the post. In the murk, the Epsom course farrier was summoned to nail the colt's shoe back on and its odds drifted from 7–2 to a more advantageous 5–1. Having followed its fortunes since its first time out as a two-year-old, this was all to the good for me. The horse had Scobie Breasley on board and won easily, my two bob each way bringing a total return of 16s 6d (about 82p). I ran through the figures in my mind, though it occurred to me there were better things to be doing with my A-levels five days away.

Exams were also going on now at the universities. For theirs, the young women of Somerville College, Oxford, were banned from wearing miniskirts on the grounds that they would distract the men and embarrass the examiners. William Mills, 21, a student of Pembroke College dismissed this as ridiculous, saying short skirts were 'an inspiration' to male students. No such strictures seemed to apply in Brighton, which I felt I knew quite well from my grandparents' *News of the World* outings. The Jay twins, Helen and Catherine, were often pictured flaunting their Biba minis at the new university of Sussex. Strangely, they were the daughters of Douglas Jay, Wilson's trade minister, who wore baggy old suits. Jay strongly opposed going into Europe, favouring instead forever doing business with the old colonies. His daughters, on the other hand, appeared leggily free of ancient encumbrances.

Not that we heard much about universities. At speech night, our teachers wore their robes from the different colleges they had attended, parading before us like members of a secret order. They never spoke about their experiences, or encouraged us to follow them. I would not have known what a 'redbrick' university was. Peter Dick, both our school's captain and skipper of its football first XI, stayed on for an extra year in the sixth form to take the Oxford entrance exams, but Peter was the durable son of a bookmaker from near Old Street. Many of us would later go to see him when he captained Oxford versus Cambridge in their annual football match at Wembley.

With his embroidered waistcoat, drums and copy of *The Guardian*, John Crowley was a more delicate flower. Cambridge set the nonsensical condition that he had to learn Latin in a very limited time before they would consider him. Otherwise we, his classmates, took care of his misplaced aspiration. Though he was well liked, we jeered at him, and on some days he was liable to find himself in the corner of the classroom under a pile of furniture. The last I saw of him was about five years after leaving school when he was working in a boutique in Kensington Church Street selling hot pants and loons. When I mentioned his wanting to go to Cambridge, he laughed the thought away.

On the whole, whether by parents or teachers, it was felt that grammar school was as far as we needed to go. Safe clerical jobs were what we were destined for. When a jobs counsellor visited the school, the best that came out of it for me was the suggestion of working behind the grille of a bank. You did not need to be careers counsellor to know that was a job readily available to pretty much anyone. I was constrained from mentioning professional gambling, given that my experience in the bookmaker's was, at the age of 17, acquired illegally.

When I wasn't in Droy's, much of my time I went to the dogs: Harringay on Monday and Friday nights, Hackney on a Saturday. If I had money left for more than the bus fare home from Hackney, my mate Ernie and I might scrape together enough for fish and chips at the café opposite Clapton Pond. Coming back on the 38 one night, we met Freddie Drew, a kid who had been at our primary school. He lived near us in City Garden Row, a near unmentionable location in our family. With Ernie, Freddie had been another of the school's best swimmers before he went on to Barnsbury, graduated to shoplifting and had been caught in Gamages in High Holborn with his pockets full. He told us that he had an arrangement with his bookie to bet on credit and made it sound like a matter of high status.

On one night at Harringay, I saw Dennis Evans, an old Arsenal footballer in the crowd. He had been a full-back during the club's fruitless late fifties and was remembered for a game against Everton when Arsenal were, unusually, 4–0 up at the end. On hearing the whistle, Evans had turned and blasted a celebratory 20-yard shot into his own net. Unfortunately, the whistle had been from among the fans and the goal stood. Now retired, he was chatting to members of the Harringay crowd. To them he remained a celebrity, but I only had to compare his overcoat with the expensive sheepskins of the bookies taking bets at the rail to have some pause for thought at what I was doing there.

I had my Barclays interview in their offices near Trafalgar Square. The Mekon was right. When the personnel man asked what newspapers I read, I answered *The Times* and *The Telegraph* and was offered a job. Banks still worked Saturdays, however, which did not appeal. My granddad suggested I should be a chartered accountant, peculiarly warning me that if I became one I was not to take bribes. Islington Borough Council offered places in its accounts department, so I applied and was accepted there. I also fixed up a summer position at the Tote, where I would be able to follow horse racing for a few spare weeks between the family holiday and starting my 'proper job'. The latter I was not looking forward to. The town hall on Upper Street looked like a mausoleum. Peter Edmonds agreed. 'You might as well be buried alive,' he said. It was OK for him. He was a cert for art A-level and was off to Chelsea School of Art in the King's Road. Both were the coolest places imaginable. Bobby Blake had got into Sussex as long as he did well in his English, which he was bound to do. These were the only kids from the arts bit of the sixth form going on to further education: the one with the divorced parents, the other a Caribbean immigrant, both of them the outsiders among us, who had an extra element of push.

The news, meanwhile, reported another killing 'by the gun gangs', this one at the Old Street end of New North Road. Ernie Isaacs, a street trader, was found shot dead in his terrace home in Penn Street, Hoxton. He had last been seen alive in his local pub, the Merry Monarch, near Murray Grove. Tom Newby lived in Murray Grove, where we generally hung around outside his parents' council flat waiting for him when we went to the Marquee. The police claimed to have no idea who did it, while the reports said Isaacs had been on first name terms with the 'South London mob' and George Cornell. By coincidence, the Met announced the same day that it was prepared for the first time to recruit policemen who wore glasses.

Cassius Clay came to Islington to fight Henry Cooper at Highbury stadium. The press could still not get used to his Black Muslim name, *The Mirror* referring to him as 'MACC' for

Muhammad Ali-Cassius Clay. He won the fight comfortably and the paper called him 'SuperMACC', no longer seeing him as the objectionable loudmouth that he was regarded as when he had come to fight Cooper in 1963.

A British former star of the ring died a few days later. Randolph Turpin, ex-middleweight world champion, had gone from such heights in the early 1950s to being bankrupt and had committed suicide in his home in Leamington Spa. His father had come from British Guiana, fought in the First World War and been badly gassed at the Somme. At the end of May, British Guiana gained independence, renaming itself Guyana.

On the suddenly very hot Whitsun Bank Holiday weekend, the police had mobilised special Mods and Rockers patrols along Britain's seafronts. Nothing happened. Cathy McGowan, who introduced *Ready Steady Go!* on Friday nights on TV, had declared that the Mods had won the 'cultural battle'. Following a recent school cricket match in south London, I was wandering home along Kingsway with the rest of the team when Cathy appeared at an upper-floor window, presumably that of the *Ready Steady Go!* office, and began waving to us. A group of her female mates rushed to join her. I thought, 'Why are they waving at us?' We had our ties and blazers off, so maybe they didn't know we were still at school.

The exams were a disaster. On Metternich I had read around the subject rather than on it, having found a biography of the Austrian count by Barbara Cartland in the Essex Road library. This had escaped the attentions of the men down the street, whose practice had been to stick lewd pictures over the author photograph on the back cover. Here, she was to be found as usual in a bright-pink ballgown. I quoted liberally from her work, but statements of the type that Metternich had 'entered the room a boy and left it a man' were inappropriate for the Congress of Vienna.

For Brecht's *Life of Galileo*, our teacher – the formerly unhappy builders' labourer – told us that the author's intention was to maintain his audience's emotional detachment from the play. Brecht achieved his end with me. With Kafka's *Metamorphosis*, I understood that the boy in the story, Gregor, had had what he thought was a bad dream. In it he had turned into a cockroach or some other form of lower existence only to awake and find it was true. It was pretty much how I felt as I emerged from the exams. *Es war kein Traum*, 'it was no dream', was the one quote I could remember from the play, and I repeated it several times in my answer.

The night before we went on holiday, my dad took me aside. I had planned an evening at the Marquee and he asked whether I was seriously considering going out to the West End in my jeans. I was. He told me that he would never wear jeans, except possibly on a building site, and even then he would make sure to change out of them before the journey home. As for a pair with large bleached white spots on them, he could not find the words.

Having scrounged my pass-out at the Marquee door, I missed the excitement outside. Around the corner in Old Compton Street, Billy Graham turned up in a large maroon car, climbed on its roof and addressed a fast gathering crowd. 'I have come here to tell you that God loves you,' he said, according to accounts of the US evangelist's visit to Soho. In a powder-blue blazer, he clutched a large Bible. A film called *Orgy at Lil's Place* was showing at a small cinema nearby and a blonde stripper in a mini-dress tried to climb on to the car with him but was pulled back by his bodyguards. To cheers and boos, Graham left after a few minutes. He was appearing at Earls Court, where Cliff Richard had joined him to reveal that he had become a Christian. Richard had been Britain's hip-swinging version of Elvis Presley at the end of the fifties but, far from *Jailhouse Rock*, had softened into making singalong films like *Summer Holiday*.

The Tories had demanded the script of the first in the series of *Till Death Us Do Part*, a comedy about a fictional East End family. Warren Mitchell, who played the bigoted head of the household, had in his youth taken acting lessons in Walthamstow. His character in the show was an ardent supporter of West Ham and had pictures of the Queen and Bobby Moore over his mantelpiece. Despite that, the programme also seemed to have embraced Labour's policy of comprehensive education, and the Conservatives were enlivened again over the image of their leader Edward Heath, who had been referred to as a 'grammar school twit'. The Tories wanted to see what action they could take under the censorship laws.

BIRTH CONTROL ON THE RATES read a headline about a bill introduced in the House of Commons for local councils to run family planning clinics, to be paid for out of local taxes. Leo Abse, the Labour Member for Pontypool in Wales, was one of the bill's sponsors. He also would be sponsoring a bill to liberalise homosexuality shortly, he said.

Women's issues had risen to the fore in connection with the World Cup. The Married Women's Association complained of the BBC's plan to screen more than 50 hours of the tournament across its 21 days. ITV sympathised by saying it would limit itself to 16 hours; unlike the BBC it would not 'go overboard' with its coverage.

The England team's summer tour was traditionally a time-filler in the lengthy gap between the end of one season and the start of another. This one had more importance than normal because of the World Cup's imminence, and the omens were not favourable. England's junior squad had been eliminated from the youth World Cup in Opatija, Yugoslavia. With the formality of one more game to play, they were competing 'for their pride', said their coach, Pat Welton, seven years on now from when he had trained us at Wadham Lodge.

Sir Stanley Rous turned up to speak as guest of honour at a sportwriters' lunch at the Café de Paris in London and sounded less than enthusiastic about England's chances. So were the sportwriters, who presented him with a jar of pickled onions as a memento of the occasion.

We drove down to Siena in two or three days. On our excursions to Italy when I was little, I had taken a bat with me and taught Luciano, the boy of the family that we stayed with and who was a little older than I was, to play cricket – this was possibly the only time the game had been staged in the medieval heart of Siena, where they lived. It being summer, I would not have thought of taking a football. In return, Luciano showed me how to throw large lead-weighted flags up in the air and catch them, as we paraded the streets in support of his horse in the Palio. Nowadays my family passed the time walking the main square or around the city walls. We visited the fort and my dad would point out the room in the far corner on the right where he had been billeted. My sister and I did our best to be interested. At night we ate with the family. A decade ago they had been poor but now had moved to an office block, where the father was concierge, in the square overlooking the football stadium. They were much better off than they had been and Luciano was already living away and at university.

From there we gravitated to Sistiana, near Trieste, and stayed in a small hotel recently built by the bay where my father had been based. It was simple, with cool marble floors affording escape from the Adriatic heat. My dad said, on hot nights in the war, the soldiers had swum out a good half-mile to find cooler water, and fortunately no Slovenian guerrillas were coming the other way. By now the area had a large and modern campsite, which played host to war by other means. The Germans were easily winning the battle against the Dutch, and others, of 'who has the biggest tent?' They also queued at a water hose every day to wash their Mercedes and BMWs. My dad left the Zephyr outside the hotel with its accumulated grime from the *Autobahn* and *autostrade* and washed it only once before the return journey.

The British newspapers that belatedly reached us said Arsenal had sacked their manager Billy Wright on his return from holiday in Italy. Only a little over four thousand people had turned up for one home game at the end of the season in protest at the team's performances. The club said it wanted a big name for the job, while having no idea who that might be.

The seamen's strike had been called off from 1 July. Wilson, challenged to 'name names' of the agents of the Soviet Union who he claimed had infiltrated the strike, had devised a list. I only recognised Jack Dash, chief union organiser around the docks of Wapping and Shadwell Basin in the East End.

Stockbrokers and industrialists invited Dash to speak at their functions. He ended his talks with a courteous Cockney 'thank you for listening' and to applause from audiences who could not help liking him. Wilson's list did the trick, however, as the union took fright at being seen in the eyes of working people as in the pocket of Moscow.

I suggested to my parents that we head back from Sistiana early. They agreed but then, on the last day, I was beckoned by two Italian girls who came running over to me as I was walking through the camp. We sat talking for half an hour, in what for me was an entirely new experience, and they suggested that we get together for a longer spell tomorrow. They were not girls I had seen from the local area. If anything, they looked Romany, familiar and with ready smiles. When my parents asked why I had changed my mind, I gave no convincing answer, guessing that my willingness to be sold into white slavery, if need be, would not be regarded as one. My dad, who enjoyed little more on holiday than putting his foot hard on the Zephyr's throttle, said we still had the Channel to worry about. We needed to make sure about getting back across it.

England's tour involved three kick-about matches against the minor football nations of Finland, Norway and Denmark. The team notched 11 goals without Bobby Charlton hitting the back of the net. He was a perplexing player who switched from world-class performer to the standard 'of an apprentice', complained Ken Jones. Greaves managed to score four goals in a 6–1 win against the Norwegians, but correspondents remarked on his otherwise 'poor attitude'. England's top stars – and, indeed, members of the team in general, the press urged – needed to find their true selves.

On 5 July, Parliament staged its first debate on the bill to loosen the law against homosexuality. The Labour party had not mentioned it in its election campaign in March. Outraged Conservatives said such a measure should not be slipped into law by stealth but tested in the court 'of public opinion', which they knew was against it. Sir Cyril Osborne, MP for Louth in Lincolnshire, said the bill's claim that there were a million male homosexuals in Britain 'darkens' the image of the nation. He had met no 'homos' himself during all his 20 years in Parliament. Leo Abse, the bill's sponsor, who was apt to turn up in the Commons in garish, if impeccably tailored suits and high collared floral shirts, sat smiling opposite him.

As the debate was going on, England began the final game of their tour. This was in Poland and the return match following the draw between the two countries in January. In a composed win, and one that contrasted with the team's efforts in Scandinavia, Roger Hunt scored the single goal, with Ramsey calling the performance 'full of spirit'. Privately, the players agreed. They had played with a bonding hard to achieve in an international team. Ray Wilson later recalled that England's control had suggested to them that – with the World Cup about to start – they might yet come out and surprise people.

But the court of public opinion dictated that for now they keep such views to themselves.

# During

# Chapter 9

# WORK

I started work on the day the World Cup began. Heading off for my job, I gave my mum a conventional peck on the cheek. My dad was late going to the site that day after our midnight return from the Channel and was washing himself at the kitchen sink. He turned his head away. Nothing was said, but we laughed. 'You're in a man's world now, son,' was the message.

Everyone worked, even most of the men in the Bray family down the street who had been in and out of prison, but we did not speak much about them. Along Colebrooke Row, in Elia Street, the son of one of my grandma's best friends did find it difficult to hold down a job. He was small and wanted to be a jockey, something Islington had little call for. My grandma and mother talked about him only in whispers. The latest unemployment figures told the story. In June only just over a quarter of a million people were out of work, about the lowest rate ever. It was mainly comprised of people who had left one job and were moving to another. Virtually everyone I knew did a manual job, my mum among them, in the print factory at the corner by Colebrooke Row, run by Mr Lowe. In the early sixties, the factory printed baggage labels for a company called 'See Spain', a destination known only to a few. My mother brought boxes of the labels home and she, my sister and I looped a string through the small hole at the end of each for £1 a thousand. My grandparents had not liked her continuing to work after I was born. My father, too, had felt that it badly reflected on him – men 'kept' their women, in housekeeping money and at home. My mum said what she earned paid for the holidays.

The factory on the opposite corner, like Mr Lowe's, faced the street with a bare wall, the windows of which had been bricked in. Its clanking machinery produced a widget of some kind that was appropriate to Britain's primacy as an engineering nation. If we dared kick a football against the wall, the foreman in collar, tie and brown overall came out to chide us for interrupting his workers' concentration. He had probably been a wartime sergeant major or a corporal, there often being someone around like that who would put you straight, according to their line of thinking. Mr Lowe, a foreigner, was more tolerant.

My friend Ernie's dad, Mr Michael, had his engineering workshop job in the alley at the side of the Mods' amusement arcade. Walking past with us on a winter's night after an Arsenal match, he would groan at how cold in the morning the steel, the vices and other metal objects around his workbench would be until he got a few gas taps going and a kettle boiling. He, and quite a few like him, worked near enough to come home for dinner – dinner was had in the middle of the day, tea in the evening. We did not know anyone who had 'lunch', except if they had sandwiches packed up to tide them through between proper meals.

Much of that was changing as efforts to clean up the air after the smogs chased a lot of local workplaces away. At the bottom of our street the British Drug Houses – the BDH – had regularly stank out our junior school by St Peter's Street. On some days you could still smell it right across Danbury Street and at the top of Noel Road. New residents, who had perhaps viewed their property with thoughts to buy on breezier, clearer days, must have wondered what they had walked into. Some 20 years later the building was turned into bijou flats overlooking the canal, but I imagined the smell still haunted the place.

My father missed manual work and had only given it up at the bidding of my mother. He was persuaded that he did not want to spend his winters on high, exposed scaffolding. Also, when he was elevated to the site office in the early part of the sixties, foremen and above earned more than the average brickie. He still picked up a trowel at any opportunity to show 'how it's done' to those he supervised. As well as his apprenticeship, in the fifties he had done his City and Guilds at North London Poly in Holloway Road. For his passing-out exhibition he built a pulpit and a sundial. We went to see them and the sundial, made of small delicate brick, found its place in our backyard.

Bricklayers today could earn more than my dad had, or did, and none had anything like his training. For both reasons, he took a special interest in their walls and often ordered them to knock them down. While he was working on one of the new hotels by London airport, the site agent – who, in general, had to defer to the clerk of works – respectfully asked if he could loosen his demands a little because the project was falling behind schedule. I was not sure that he did, because on one occasion he heard a young type was on site calling himself 'the Golden Trowel'. My dad went round to see him, pointed out he hadn't turned a corner too well, and the bloke took offence. 'You do your fucking job and I'll do mine,' he told my dad. So my dad did, and sacked him, or as the phrase had it, sent him 'down the road'. The best brickies nowadays, he said, were those who had been to prison. In the Scrubs or on the Moor, they had been given at least a six-month course.

*The Mirror* advertised a full page of jobs available on the World Cup's opening day. A company in Harlow, Essex, wanted glass inspectors for £20 a week 'with a house'. Pipe benders on shift in Derby and Sunderland were told '£30 a week possible'. Crawley, the new town in Sussex, needed coded welders; if you were one, you presumably knew what that was. The Initial laundry sought to attract women out of the house with £9.12s.4d (about £9.62) for a five-day week with 'day nursery available for children between 2 and 5'. During the years my dad was out late at the poly, my mum worked nights at the Initial in City Road. My grandma and granddad dropped in to see if my sister and I were sleeping OK.

On the fourth floor of the Tote building off Fleet Street, by St Bride's church, I had to report to a Mr Felix, the man in charge, and his assistant, Madge. In his office, they looked again at my application letter, written in longhand assisted by our school handwriting classes. 'Let's see. How old are you?' asked Felix, who wore a navy pinstriped suit, which marked him out from any of the other men I had seen around. Both he and Madge whooped 'congratulations' when they saw I had been 18 the day before and announced the fact as they escorted me out into a large main hall.

It was almost empty of people but lined with ranks of desks and phones. Nearly all the staff I could see were men. My boss, Tony Barker, was from Upminster at the end of the District Line and smoked with a rolled cigarette on his lip. He had consistently to relight it, which he did without burning himself, even when it had nearly disappeared. Younger than my dad, he had a National Service background – that was to say he had been forced to join up after the war – and had been sent to the Far East. He was delighted to have a starter from a grammar school: 'I'll teach you everything, son.'

I already felt bad. I had not told him or anyone else there that I would only be at the place for a few weeks. Though abundant, work was a prized thing for those who recalled the thirties or forties. All employment had to be approached as if it was the only job we had dreamed of, and that we craved it for life. Anything less would have seemed ungrateful, something we were often regarded as being.

The office was quiet in the morning, as we balanced the previous day's bets from the racecourses. What had been paid out had to match what was due to be paid. I had gone into work in jeans. Ron, who had left school at 16 and was younger than I was, had a grey suit that he wore every day. An elderly man named Jack smoked heavily and said little as he huffed around in a sports jacket. Ron was diligent and friendly. Mike Cole, on a desk by the window looking over a Ludgate Hill bomb site towards St Paul's, dealt with forecasts: bets forecasting the first and second in a race. The work required specialist calculations and Mike wrote his numbers in his own calligraphy, with flicks of a well-sharpened pencil. He was courteously friendly and spoke in an abrupt, slightly affected accent: 'Thang'kyo!' He was not interested in the World Cup. 'Tennis is my game,' he told me.

Informed I could take an hour's break in the top-floor canteen at any time from 11.30 – as long as I was back by the time the racing started – I was surprised, on my return, to see a large number of women arriving. A big lady named Ivy from the East End worked a clunky adding machine near us on a section called Silver Doubles. I never did find out what that was. The other women worked part-time in a room next to our area filled with more adding machines. They all seemed to come from east or south London and several were called Jean.

An elegantly dressed woman, Daisy, was their boss. Two girls of about my age were also among them. One, Terry, had her blonde hair in a Mary Quant style, and both had their moments of staring at me through a small window on the wall that separated us, not that I didn't initiate or reciprocate. They and the Irish lady serving in the canteen, who had kept chatting to and winking at me during my break, provided my first close contact in a daily environment with members of the opposite sex. It felt like life had begun.

A band of men poured in for the racing. Several had slicked hair and red faces, like they had just shaved. Many had. They had two jobs, and worked the night shift at one of the Post Office's many telephone exchanges. Featureless red-brick buildings, each one served a different area of London – Canonbury, Putney and so on. Some exchanges had strange names: 'Terminus' was for numbers in the City. Chelsea's exchange was, for some reason, called 'Flaxman'. The men, I learned, had been in their jobs for some while and had risen up the career ladder; they put people through for long-distance calls abroad, to the US or elsewhere, though whatever skills this required did not seem to include another language. The Post Office advertised for women to handle domestic long-distance calls on considerably lower money.

My first day, there were three race meetings: Windsor in the afternoon and Nottingham and Stockton-on-Tees in the evening. Geoff Lewis, one of the leading jockeys, was managing to ride at both Windsor and Nottingham. Evening racing had only been a feature at London's Alexandra Palace – the 'Ally Pally' – until recently, but the country was becoming yet more entangled in the bookies' web. The Tote itself was not there to make a profit. Once it had paid its expenses, whatever was left over went into horse racing and, ostensibly, into giving pleasure to the millions gripped by it.

The money flowed in, and some of the bets were enormous. One Tote punter bet £300 on every favourite whose odds narrowed with the bookies to 1–3, or 'three-to-one on'. That translated as £3 being staked to make a gain of just £1. This gambler did not take his huge punt, however, on the horse winning the race, but on it making at least the minor placings of second or third. Such a hot favourite, you'd have thought, would surely do that. The punter's return would be very small but he had no doubt calculated that it added up over time. Or that was what several of my colleagues assured me, variously nodding or tapping the side of their nose at the shrewd people who populated our world.

With each race run, we had only a few minutes to work out a preliminary figure for what had been won and lost. To calculate the pay-out on each horse, books similar to the logarithm tables we had at school were available. My colleagues had little use for them, Tony none at all as he rapidly did everything in his head. Paper passed from hand to hand and piled up on the tables. Cigarettes were lit in rhythm with the pace of the afternoon. Everyone except Mike the tennis player and me smoked. 'Do not throw cigarette ends in the stalls,' said a printed sign in the gents. Someone had scrawled: 'They get soggy and difficult to light.'

I was put with Dick, a squat Cockney with thin Brylcreemed hair parted in the middle. Dick wore black horn-rimmed glasses and a dark-blue suit and worked with Chris who, in his sports jacket, had an accent of cut glass and was the only person who could understand Dick in full flow. They operated a few feet from everyone else, over by the window that looked through towards the women, which gave me the chance to peer in at Terry and her friend. One of the Jeans, all of a rush, delivered a machined list of bets, the last on each race. Many were very large and placed late as punters weighed the odds. Dick rattled off the bets to Chris at the speed of a tobacco auctioneer. This list had to be accurate and was 'blown' late to each racecourse. That was to say, its figures were reported over the phone – the blower – and comprised the final input for the people at the course who calculated the Tote's own starting prices. At Dagenham dogs two years earlier, someone had blocked the phones to prevent bets getting through and landed a coup on the distorted odds. But not for long: the scheme's organisers were caught and jailed.

In World Cup terms, the day had been subdued. *The Mirror*'s main front-page story was of a lost trawler from Grimsby found in the North Sea with five crew members missing. One suggestion was that they had mutinied in the seamen's strike. Another said they had paddled away in a small boat in the direction of East Germany. Had they defected to the Communist bloc? More likely, it was the latest in a series of incidents affecting the Grimsby trawler fleet. A disciplinary committee had been set up to deal with a spate of hooliganism. One crew had recently got drunk and thrown its lifeboats overboard. I was reminded of when Grimsby Town were passing through London on their way from a game on the south coast and making their late-night connection home at King's Cross. Some of the players were so merry that they could only scrawl their signatures, whether from celebrating victory or relieving the sorrows of defeat, I couldn't recall. One or two were incapable of holding a pen.

A small report on the front page of *The Mirror* at least nodded in the direction of the event of the moment. The Brazilians were anxious about drug tests being introduced for the first time in a World Cup. They might test positive with all the coffee they drank and wanted the same to apply for England and their cups of tea. Actually, this view was becoming a little outdated; more people I knew were beginning to drink coffee. In the fifties, all we'd had around was the black gooey liquid called Camp coffee, which you mixed with hot water. For some reason it was made with chicory. It came in a thin bottle with a picture of a Scottish soldier from the days of empire sitting outside his battle tent in his kilt and saying, 'Aye, Ready.' These days, though, even my grandparents might have the occasional cup of instant.

At the back of the paper, Greaves was pronounced as England's 'Ace in the Pack'. He was shown smiling and smoking his pipe on a child's swing, his feet high and large at the front of the picture. THESE BOOTS ARE MADE FOR SCORING said the headline, a pun on 'These Boots Are Made For Walkin'', the number-one hit Frank Sinatra's daughter Nancy had had earlier in the year. The consensus view was that the Uruguayans – a small nation of meat eaters – were strong but beatable. Their youngest player Milton Viera, 20, was shown praying at a church in Harlow, where the team were based. A photo of the England team had Jack and Bobby Charlton and others relaxing over a game of cards at their hotel headquarters in Hendon. England had a short trip along the North Circular to get to Wembley. From way out to the east, Uruguay's bus would crawl across London.

As I arrived back from work, I just had time before the game to put in a quick call to Ron Burgess. The Bedford Town manager would be at his home number and I wanted to ask when we were to start pre-season training. It would usually begin in mid-July, about now, yet I hadn't heard. Bedford had just transferred Derek Bellotti to Gillingham, a fully fledged league team. He had made his way into the professional world and would go on to play for Southend, Charlton and Swansea around the lower divisions until the mid-seventies. Maybe this would open up a path for me: a spell in the reserves, a nice bit of cash in the boot after a game, a chance to climb up and, perhaps, attract the interest of a league side.

Burgess would be settling in for the game himself, re-living a few memories of the big matches he had played at Wembley: those for Wales, and the one when he had skippered the Rest of the World; just a minute stood between him and leading the first foreign team to beat England at Wembley. Ramsey had got in the way.

We had a chat about prospects for the game and how our summers had been. I thought he sounded a little distant and finally, when I asked about training, he politely told me that I need not turn up. No reason was offered. I did not know what to say and just had to take it that he was reassessing his goalkeeping situation. Not only was he a former captain of club, country and world status, but also he knew his goalkeepers, and I was not up to being the next Pat Jennings. I went up to number 7 to watch the game with my granddad. I didn't mention to him that any lingering ambition I had of making it in football had ended a few minutes before England kicked off in the World Cup. He'd have nodded, possibly without comment. Life had its disappointments, and his view would have been: 'So, you'll do something else, then.'

The royal party arrived a quarter of an hour before the kick-off to declare the competition open and meet the players on the pitch. The Coldstream Guards had provided 30 minutes of marching and martial music, in what turned out to be the night's most spirited play. What a 'dreary dish to set before the Queen', one report of the match would say. I read that a vicar in Newmarket had written in his church magazine, before the World Cup, that he hoped players would desist from the 'ridiculous craze' of hugging and kissing when celebrating goals. His prayers were heard; the match ended 0–0.

The quiet confidence generated by the England players in the Poland game deserted them, as it apparently did Ramsey. He put aside his unusual tactics, dropped Peters and brought in

John Connelly of Manchester United. Connelly was a winger. What was Ramsey doing?

What the Uruguayans were up to was looking for a draw; they packed their defence from the first whistle. Greaves' shooting boots went missing, Bobby Charlton was anonymous and most of the 87,148 spectators who turned up hooted their disapproval.

Relieved that England had not lost, I was unaware that my mood had deteriorated as a result of the general evening's events until after the final whistle. You misjudged a high ball or a low one slipped under your body, but you either suppressed your feelings or found a way to let them be. Not so Uruguay's captain and goalkeeper, Ladislao Mazurkiewicz, who danced around in his penalty area doing a polka of delight. Wasn't that just like the Latins? And what did he have to celebrate? Did he think getting a draw against England was a big deal? With my granddad around I couldn't, but in my head I shouted at him: we were 'never going to win the World Cup anyway!'

In other news, the British car industry was also going down the pan. Next morning, Jaguar and BMC – the British Motor Corporation – announced that they were to merge. Douglas Jay, in charge of UK trade, said the government would not get in their way. Sir Jack Lyons, the founder of Jaguar, said it was far better than selling out to the Americans. But BMC was already a defensive alliance against foreign invaders. It combined Austin and Morris and, in turn, Morris had under its mantel other old names like Wolseley and MG. My dad insisted he would do his bit by never buying Japanese, thanks to what Uncle Reg had contended with in Burma. The Zephyr was from the huge Ford plant at Dagenham, and that was as good as British.

It hardly mattered anyway because the roads were seizing up. An official report said it would happen in 15 years' time, although it skewed its findings. Increased car ownership in the suburbs was the problem, it said, not central London. Had its researchers been to Noel Road in these Kaganite times? The report proposed a new ring road around London, the one that eventually would be called the M25. Transport minister Barbara Castle, meanwhile, said the experiment of a limit of 70 miles per hour on the motorway system would stay for another year. Future M25 and other motorway users would often dream of such a speed.

We had warnings of a 'credit squeeze' during the week. This related to the Bank of England's messengers running around as the bank rate rose 1%. It went up to 7% to 'keep prices to the consumer down'. How? I could not see the connection. By, it was explained, reducing borrowing from the banks. No one I knew borrowed from the banks. My granddad refused to.

In some related way that was difficult to fathom, Barclay's chimed in by saying it was not necessary to get money from a bank at all. Maybe I would have understood if I had gone to work for them. The bank said you only had to show shopkeepers a plastic card it had invented and they would hand over what you wanted. Large adverts in the papers told us not to be suspicious, even though our money would move around now without anyone seeing it.

It could have been that the people doing the borrowing were those moving into our street and the surrounding areas. One of the latest things was to have their doorsteps nicely re-levelled and cemented by Brian, an acquaintance of my dad, though younger. Brian had given up on building sites, 'gone out on his own' and was nifty with a trowel. Only a few years ago, with the delayed effects of the war, the street's front doorsteps had been collapsing into the kitchens or bathrooms beneath. Brian gave them support and a smooth veneer, working alongside his transistor radio. He tuned it to the classical BBC Third Programme, creating a good impression for the newcomers and the right result. 'He's good,' said my dad. 'And doesn't he charge.'

Paul Jones, lead singer of Manfred Mann, had moved in by St John's, the Catholic church in Duncan Terrace, and had a child's rocking horse in his front-parlour window, another symbol of arrival. He made the front pages on the World Cup's second day. With Jean Shrimpton, the model, he was to star in *Privilege*, a film to be shot in London and Brighton 'in colour', said the reports, implying this was especially daring. Shrimpton, who had taken modelling out of the frumpy fifties feel of the early years of the decade, had given way to Twiggy as the face of the 'sixties' proper and said she had wanted to get into films for a while. Her contract was worth £25,000. No figure was given for what Jones would get but it was enough for him to announce he was giving up Manfred Mann.

At the Albert Hall, Bob Dylan had brought his electric guitar to the South-East for the first time and prompted howls of disgust from his folk-singing fans. They were a rare bunch, judging by the couple of older kids at my school who had organised Friday-night sea shanties and similar in a room over a pub near Highbury Corner. Why were they so keen to keep Dylan to themselves? A lot of us enjoyed mouthing along to hits like 'Subterranean Homesick Blues' without any idea what he was getting at. Why, for instance, had we better 'stay away from those that carry around a fire hose'?

Pelé and the Brazilians put the World Cup properly into motion with the tournament's opening goal. In their game against Bulgaria, Brazil won a free-kick on the edge of the opposition's penalty area and Pelé bent the ball through a gap in the defensive wall. Garrincha, too, was spectacular, and the champions looked on course to retain their title.

Jack Dunnett, a football-loving MP for Nottingham Central, had already seen enough to make up his mind. Although his parliamentary seat was in the East Midlands, he somehow managed to be the chairman of Brentford Football Club in west London at the same time. Once the World Cup was over and all the teams had gone home, Dunnett said, sadly, we faced the prospect of very few overseas players gracing our shores again. If overseas footballers wanted to get on the books of an English club, they had first to live in the country for two years. During such a time they'd have grown too rusty or old to be able to play. He was going to ask the Ministry of Labour to loosen its restrictions on work permits for foreign footballers.

In Brighton, students at the university Bobby Blake said he was heading for had made their own protests over Britain's stance on Vietnam. They were outside the Corn Exchange as Harold Wilson arrived to receive an honorary doctorate from Sussex University. It was difficult to know what Wilson's stance was, although the US had begun bombing Hanoi, the North Vietnamese capital.

The Jay twins received their degrees, among the first awarded in Sussex University's three-year history. In ancient Cambridge, however, Robert Harbinson – described as a brilliant student who had failed his eleven-plus, gone to a state school and on to Corpus Christi College – was refused his degree after police found drugs in his room, including £10 of hashish. He was told to take psychiatric treatment and put on probation. The impression Bobby had given of the university he was bound for was that if the police had raided there, Wilson would have been one of the few 'graduates' leaving Brighton that day with their certificates.

The prime minister was otherwise engaged in reorganising his cabinet. Frank Cousins, the union leader, resigned from the Ministry of Technology protesting at the prime minister's policy of keeping wages down. Wedgwood Benn, far less radical in the cause of the worker, replaced him. My telephone operator colleagues at the Tote spoke of the all-number system that would allow direct dial calls all over the world without any realisation that it would render their jobs useless. Wedgwood Benn now moved from Postmaster General to being, in effect, the minister for British industry. One of his final acts in his old job was to have tea with the Queen at the top of the newly opened Post Office Tower near Tottenham Court Road. Its revolving restaurant had views all over London but members of the public complained that, unlike the Queen, they could not get a reservation. Its phone number was ex-directory.

Ramsey was also moving his team around, but remained tentative in the way he went about it. For the approaching Saturday's match against Mexico, he dropped Connelly and brought in Terry Paine, the Southampton veteran. A Paine goal against Leyton Orient to seal a 1–1 draw had just won Southampton promotion to the first division and condemned Orient to the third. That was hardly World Cup calibre and, yet more confusing, Paine was another winger. You couldn't fathom it.

Kick-off against Mexico was only a couple of hours away as I drew my first weekly wage packet – £15. That was as much as a merchant seaman made and, with no tax to pay as I worked off the unused part of my annual allowance, I celebrated by visiting a new 'hairdresser' in Camden Passage. Not too long ago, the passage had contained a pram shop, a toy shop that specialised in model railways, and a lean-to occupied by a cats' meat man. Our area had had two, the other one peddling his bike out of the same yard as the Frome Street scrap-metal dealer. Both had seemed to vaporise with the last of the smogs.

England's second match was going the same way as the first as the Mexicans withdrew around and into their own penalty area. Half-time approached with minimal sign of England making any impression when Bobby Charlton suddenly exploded into the game. Once a striker and drafted by Ramsey into the role of midfield craftsman, he had seemed uncertain during a long lean spell of games about what function he was to perform. Here he chose to combine the two. Picking up the ball near the halfway line, he set off on an individual run straight at the opposition defence and, from 30 yards, hit a shot with his unfavoured right foot.

My parents had gone to Bedford for the evening, and I had prepared myself a plate of spaghetti for the occasion. I half shouted and half choked on a tightly twirled forkful as the ball flew on a rising trajectory into the top-right corner of the net. Charlton had imposed himself at last. And something changed.

# Chapter 10

# CRASH

Harold Wilson missed the Mexico match. He had flown to Moscow that morning for talks. Bringing peace to Vietnam was on his agenda, which was getting less and less easy. The Russians backed Ho Chi Minh, who had called up his military reservists. The Americans had intensified their bombing. I had heard Bernard Levin talking about it. Levin was the brilliant character in tightly buttoned suit who had been part of the satire wave two or three years ago with David Frost and others on *That Was the Week That Was*. He said he supported the US bombing, for which they were using a new kind of weapon called napalm. The Americans aimed to destroy trees rather than people so they could see better the enemy they were fighting.

As Wilson shuttled between the sides, he sometimes looked a bit lost for a role, for himself and for Britain. But his response remained: when in doubt keep moving. This gave the impression of doing something when there was not very much he could do, really. In a sweltering Moscow, his hosts applied the brakes for him, putting him up in a guest dacha on the city outskirts. He sat alone on the Saturday evening watching – not football – but the Russian version of *War and Peace.*

On his trip, he was due to meet Alexei Kosygin, the USSR's deputy leader. They were attending a British trade fair that was exhibiting UK factory machinery. Our exports to the Soviet Union had been going up, even if, as we heard, they were not to the rest of the world. Big new orders were expected from the Russians, who were ahead in the space race. Just three months ago they had beaten the Americans in landing an unmanned spacecraft on the moon.

In the end, England had run out 2–0 winners against the Mexicans. The crowd of getting on for 93,000 was up on Uruguay, possibly because people enjoyed their football more of a Saturday than a Monday. Hunt popped in the second goal from an easy chance. There were other things to celebrate. Brazil were struggling, having lost the night before to Hungary at Goodison Park. Pelé was unfit and unable to play and the Hungarians capitalised to win 3–1. Their second goal – from a long diagonal cross from the right wing by Flórián Albert, and a János Farkas volley on the run – was spectacular. I watched the game with Ernie in his small TV sitting room, his dad finishing off his regular third packet of Woodbines for the day. The fug allowed the sense of watching the Magyars through the mists of '53.

Then again, some dubious scheduling had helped. Pelé needed time that he did not get to recover from an injury incurred in the Bulgarian game. Fifa and Sir Stanley Rous had fixed the match dates such that the Brazilians had only from the Tuesday night Bulgaria clash until Friday evening to prepare to face the Hungarians. England had played Uruguay on Monday and did not face the Mexicans until Saturday, two days more in which to recuperate from any aches and strains.

CRACKERJACK CHARLTON read the top of the *News of the World*'s sports page next morning, a possibly confusing reference, since it was Bobby not his brother Jack who had scored. The headline writer may have already edited the Sunday evening's TV schedules on an inside page. The jovial chat-show host Eamonn Andrews would be in his usual 10.30 p.m. slot. He had made his reputation years ago on the children's show *Crackerjack*, when kids who answered questions correctly won prizes and, if they didn't, took home a cabbage. Andrews looked now like he was handed one every week. Young sixties upstarts like David Bailey, the photographer and ex-boyfriend of Jean Shrimpton, were joining him on Sunday nights and taking advantage of the fact that the show was live by making lewd comments to inflame the censor. Actor Laurence Harvey had told an obscene joke about a camel.

Greaves had shown a spark of revival in the Mexico game. With 15 minutes left, linking well with Charlton, he put in a good shot across the face of goal. The keeper, diving low, only managed to palm it out but into the path of Hunt rather than Greaves. Jimmy might have settled into the tournament nicely, if it had come to him. There were general signs of things stirring, as by the end a few choruses rang out from the Wembley terraces of 'When the Whites go marching in'.

Was this an indication of the three lions on England's shirt starting to roar? Not quite, suggested another news item. Three lions had escaped from their cage on a flight from Frankfurt to London at the weekend, though one of them was only a cub. Percy, Olaf and three-month-old Sheila slipped out and made for the cockpit on their way from Ethiopia to the Marquess of Bath's wildlife park at Longleat. The co-pilot held off the animals with an axe until an emergency landing at Brussels when 'Tommy-gun wielding police' surrounded the aircraft. The pilots escaped through a cockpit window and a net was thrown over the front of the plane.

Elizabeth Taylor and Richard Burton were also flying into London, following the death of the actress's sister in Rome. Burton and Taylor's film *Who's Afraid of Virginia Woolf?* had opened to the acclaim of critics. Others would find its story of a relationship in collapse harrowing. When I went to see it, I gave myself no idea what to expect through any advance reading and, if anything, anticipated a comedy. Burton and Taylor, who married and divorced each other twice, may have been living rather than acting the parts.

Divorce was always news. Only the wealthiest people could usually afford it and their secrets made good material for the papers. Blame had to be proved and it was very expensive to do so. Recent cases included bandleader Jack Parnell, who denied having an affair with the hostess of 'Beat the Clock', the family games part of *Sunday Night at the London Palladium*. In another court deliberation, Justices Diplock and Scarman decreed that it was less harmful for a dustman to lose his wife to a baron than the other way around. They had before them the matter of an engineer's wife who had run off with a wealthy businessman. The latter had to pay the engineer damages of £7,500 but, on appeal, the judges said the engineer's relatively modest lifestyle meant he could get by with a third of that. Another case was of a wife who 'yearned for gay Vienna'. An Austrian woman married to an Englishman had missed the gaiety of her home city, made regular visits back and had an adulterous affair while there.

Family break-ups were now less remote than they had been; in our area the old order was breaking down. One of my uncles and his wife had separated. It was upsetting and we didn't talk about it. Our next-door neighbour to our right vanished with the wife of the man two doors to our left. Divorce was suddenly all around us, in the world of ordinary people.

The *News of the World* had turned itself to the matter of the 'blue pencil'. This was what the official censor was said to use when cutting something from a film, newspaper, book or magazine. The Lord Chamberlain censored the theatre, the police scrutinised books and magazines and the Secretary of British Film Censors ran his eye over the cinema's alleged dirty bits. Parliament would soon study the matter. The *News of the World* cited the public criticism about *Till Death Us Do Part* which had mocked such 'sacred cows' as Edward Heath and 'football fans'. I did not get this. What was sacred about Heath? That he was a dab hand on the organ in Salisbury cathedral? As for football fans, I had no idea that we were so highly regarded. The writer was probably just fed up with the suddenly large number of live World Cup games on television (normally we only got the FA Cup final or the occasional England match). The paper professed to care that so many people were gravely concerned 'at the trend towards greater freedom of expression'. Did it mean we were heading for a brave new world, it asked, or the 'decadent dung heap'?

Top of that pile as far as Harold Wilson was concerned were the 'Gnomes of Zurich'. As the World Cup entered its second week, the pound dipped and the Gnomes hawked sterling for any alternative currency. Wilson used the term to summon the image of Swiss bankers – small and industrious people, no doubt – busying in their mountain caves to mess up other people's economies. The cry went up to 'defend the pound', but what did this mean? Were we to sell more planes, lathes and a rocket part or two to the Russians? Maybe we should allow fewer Japanese motorbikes into the country and return to the days when British-made Nortons ridden by Geoff Duke dominated the Isle of Man TT?

The *News of the World* provided the answer. The morning after Crackerjack Bobby hinted at new possibilities for the England football team, the paper ran an article about the state of modern Britain by the Conservative MP for Worcester, Sir Gerald Nabarro. Sir Gerald often appeared in the papers, on the radio and on TV, with his handlebar moustache and manner in which he declaimed rather than spoke. Referring to a row, say, among MPs, he was likely to smile widely and deride it as a mere 'brouhaha'. His story told us why we were in a mess. Last year British production had been static but earnings had risen by nearly 10%, or two shillings in the pound. But was this not a good thing? Employers, or 'governors', as we tended to call them, were only showing their appreciation for our efforts. Apparently it was not. 'There is gross overfull employment,' said Sir Gerald. The newspaper, for which my grandfather had worked for so many years, itself went on to explain that we had 'rigidly held views on the need to maintain full employment'. In short, we had entered a world where too many people worked. Those, like my granddad, who had kept himself employed through the Depression, had laboured under quite the wrong idea. So had the people at the Tote who did the telephone nightshift, and so had I in getting a summer job. We were out of time with the world and its demands. With us all in work, an employer had to pay us more than he wanted to in order to attract us into another job or to keep us in this one. It was staggering how my family and almost everyone I knew had deluded themselves for so long. The one who was doing it right was the kid two streets away who wanted to be a London jockey, when the Ally Pally only staged a few night meetings each year.

'Stand firm, Wilson,' insisted the *News of the World*. He had railwaymen, coal miners and the dockworkers led by troublesome Jack Dash lining up with pay and pension demands. The prime minister was reminded that he would have a lot on his plate when he got back from Moscow.

Ramsey appeared nervous approaching the France game for the following Wednesday. He dropped Terry Paine and brought in Ian Callaghan of Liverpool, yet another winger. That was three now in a row – Connelly, Paine and Callaghan, all good players, but did they fit the bill? What bill was the England manager trying to fit them to? England only needed a draw against the French to qualify for the next stage of the competition but Ramsey's many advisers in the press told him that he 'must not play it safe'. There were very good reasons for that. Brazil had gone out the night before, clogged by their cousins from Portugal. Pelé came back, not fully fit, and the Portuguese defence hacked at his wounds. He hobbled off, holding his boots and making his way painfully around the Goodison touchline, almost in tears. Portugal's star Eusébio was now the striker to watch. In Middlesbrough, Italy went out shockingly to a 1–0 defeat by North Korea. In the celebratory pitch invasion at the end, a burly Teesside steelworker lifted Korea's tiny goalscorer Pak Doo-ik high in the air. Italy took flight home under cover of darkness, angry fans still turning up at Genoa airport to pelt them with tomatoes.

England beat the French 2–0. Wembley was getting near capacity at 98,270, the crowd's curiosity aroused. Largely against the run of play, Hunt scored both goals. One came after a Jack Charlton header did all the work, hitting a post and bouncing back such that Hunt could not miss. The second was an easy header which he bungled by nodding the ball straight at the keeper, who fumbled it in.

Qualification from the group stage meant England had evaded humiliation. What chance we had of going further, I was still deciding after the final whistle when Wilson cut in to the *Horse of the Year Show*. Back in the country, he appeared on television to announce dire economic developments. It was time to 'call a halt', he said, without precisely saying to what. We had heard this before from him. Just as we were getting things going, the prime minister was telling us to stop again.

Not necessarily to clarify matters, another Wilson weighed into the debate next morning. What mistakes had we made and what of the future? Indeed, did we have a future? Or was this truly when everything ground to a halt? These were the questions exercising the minds of the majority of people, certainly among the male members of the population, and it was not Harold, but Peter Wilson, *The Mirror*'s chief sportswriter, who addressed them in his role as the 'man they can't gag'. England's performance against France, he reported, sent you away from Wembley 'not wanting to sing Rule Britannia'. Yes, England had moved from the first group stage of the competition to the knock-out games of the quarter-finals, but what hope was there beyond? Not much, and the victory against France had been like 'shaking hands with an empty glove'.

It had been a night for gloves. Banks had his on to handle the slippery ball. Wilson wrote that the teams played the match through a 'grey skein of rain' (I made a note to look up 'skein'). Keepers only wore gloves in the wet, generally wool or a stringy variety that my dad called oiled-cotton. I had used old pairs of his, while Banks, I imagined, bought the ones he wore from Marks and Spencer's. In part, England had won last night because of deficient gloves. That was why the French keeper had let Hunt's header slip through his hands. It would take until the seventies and Sepp Maier of Bayern Munich before goalkeepers started appearing in the all-weather glove, which was another facet of the German revival. I wished I'd had them at Brisbane Road. They made your hands feel bigger.

The contest with the French, said Wilson, had threatened to develop into one of those 'cobweb matches where theory strangles an essentially simple game'. Here he betrayed that he was not making the transition from the old to the new English style of play. Until fairly recently, teams lined up on the field in a pyramid of goalkeeper, two full-backs, three half-backs and five forwards. This was so normal that neither players nor fans noticed. It was just the way the game was. Any theory behind it amounted to someone at the back hoofing the ball up to someone big at the front. This would be the giant centre-forward, who bore down on the opposition goalkeeper with licence to assault him.

Now we had gone cobwebby, and had teams lining up in strange formations. Ramsey and Dave Sexton were in the vanguard of the movement. Were we ready for it? Would it be effective? Maybe such questions had troubled Ramsey into being so tentative in the first three games. It was OK away from home on a winter's night in distant Madrid, but maybe hard to put on show at Wembley in full public view.

A lot of mental cobwebs would have to be cleared for the next game against Argentina, in the quarter-finals. England had only two days to prepare for the team billed as the world's major proponents of negative football. The Argentines' match at the group stage against West Germany had deteriorated into a riot, with one of their defenders being sent off and their training staff invading the pitch. Against such a force, did we have the mentality to push on? The tournament was now getting serious. England's best ever performances had always been in one-off friendly games that did not matter. Were we so used to failure that we did not want success? England were going to have to show as yet unrevealed qualities against Argentina and display, Wilson concluded, the 'air of those not afraid to be hailed as champions'.

Next to his article was a tiny piece in a box about an inch square. It bore the peripheral information that Greaves had been injured against France. He had some stitches in his shin after a clash in the first half but had played on and presumably would be fit again in no time. The article ended with Ramsey saying England had been 'far too casual' against France and had not played as well as in their first two games. This came as news to many fans, who thought that in those early matches England had been rubbish.

The respectable element of the population, meanwhile, had been stunned by Wilson's words – Harold's of the night before, that was. People who generally did not think much about football were all of a quandary. Industrialists, stockbrokers and retailers wondered 'what now?' Down among the sacred cows, I struggled to comprehend how the world had changed. DEEP FREEZE blasted *The Mirror*. Wages were to be frozen for six months, prices for a year and, at last, we had a 'government with guts'. After 15 years of erosion – 13 under the Tories and two under Labour – our punishment was allegedly justified: '40 whacks,' wrote the paper, as if the population had been on a thieving spree several times worse than our school's trip to HMS *Victory*. 'You've had the beano, now comes the headache.' I did not get this either. Beanos were coach trips that catered to a pre-war audience. Wallace Arnold up at the Angel, or possibly other companies organised them. They started at the public houses open first thing in the morning in Smithfield market for the meat porters and travelled to others in the southerly direction of Brighton or towards Southend in the east. They ended up late at night in Smithfield again as the pubs reopened at the start of the porters' shift. Beanos were dying out and were for people who either could not manage a proper holiday or went hop-picking in Kent. No one I knew went on them, and the implication that large numbers of ordinary people had been living life to such excess was insulting. My grandma used Wallace Arnold to book day trips with my granddad to places like Margate. She said it was one of the few ways she could get him to come away.

To make matters worse, petrol was to go up sharply by 4d (about 1½ pence). Another penny was going on a pint of beer and an extra 3s 5d (17p-ish) on a bottle of whisky. The latter worked out as 2d on each single measure: 'tuppence on a tot!' A rise in purchase tax added 18s 9d (about 94p) to the price of a television, but it was difficult to see what effect that would have. A black and white set cost £65 and, what with that being more than a month's take-home pay for most people, many hired TVs. (We did, from the Radio Rentals shop on Upper Street by the Union Chapel, and had done so for years. I had won a football there by forecasting the correct result in the 1959 Cup final which, since my uncles' team Luton lost 2–1 to Nottingham Forest, was controversial. Roy Dwight, Elton John's uncle, scored the first Forest goal.) You also rented a television because they broke down a lot. If it was your own it might disappear for a fortnight. You needed to know how the thing worked, when all you wanted to do was watch it. It was better, therefore, to have the Radio Rentals repairers come round free. The company was running adverts of its people lined up for a picture on the Wembley turf. They formed up in their work gear like a team photo in my old scrapbooks: 'Don't take a chance at World Cup time. Perfect viewing for 7/8d a week [about 38p].' Not that Pye, the Cambridge television maker, had lost hope about the future of colour. When it had the government's go-ahead, it said, it would sell the first mass-produced sets for a guaranteed £260 each. Who to? My dad had got that for the Classic when he traded it for the Zephyr.

Wilson's measures, I read, were to take 'five hundred million pounds out of demand'. All very well for him with his terms but what did that mean? Normal Islington people did not walk around thinking, 'I wonder what I need taking out of demand today.' We were suddenly in an age where it was assumed we knew about such things. Apparently, demand was what we did when we came within reach of a shopkeeper, although not necessarily around our way. If I'd have 'demanded' this or that of Bert or Mr Millard, the competing grocers in Danbury Street, when presenting them with my mother's shopping list, I'd have been told to be more polite in future.

What the five hundred million 'out of demand' meant was that the government wanted us to stop spending money in the less than reckless way that we were. We were doing far too much of whatever it was that we were doing: first it was work, now it was modest levels of spending. I had had just over a week of the former and – since my first wage packet – five days of the latter. So far I had 'demanded' some tomato sandwiches off the Irish lady in the canteen – 'We normally only do cheese and tomato,' she winked – a few tube tickets between the Angel and Blackfriars and a Camden Passage haircut.

So who were the reckless spenders? Viv Nicholson, the Yorkshire housewife whose husband had won £150,000 on the football pools in 1961, had said at the time she was going to 'spend, spend, spend'. She had been so true to her word that, five years later, she was just about to run out of money. But she hardly spoke for the generality. Apart from on defence, the big money was being spent on hospitals, schools and public housing. My parents' generation had learned, often warily, that this was among their rewards for the war.

As for pointers towards a new future, several large finds had been made in recent weeks of oil and gas in the North Sea. This was giving the City of London something to do with all its spare time. The new investment of Unit Trusts was launched and tied to the discoveries.

In health matters, the US had tested magnesium pemoline, a new drug 'to restore memory to old people'. With people living longer, a greater prevalence had been noted of people like my grandma Chapman, who forgot who or where they were.

At Westminster, Wilson both had a prodigious memory for detail and composure in debate that had him easily outwit Heath in their House of Commons confrontations. The newspapers ran advertisements for Sanatogen, the tonic that claimed to transform people from 'bundles of nerves'. The satirical magazine *Private Eye* said Wilson was a Sanatogen addict. It made him happy, despite all the problems he had.

But, frankly, what was the big deal or even 'very big deal' with these problems of his? I had used either term since reading *Catcher in the Rye* and quite a few people were beginning to, regardless of whether they knew anything about Holden Caulfield and his stream of consciousness. What was all Wilson's urgency for? He could not sit down for five minutes without leaping up again with an emergency proclamation. When he was not dashing out of halls to sort out the Rhodesia question, he was rushing back from Moscow to convene the 'longest cabinet meeting since Suez'. Why? Who were we going to invade? We did not do that any more. The Australians had sent troops to Vietnam but we had not followed their example. Wilson himself had told black Africa's leaders that it would be futile attempting to overthrow the Smith regime in its landlocked country by having troops ferried across the Zambezi. But now the prime minister had found himself as penned in as the Rhodesian whites. He had campaigned his way to power in 1964 on the wasted years of the Tories and the disaster of the Balance of Payments and said he was going to sort it out. Allies and opponents alike now turned on him and told him to get on with it. On the one hand there was Sir Gerald Nabarro, and others like him; on the other even the *Daily Mirror* proprietor Cecil King was developing his idea of an emergency 'national government', something along the lines of how General de Gaulle ran matters in France. King's idea was for Wilson to step aside and for the newspaper magnate himself to move into a leadership role.

Whether we had our eyes on the football or not, few of us knew it but on the World Cup's second Wednesday, right in the middle of the tournament, everything in what some people called the 'post-war consensus' changed. As England advanced to the next stage of the competition, the final whistle sounded for the unwritten agreement that society was to be run in a particular way. The war had been hard on ordinary people, as a result of which, rulers and ruled had both decreed that there should be health and education for all. 'Demand' was to be maintained by the Bank of England pumping pounds into the economy in order that everyone of working age could stay employed. From now on, the emphasis and the talk would be transformed to that of shedding jobs, tight control of the supply of money and, 'Sorry, we can't afford it.'

Wilson felt better for having got the crisis off his chest. All of us, he said, were prepared to display once again to the world that 'when Britain is up against it we are at our best'. It was more Dunkirk and, in *Private Eye* terms, it sounded like Wilson had been at the Sanatogen. He made off to Liverpool and to a far better reception than he had had during the seamen's strike. His destination, the Cavern club, had closed since its days of launching the Beatles and Cilla Black, but was reopening. The prime minister went as guest of honour for the occasion. The Cavern was full and he was amazed at how people cheered and wanted to shake his hand.

# Chapter 11

# PUNDITS

Word was doing the rounds that more and more women were becoming football fans. The World Cup was 'common gossip', I read, in supermarkets and ladies' hairdressers. I remained unconvinced. My mum and sister were not at all interested and certainly would not have talked about it when they went to Chapel Market or had their hair done.

One factor said to be getting women interested was the new idea of the TV football pundit. With so much action put in front of them, viewers needed guiding. The BBC had created a two-man team, one of whom was Billy Wright, who had represented England over a hundred times – the first player to do so – and recently had managed Arsenal. Wright was the nearest thing to a celebrity footballer. A former England captain, he was shy, polite and married to a member of the leading girl group in the land. His wife Joy was the elder of the three Beverley Sisters, who were not my generation, but many people had liked the way they danced and sang in their wide fifties skirts and petticoats. Billy gave off an air of vulnerability and had married Joy only very late in his career. She was said to have been his first girlfriend.

His fellow expert was Joe Mercer, another former Arsenal man; as captain in the early fifties he had led them to two FA Cup finals and the first division title. After the Cup victory in 1950, my parents had taken me in my pram to the celebration parade outside Islington Town Hall. I couldn't remember it, but it was probably the reason I supported Arsenal, who'd won nothing since. Mercer, now manager of Manchester City, was the acerbic one of the pundits and revelled in highlighting things that the ordinary fan would not know, like what the players were up to in a sneaky way.

Mercer was the first to point out the activities of Antonio Rattín, the Argentine captain. Mercer considered him the perfect leader, always thinking of his team first. 'Just look at him as he follows the ref around,' Mercer said, with a look of cheeky admiration. 'See how he is always talking to him, taking charge on his side's behalf.' Rattín was lean, tall and dark-haired, commanded Argentina's midfield and defence, and could put in a decent shot on goal. 'England had better watch out for him,' Mercer warned; thanks to him, the Argentine skipper became the man to watch over the next few days.

We knew we had to beat Argentina. The quarter-final was a knock-out game, possibly literally so. Argentina played a different kind of game to us – shirt-pulling and spitting at opponents behind the referee's back. We played in manly style, with full-blooded tackles from behind, sweeping a rival's legs away in the effort to get the ball. The Argentines thought that a far more dirty way of playing. They seemed very foreign; as football teams, we did not understand each other.

As a nation, we knew Argentina quite well. A lot of our beef came from there. During the seamen's strike, a ship from Argentina had run aground in the distant South Atlantic and, just down from us, at the end of St John Street, prices in Smithfield meat market had soared. One of the school radio broadcasts at my primary school had been about Argentine cowboys – *gauchos* – who rode the wide grasslands called the Pampas. They wore hats different from the Wild Western norm and had a lasso that was not of the type used by Hopalong Cassidy. It had weights at the end, was called a bolas and brought their cattle crashing to earth. Their footballers, incidentally, could scythe your legs away just as effectively, whatever claims they made about our players' tackles.

I had pictures in an old football album of England on one of their summer tours in the early fifties, which had taken them to Argentina – an adventure, given the novelty of flying. When they reached there, it was not summer at all but mid-winter and the game had been rained off. Buenos Aires, the name of the Argentine capital, translated into something to do with the good quality of its air. In London, on the other hand, we had thousands of people die each winter from bronchitis and other complaints. That's what growing up in a city was like. Once the smogs came in October, my mum's uncle Sam, who had been gassed in the First World War, went to bed for three to four months. When I was about seven, I had leaned back during a shower one February to drink the rain and a few days later went down with a mysterious disease. When my dad got home from work, he recognised it from his experience in Africa and Italy as dysentery and carried me to the children's hospital in Hackney Road. They kept me in for three weeks.

My mum told me about Eva Perón coming here at some stage in the 1950s. She was an actress who had married Argentina's president, had arrived on a plane, stayed briefly, attracting great crowds, then flew off again to Paris and Rome. She was a woman leader in her own right, the chances of which were quite unlikely here. Barbara Castle had been in an ITV debate during the approach to the World Cup on the subject of women's role in politics and said, in spite of there being a lot of prejudice, she remained hopeful. It would suddenly become the 'most normal thing' for a woman to be a prime minister, she commented.

Eva Perón's husband, Juan Domingo Perón, had been a military dictator. Argentina had them sometimes and liked a strong man in charge. The news in the days approaching England's game against the Argentines was that their camp was having trouble between its two strong men. Their manager, Juan Carlos Lorenzo, did not really have control over his players, and Rattín was the one who had taken on the role of strong leadership.

One thing about the Argentine team was their European background. They had no black players, as their neighbours Brazil did, or other Latin American countries, like Peru. Several players had Italian names. Roberto Perfumo was one. He had been involved during the uproar when they played West Germany. Antonio Roma, their goalkeeper, was another. But Argentina's Italians by and large did not come from Rome. They were descended from the Italian south; Naples had more likely been the home of their grandparents.

We had been to Naples four years before. It was my mum's idea and my dad had said we wouldn't like it. 'See Naples and die,' people said dreamily. That was what he was worried about, my dad told me. We arrived in the early evening, and it looked incredibly poor. People crowded around the car when we pulled up outside a hotel in the city centre. They stared while we opened the boot to take out the luggage. There was no hotel garage, so we had to unload everything off the roof rack. In the Spaccanapoli, the old central area of the city of narrow streets and lanes, where my dad and I went looking for bread, people looked down at us from the tenements. When we went for a walk the next day they came right up to look, particularly at my sister's miniskirt. Even my mother's skirt, barely an inch above the knee, attracted attention. They muttered things that my dad could not catch in the local dialect, or that he would not translate.

The mood of the Wembley crowd was going to be vital for the match. The fans were not used to this kind of thing any more than Neapolitans were to the miniskirt. England had qualified from their group to find that no less than Brazil and Italy were out of the competition. Win this next game and England would be in the semi-finals of a World Cup, with a good chance of going further.

It was too much to imagine, so I did not think about it. England supporters in general found they had a ready-made excuse to give up now if the stress was getting to them. The news was that Greaves was out of the Argentine game, the gash on his shin having not yet healed. Home fans could throw up their hands and say that was that: another hard luck tale of the fates stacking up against us. To what extent, then, were they going to get behind the team? In particular, would they ever warm to Ramsey? He had never said or done much to endear himself to the spectators, and no emerging science of public relations was in place to guide him, even assuming he would have let it. But the football establishment unwittingly did a lot to help. It made the mistake of trying to push Ramsey around, as Nobby Stiles became the centre of debate following a bad foul he committed on a French player during the damp match in mid-week. The referee had not seen it but Peter Wilson had. The Frenchman was left 'inert on the green blotting paper grass', Wilson wrote, adding that Stiles was lucky not to have been sent off. Fifa gave the English wing-half a warning that if he did that kind of thing again he would be out of the competition, but Ken Jones reported that the powers that be in the English FA were putting Ramsey under pressure to drop Stiles from the team. An England player could not act like this, they were believed to have said. It was not how we 'played the game'.

To what extent this was true, few people knew, but FA headquarters at Lancaster Gate had never liked the way Ramsey seized control when he became manager. This latest development had the smack of the officers' mess attempting to wrest back power from the men. It was no time, however, for ancient Corinthian attitudes. Even cricket had made efforts to sweep those away when it ended the Gentlemen versus Players game at Lord's a few seasons earlier. The Gentlemen were amateurs, the Players professionals, and most of the amateurs were good batsmen in the style of when the game was first played. In those times, lords of the manor challenged each other to batting contests and brought along a trusty servant who knew how to bowl a ball on a length and at a huge speed. In the last Gentlemen v Players contests, the amateurs could not find a decent bowler and Brian Statham and Fred Trueman, for the professionals, had taken the upper-class batsmen apart. The game was dropped as a contemporary irrelevance.

Ramsey decried the attempts at 'gross discrimination' of his player and threatened to resign. He chose the team, and Stiles was staying in it, he said, and the crowd hooted again, this time in support. At the Tote, the argument divided along age lines, older blokes I worked with reflecting the 'drop Stiles' idea. Younger ones regarded him as someone we needed in the team, if we wanted to win. Suddenly, I felt that, too. Winning? What a funny thought.

Besides, I knew Stiles was not the hard character that some claimed. Substantiating the point, he was photographed after training at Hendon relaxing with a game of cricket and awkwardly bowling a few spinners. More intriguingly, innocence itself, he was wearing glasses. It materialised that he was near blind as a bat, and when he played football he wore contact lenses. Indeed, as an early user of them, he was at the frontier of optical science. It may have explained not only how he had come to clobber the Frenchman, but also why he was so startled when, looming up at his shoulder, I had tackled him on the Highbury pitch. To my mind, Stiles was a pussy cat.

But pussy cats could turn. The day before the Argentina game, Parliament held its first debate on the Medical Termination of Pregnancy Bill, which aimed to loosen restrictions on abortion. Friday sessions in the Commons rarely caused any stir, as MPs prepared to leave for the weekend, but this one turned into a huge row. Norman St John-Stevas was the Conservative MP for Chelmsford. I had known him as the mild type, one of those with detachable collars and striped shirts who appeared on *That Was the Week That Was*. He would discuss such subjects as whether clichés were an important part of our language.

St John-Stevas denounced the idea of legalising abortion as 'barbarous' and an 'abomination'. Jill Knight, his fellow Tory MP, joined him. Many couples felt they could not cope with elderly parents: 'Were they to be put down too?' She represented the well-off Birmingham constituency of Edgbaston. A few hundred yards or so beyond the back end of its cricket ground was Balsall Heath, one of the city's red light areas.

In London the scene was comparable. The south London slum of Battersea lay across the river from affluent Chelsea. The BBC had got into trouble earlier in the year for showing *Up the Junction*, the play by Ken Loach (adapted from Nell Dunn's short story collection) that featured a young girl having a back-street abortion. The name of the play alluded to Clapham Junction, a district I was familiar with only in that its name was on the destination board of the 19 bus that I had taken home from school. Now the area became known for something other than its belching power station and, so I learned from a quiz, having England's busiest railway station. But while on the one hand the BBC came under attack for showing such 'kitchen sink' drama, on the other, and thanks to the debate having reached Parliament, it was being urged to show *Up the Junction* again.

David Steel, a 28-year old Liberal party MP for Roxburgh, Selkirk and Peebles, a Scottish constituency some way from London permissiveness, introduced the Bill. Roy Jenkins, and more importantly my mum, backed it. We had had the case of Jeannie, a woman in her twenties from Rheidol Terrace, who, some people said, was 'Mongol' (Down's syndrome being unknown). In local parlance, she had been taken advantage of by someone and was bringing up her baby with her mum, who herself had struggled for years to bring up Jeannie. That whole episode was 'a shame', said my mum, a sign that she went along with the Steel and Jenkins view.

On the same night as the debate, Argentina went to the dogs. They were stopped at the gates of Wembley stadium and told, sorry, they could not train there as was permitted by World Cup convention. They would interfere with the greyhound meeting scheduled for that evening. On the night before a game, visiting teams were allowed a feel of the turf they would be playing on the next day – especially vital in the case of Wembley, since its velvet-like surface, we had always been told, was unique. The Argentina squad left sensing a conspiracy against them. Latin Americans from several parts of the region told me some years later, however, that Argentine people did sometimes turn up in your country acting as if it were their own. They could be annoying.

Fifa had chosen a West German to referee the game. Rudolf Kreitlein was from near Nuremberg; of a region, and generation, hauling itself from the ruins bequeathed by a dictator. By trade he was a master tailor, a man who worked along fine lines that should not be cut across.

Circumstances had swung England's way without anyone realising. Ramsey brought in Geoff Hurst to replace Greaves, on the face of it a journeyman for a genius. The manager stood Callaghan down from the wing; Martin Peters could play there as part of his free-roaming role, depending on the flow of the game. What he did at Upton Park, he could do at Wembley. By accident or design, therefore, Ramsey had his team as per the desired blueprint. They were wingless, if something less than wonderful.

I went to the Tote for a normal Saturday and, assigned to the racing at Ripon, was put near Ivy on Silver Doubles. She had a television at the side of her adding machine but, big lady that she was, I needed to rely on her for commentary. Under normal circumstances she would not have professed to know what she was talking about, but these were not normal circumstances, and she was both a fan of Billy Wright and had been listening to Joe Mercer.

'Come on, stop him doing that,' she shouted, only a few minutes into the game. She did so again a little later. Each time I looked up and around her, I could see a tall, dark-haired character in tight-fitting Argentine shorts and stripes following the German referee around. Rattín towered over Kreitlein, talking to him up close and staring intently at him. The game itself was going nowhere. Argentina looked composed and in capable hands. We looked flustered in the heat and were committing more fouls than they were. This was presumably what Rattín was complaining about.

Any rise of tension before the game was matched by the heat on the day. Some 73 degrees Fahrenheit (23 degrees Celsius) was expected, which in the bowl of Wembley translated into a lot more. Though Wembley internationals were quite formal affairs, many spectators had their jackets off and had stripped down to their collars and ties. They were baying at the dual struggle for power going on before them: between the teams, and between the ref and the Argentine skipper.

As much as I directed my attention to the 3.30 Billy Butlin Holiday Camp Handicap for three-year-olds, I kept being drawn away. Ivy erupted: 'That's right, get 'im off!' Several of us ran to the TV to see Rattín looking mystified and Kreitlein making short sharp movements of his right hand as, like the conductor of an orchestra, he pointed the Argentine captain towards the touchline. Rattín stayed, staring and talking, as if this might do any good, but after five minutes he trailed slowly off the pitch with the look of someone who had no idea what he had done.

Argentina did not collapse into chaos without him, but had lost their central player. When ten minutes of the game remained, Kenneth Wolstenholme talked of it going to extra-time and – if still a draw – the toss of a coin being used to decide the winner. But soon after he said this, Ivy's betting slips went flying. Hurst had scored from a Peters cross.

With no television replay, I saw the highlights that evening. Peters beat two men near the touchline and his cross from the left had come out of the sun. Hurst was looking straight into it when the ball, as if from the skies over Green Street, had flown in his direction. It was the moment he had imagined and been waiting for. Sprinting to lose the defender near him, Hurst's glanced header brought the winning strike in the most important international that England had ever played.

Just shortly before the game, the Post Office had announced that, at the request of the newly formed Race Relations Board, it was going to stock complaint forms and leaflets entitled 'Race Discrimination – How to Complain'. Mark Bonham Carter, the board's director, denied that the body was encouraging people to air unnecessary grievances. Prejudice could come in different guises. The Birmingham police told a Pakistani man from Leamington Spa that he could not join the force until he spoke properly. He had passed all his tests but was advised to take speech lessons and come back sounding like a Brummy policeman. Other forms were less subtle, even if most people were still inclined not to see anything wrong with them.

LATIN LUNATICS PLUNGE SOCCER INTO CHAOS screamed the headline over Peter Wilson's column following the Argentina match. The 'South American bandits' should accept the condemning judgment of the sporting world, he wrote. Fifa fined the Argentine team 1,000 Swiss francs for abusing referee Kreitlein after the game, but at the prevailing exchange rate that was a paltry £83. Argentina should be banned, said Wilson, from the next World Cup, scheduled for Mexico in 1970.

Rattín's offence remained unclear. Kreitlein said the Argentine captain had tried to dictate the running of the game. Not a Spanish speaker, he could see Rattín's intent 'in his eyes'. Ultimately, there was little reason for the dismissal other than Kreitlein saw matters from the point of view of a German and northern European, and Rattín was acting in the normal ways of an Argentine.

Surprising was the fashion in which Ramsey acted out of character. Following his furious intervention to stop George Cohen swapping shirts with one of the Argentine team, his claim that the opposition had played like 'animals' translated badly in Buenos Aires. The Argentine press responded that Ramsey, out of keeping with someone from England, was not 'a gentleman'. He was, on the contrary, 'a gypsy'. Suggestions had been made at home in the past that Ramsey, who had slightly darker skin colour than the Anglo-Saxon norm, was of Romany stock. He had denied it.

As for England's winning goal, it had come from a long-familiar formula in the most traditional reaches of London's East End. When Hurst had first joined the England squad in February, Ramsey reprimanded him in training for being over-elaborate: 'I selected you to play in the way you do for your club,'

Ramsey had told him. Hurst and Peters had worked their move successfully more times than fans at Upton Park could recall: the fast ball from the wing, the dash to the front post catching the defence unawares.

The next opponents were Portugal in the semi-final, and such excitements were distracting many people from the supposedly dire condition of the economy. Sterling had recovered only slightly to $2.95 to the pound since the prime minister's drastic statement on Wednesday. Not that the information would have meant much to many people anyway, since popular lore had it that the pound was still worth four dollars, the rate that existed at about the end of the First World War. Few people ever went to the US, or otherwise needed to know. Five shillings (25p) was a 'dollar', or in Cockney slang an 'Oxford', for 'Oxford scholar'. This meant half a crown was ''arf a dollar', though not, as I had ever heard ''arf an Oxford'.

Harold Wilson was taking satisfaction from the unemployment rate, which had risen by 3,000 since its low point in June. James Callaghan, the Chancellor of the Exchequer, said he could see nothing wrong in it increasing to half a million, almost double its midsummer number. Callaghan had also appeared on television to say that from November we would no longer be allowed to take more than £50 abroad each year. Smiling in the manner that earned him the nickname of 'Sunny Jim', he suggested we take our holidays at home. If I had not been so much taken up by the World Cup, his statement would have infuriated me. As it was, I felt merely angry. No government had the right to stop us going and taking a look elsewhere.

In addition to what we travelled with, everyone's pay at home was under scrutiny. Wilson insisted that company directors had to reveal their bonuses and that these, too, would be frozen. *The Mirror* threw in the argument that since most men's wages were public knowledge, women should reveal theirs to their husbands. 'Come on, girls,' said the paper; with four and half million women in the workforce, this mattered. If any women had done this, one possible success of Wilson's incomes policy would have been to show husbands and wives alike how much less women earned, even for comparable work.

The subject of equal pay was not raised in any conversation that I heard involving the older women I worked with at the Tote, but some of the younger ones – like Sandra and Doreen from Stratford, who'd started working there for the summer – were more likely to bring it up. When I took my break with her one day, Doreen told me that the women's pay was far lower than that of the men. Daisy, her boss, had passed this on to her and said it was wrong. Doreen also said her mum, who worked as an early morning office cleaner in the East End, was on a much lower rate than the men alongside her. Such facts of life I learned on the first occasion I had lunch with a girl, while the men around us talked of the World Cup.

With the semi-final pending, the Portuguese combined a lot of skill with a mean streak. In their game against Brazil, they had kicked Pelé off Goodison Park. On his way back home from Liverpool to São Paulo, Pelé had arrived at Euston saying he was so depressed by the treatment Portugal had given him that he would never play football again. But their star, Eusébio, was world class and had hammered four goals in Portugal's quarter-final victory against the North Koreans. He had seven in the competition so far. Hunt was our leading scorer on three.

Eusébio's club, Benfica, had discovered him at an early age in Mozambique, one of Portugal's African colonies. No one black or from the old empire was remotely near to playing for England. I had an old Leeds team photo signed by both Jack Charlton and Albert Johanneson, a South African left-winger, the only black player in Britain I could recall. That was from several seasons ago, when Leeds had been in the second division.

In the early sixties, Benfica had been the first team other than Real Madrid to win the European Cup. They beat Barcelona. The following year, 1962, they swept Real Madrid aside, Eusébio scoring twice in a 5–3 win. But the Portuguese champions had since been under a spell. After an argument, Béla Guttmann, their Hungarian coach, had left claiming to have put the evil eye on them and saying they would never win anything big again.

In their favour, England had the rising spirits of the crowd. Martin Peters said with the Argentina match he sensed for the first time the fans really shouting for the team. Fifa had also been benevolent with some more interesting scheduling. The semi-final was initially fixed for Goodison Park. Since Portugal had played their earlier games there, they would have been nicely settled in if England had had to travel up from London. Fifa, Sir Stanley Rous at its head, however, switched the match to Wembley. With minimal advertising at games, it was pointed out that Fifa made its income from money paid by spectators at the gate, and Wembley could cater to a far larger crowd than Goodison Park. The semi-final came to London, therefore, for what might or might not have been entirely commercial reasons.

If there was an evil eye anywhere, it was focused squarely in the right direction. Nobby Stiles, with his glasses off, had played Eusébio out of two games in the last couple of months.

In Manchester United's recent European Cup-ties against Benfica, George Best's rising star had been the one everyone witnessed, but Stiles had laid the foundation for victory. Across the 180 minutes of the two games, he had not allowed Eusébio a sight of goal.

Greaves was still out of commission and Ramsey chose the same team as against Argentina. Despite forecasts of a tetchy game, no fouls were committed in the first half an hour by either team. Following a Hunt run into the penalty area, the visiting keeper was only able to knock the ball out with his legs to Bobby Charlton who, 25 yards out, had most of Portugal's defence between him and the goal. He calmly side-footed the ball past them. Charlton scored again in the second half with a pin-point volley of such technique that it prompted Portuguese players to shake his hand as he ran back for the re-start.

His brother Jack featured in Portugal's single goal seven minutes from the end. Banks was deceived by a cross and José Torres, the opponents' beanpole striker, headed towards an empty goal. Jack stuck a hand out to stop the ball going in. 'He had to do it,' noted Wolstenholme. Years on, Jack would have been sent off and banned from the next game, in this case the final. Eusébio took the penalty and scored. Other than that, Stiles blocked him out again.

Nobby led the post-match celebrations in the centre circle, his front teeth missing as he laughed and jigged along to the chants of the crowd. Ramsey had been right to stick by him. What a game, what a player and, to think, how I had known him when he was nothing.

# Chapter 12

# OUT OF TIME

With state support I cured my addiction to gambling. At the government-owned Tote, I had quickly come to see that the betting slips that passed before me every morning made any half-crown each-way that I might have mustered look very small beer. In particular, the punter who put £300 on very hot favourites to finish in the first two or three places in a race had lost two bets within a couple of days. On occasions when he won, he received only the most minimal return; each time that he failed to, I had worked it out, he had to win about 24 times to get back his lost money. Losing twice like this, he would have to win nearly 50 times to break even. It was truly a mug's game.

Several men in the office had been putting their money on individual games throughout the World Cup. They freely told you about their winnings. One told me how he had shrewdly chosen the Russians to beat the Hungarians, even though Hungary had previously beaten Brazil. Another said he had made money on Spain getting a draw against Italy at an early stage of the competition, when the Italians were thought to be among the leading favourites. They were not so forthcoming about their losses, on which subject I heard nothing. But even the most devoted in-house punters now declared that any further bets were useless. England were odds-on favourites for the final at 8–13: you had to gamble £13 in the hope of making a profit of eight. It was not worth the risk.

England had suddenly flipped from being no-hopers to hot favourites. There had been no such time in my life. Ten years ago, we had been odds-on to win at Suez, only to be beaten by a conspiracy of war-crazed Soviets and unreliable Americans – not to mention upstart Egyptians, who had the idea they could run a canal themselves. We had been fortunate that at the same time the USSR had invaded Hungary and we could reflect on the villainy of others.

For a while, I had thought we had been top of the world during the Empire Games in Cardiff two years later in 1958. I woke each morning thinking how envious children of other nations must be of me as we ran off with more medals than anyone else, in everything from fencing to bowls. The Queen used the glory of the occasion to announce that Prince Charles would be the next Prince of Wales. Soon after the shouting was over, I realised that this was a competition organised among ourselves and the scattered dominions. When matched against everyone else at the 1960 Olympics in Rome, we had to learn far more humility.

From finding our glories in retreat, we were now going to have to lead from the front. We had, however, the very person to help us do it. Ramsey was acclaimed as a hero, and after years of abuse had won 'a nation's respect'. That did not necessarily mean that we loved him. The question remained, noted one commentator, as to 'who was the man behind the mask?' He had worked in the company of Ramsey for some good few years without being able to say that he knew him. What he did know was that Ramsey was not a person to 'offer the hand of open friendship'.

The mass reaction was to unite behind him and England. You could be forgiven for thinking the whole country was united behind football. Frantic goings-on were reported at Foyles in Charing Cross Road, where apparently there had been a huge increase in sales of football books. I found this difficult to imagine. Foyles certainly had a lot of books, but it took a long time selling them. Mrs Christina Foyle hired young people from abroad who wanted to learn English, and in return she paid them very little. Given this, she could afford to be very inefficient. In Foyles, having spent time finding your book, you queued three times: once at a desk to exchange the book you wanted for a ticket; once at a grill where you handed the ticket over and paid; and, finally, at the original desk when you collected your book. Foyles was less of a place to immerse yourself in the gathering excitement of the build-up to Saturday's final than one where you could quietly escape it.

The growing certainty was that England were going to win. My own conviction, and that of most other fans, was based on the fact that we were playing West Germany. My dad's words to me of some years before that we 'never lost to the Germans' fused in my mind both the history of politics and of football. My family had emerged from two world wars – hardened, bruised, and not with any great whoops of triumph – on both occasions on what was deemed to be the winning side. In football, the figures were incontrovertible: we had played eight, drawn one, won seven. In either case, we always came out on top.

I had been compelled to think about the Germans from an early age. For some reason, they had always been out to make trouble. When my parents lived with my grandparents, our bedroom on the first floor overlooked the remains of the two destroyed houses over the road. If you peered hard enough you could just see down to the canal through the trees that had grown up on the waste land. This had since become the home of bands of cats. Mrs Clements, who had lost her husband in the last days of the first war and lived on the top floor, fed them with deliveries from the cats' meat man in Camden Passage. In anticipation, they yowled at dawn like spirits of the dead.

War films were all around us. I saw one at the cinema next to the Lyons Corner House at the Angel, when I was about ten, which included a brief scene of some German soldiers chatting and smiling in an off-duty moment. A couple of older kids with Elvis quiffs sitting behind me started laughing at how stupid spoken German sounded, so it occurred to me it might be something to learn. At Highbury, in our second year, we were offered the option of German or Latin. The Latin master, a Mr Lincoln, was to be avoided. A clever kid in our year named Bicknell got 100% in one year's exam but was told that no one was allowed full marks, so his were cut to 90. Never let it be said he was not a fair person, Lincoln told him, however: he would also cut everyone else's by ten percentage points. Several kids at the lower end of the class were left with minus figures and presumably had to report back to their parents that they had not even managed to spell their names right.

German was the daring alternative: *Eine Fahrt ins Blaue* ('A Journey Into the Blue') as was the title of one of our textbooks, which always raised a laugh. For our first classes, we chose German names. No one fancied Adolf, and I went for Otto. It was easy enough to spell front and back. Our German teacher, a Mr Batley from Huddersfield, who was proud of coming from the same town as Harold Wilson, had us jumping up and down on chairs talking as we went along. I also chose the subject because of Bert Trautmann, the Manchester City goalkeeper and ex-prisoner of war who had broken his neck diving at the feet of a Birmingham forward in the 1956 Cup final. He had heroically played on. We would have done that, I decided – as did just about every football fan in the country – and since Trautmann was like us possibly other Germans were, too. It helped to know that those responsible for the bomb site opposite might have it in them not to do it again.

We were like the Germans in other respects too: a bit dour, prone to giving orders and taking them. Of course, we would not have allowed ourselves to be corralled by our government in such a way as to have done horrific things to Jews and gypsies, as the Germans had. Then again, from what we had learned in history at school, the Irish at the time of the potato famine might have opened a debate on that point; not to mention the inmates of the first concentration camps, which we had set up in South Africa, when my granddad Chapman had been there during the Boer War.

But there were ways in which we differed. My dad told me of the time he was in Tunisia. He was at Cap Bon in the north and shortly to sail for Sicily. The Germans had been as good as defeated in Africa, with the front now shifting to Italy.

He watched as thousands of captured Germans marched in perfect order into their prison camp. My dad admired their discipline but then, he said, it broke down. That night the prison camp erupted into a huge party, or something akin to it, which sounded at any moment as if it might turn into a riot and a mass break-out. The Germans appeared to have quite gone off their heads. In their position, British prisoners would have whistled themselves to sleep with a few choruses of 'Colonel Bogey'.

So, we may have been like the Germans in some ways, but attention was drawn to our differences straight after the semi-finals. Those watching the tournament closely had noticed that five players had been sent off so far. In the case of Rattín, no violence had been involved. The expulsion of the other four players had involved one physical act or another, but the question was asked, how violent had these incidents been? Strangely, they all involved Germans, not as perpetrators but victims. Four players had had to leave the World Cup field of play, with Germans left writhing on the ground. Was it more than coincidence? WE'RE NOT ACTORS, STORMS ANGRY GERMAN BOSS read one headline, as Helmut Schön, the West German manager, responded to claims that his players were play-acting cheats.

I had imagined the Germans too stolid a bunch to be actors. But, when I thought about it, there had been their first game of the tournament, the one at Hillsborough that the German and Swiss card players on the ferry were on their way to. It was not much of a game. The Swiss were both a weak side and had dropped three of their players because of a sightseeing tour they'd had in Sheffield the night before. Two local girls ran them around in their Mini – so all concerned said – causing the players to miss their team's curfew back at their hotel. They were sent back home and later banned from the international team for life, which seemed a bit strict, really. There was not much five people could get up to in a Mini.

So it was no surprise against the Swiss that West Germany had won easily, 5–0. Yet after each goal you would have thought they had secured the World Cup itself, as their scorers – Siggi Held, Franz Beckenbauer and the rest – ran around with huge smiles, waving to the crowd. Why didn't they just calm down and behave seriously? It was quite clear they would come unstuck before long.

'We are just as fair-minded as the English,' Schön protested in answer to the critics. He could not understand why such rumours 'are started against us', and sounded hurt. His suggestion seemed to be that the Germans were much misunderstood, far from the bunch of strutting posers that they had been characterised as in the past. The West German team, like its country, was diligent and getting on with building anew. They had already come a long way – many of its footballers were semi-pros when they had won the 1954 World Cup. Uwe Seeler, the present team's veteran captain and striker, had combined his early football days with being a furniture remover. One reporter who visited the Germans' camp said he found them 'courteous, co-operative and more modest than most'.

From any reading of the papers, the West Germans were also making an impression in wider affairs. Harold Wilson had visited them recently to tell them they had to pay more for the British army on the Rhine. The Americans also kept reminding them how expensive it was to keep Allied troops occupying their country. The West Germans' response was to look in the direction of other countries to raise revenue. The US were furious with them over news of German plans to build a steel mill in China. Washington only recognised the small island of Taiwan; the huge Chinese mainland next door, according to the US view of the world, did not exist. The Germans were sneaking in the back door.

Admittedly, the Chinese did seem to have gone a bit mad. Chairman Mao was reported to have swum eight miles down the Yangtze to prove he was neither ill nor dead, and Red Guards were waving his Little Red Book under the noses of anyone alleged to be a capitalist running dog. The first I heard of this was when Jack de Manio, presenter of the morning *Today* programme, read extracts for, as he believed, a laugh. I thought some sounded quite sensible: 'When the enemy attacks, we retreat; when they withdraw, we attack,' or words to similar effect. It was more or less how I had survived life at the stations.

My family had also opened relations with China. Roughly every couple of months we ate at a restaurant just along Wardour Street from the Marquee called the New Shanghai. My parents ordered the same thing each time: sweet and sour pork, bamboo shoots, egg fried rice and crispy noodles formed into a nest which, as you cut it, flew at many angles off the plate. They once invited my aunt Laura and uncle Geoff on a rare visit from Bedford. My uncle usually ate what he produced on his allotment, and Aunt Laura's grounding was the Edwardian kitchen that she had kept for Lloyd George. She denounced the meal as 'foreign muck', in spite of the fact that her younger brother was paying. The New Shanghai was something of a West End pioneer. The remnants of an old Chinatown existed in Limehouse, which was somewhere in the East End that my parents would never have gone to at night. One of my mum's friends said she had heard Indian food was nice and that there were some places opening up, but we never went. I much preferred Italian anyway.

Some 48 hours before the final, Harold Wilson was shown kissing his wife Mary goodbye at London Airport. He was off to Washington to visit President Johnson, although his mission was not clear. Some papers said his objective was peace in Vietnam but that had changed to his wanting to discuss the instability of the pound. Canada was also on his itinerary, so what could he possibly want to talk about there?

We also had troubles enough of our own to stay at home for. Running street battles were happening in Belfast during the Protestant marching season. It came as news for many of us that there was a marching season in Northern Ireland, never mind that it caused such problems. Catholic demonstrators, meanwhile, were demanding the same rights as Protestants on things like housing and voting. They said the Protestants fixed elections. Were they serious? Could that really happen in the UK? In the US, yes, civil rights demonstrations had been going on for three years and more. In the latest, black protesters clashed with police in cities such as Cleveland, Ohio. Both there and in Belfast, the police turned on the water cannon, and the meaning of Bob Dylan's lyrics became clearer.

With the day virtually upon us, the referee for the big game was named: Gottfried Dienst, a 47-year-old postal worker from Switzerland. No, he was not about to be delivered into the lions' den, he indicated, as photographers arranged a picture of him with the Marquess of Bath holding a cub from Longleat's game park. Whether it was one of the animals that had escaped a few weeks back on the flight from Frankfurt, the report did not say. He was pleased that two European teams had reached the Wembley final because they took discipline more readily than the Latin Americans. He would put up with no nonsense, he said. He knew all the German swear words and quite a few in English.

That was fine for his communications with the players. How well would he fare with his linesmen? One of them, Dr Karol Galba from Czechoslovakia, had a qualification suggesting he came from a studious background and may well have spoken some German or English. The other linesman, Tofiq Bahramov, was from the Soviet Union, but I did not recognise his as one of those Russian names: Rudolf Nureyev, Andrei Gromyko, Lev Yashin. Given the circumstances of recent history between Germany and Russia, at least he was unlikely to be pro-German.

For their part, the West Germans were bending over backwards to meet the highest standards of old-world chivalry. England's squad of 22 players was on a total win bonus of £22,000 and, in the event of success, would share it £1,000 per man, whichever players were in the team on the day. A representative of the German camp countered that its players would be out to win for honour alone. He made considerable play of adding that they were under strict instruction not to argue with the referee or other match officials should, the spokesman emphasised, 'anything controversial occur'. The claims made by others about the Germans' prior behaviour, it appeared, had taken effect.

For what was to be the last World Cup final in black and white, the television audience in Britain was forecast to break all records. No figures were available yet for England's games against Argentina and Portugal, but the France match had topped the viewings at seven and a half million, which didn't quite out-do ITV's *The Blackpool Show* which scored the same. ITV's Sunday evening schedule was allowing itself to think the unthinkable. The commercial channel was to show the 1956 film starring Hardy Krüger as the only German prisoner who escaped from Britain during the war, *The One That Got Away*.

Meanwhile, our neighbour opposite, Anthony Blond, the publisher who had had the luxury flats built on the old bomb site there, was in the news. Two days before the final he brought out *The New London Spy*, a book including chapters on homosexual and lesbian London, the main centres of prostitution and how much to pay for it. As you would have expected of him, this was all a bit 'canal side of the street', but that was not to deny that the street as a whole had a history. My mum had mentioned to me about the quiet lady down the road, who had no obvious man in her life but did have two good-looking daughters. She had been particularly close to American servicemen during the war. My mum said how she had 'stood' on the corner of White Lion Street and the Angel in the line of her business. Another neighbour, if more outgoing than most, Nelly Gurr, had had a relationship when underage with a man who had 'gone to jail for her'. When that was done, he came back and lived with her in the same house as her mother and everyone's life went on.

Blond's book aimed to strike a balance between not only what was fast becoming the future but also the past. It had a chapter on where London's best church sermons could be heard. The authors of each chapter were not named but this one was thought to have been written by John Betjeman, the poet and church expert. 'Pleasure' was the book's criterion, said one of Blond's publishing people.

From west London, a parents' committee in Ealing had its effort to stop comprehensive education turned down by the high court. The parents said the government should not be allowed to bring it in without consulting them. The court penalised them with a stiff order for costs of £2,500.

The nation's farmers were angry with *Mrs Dale's Diary*, the afternoon radio programme that my mother and grandma listened to, which came on after *Listen with Mother*. Portraying the fictional 'life of a doctor's wife', Mrs Dale would occasionally report of her husband that she was 'very worried about Jim'. The farmers were concerned because she had revealed that the family ate Danish bacon. There was, they complained, plenty of British available.

On the eve of the final, the cosy life as lived by Mrs Dale was not one recognised by the House of Lords. The Archbishop of Canterbury's committee led by the Bishop of Exeter had studied the painful question of marriage breakdown and introduced its bill 'Putting Asunder: A Divorce Law for Contemporary Society'. Some of our closest neighbours were among thousands of couples caught in a no-man's-land of being neither married nor divorced. Whether 'innocent' or 'guilty', the parties faced huge costs if they went to court. The bishops proposed making blame an irrelevance so that both sides involved might move their lives forward with less acrimony. Reconciliation could follow. In the House of Commons, Leo Abse said he was supporting this measure too.

At the Tote, my colleagues observed that in the high court Florence Nagle, at 70 years old, had won the battle to be the first woman allowed by the Jockey Club to hold a training licence. It had taken her 20 years, during which she had expertly schooled racehorses, with the club previously insisting she could only call herself 'head stable lad', or anything other than 'trainer'. She said she could have gone on for ever like that but had a good laugh taking the Jockey Club before a judge.

I courted controversy with Tony Barker by arranging for the day of the final off. We were allowed only one Saturday in six free and – three weeks into the job – it was not my turn. I swapped with Ron, who had no interest in football. Tony looked at me when I told him: 'A game of football? The job's the thing, son', he seemed to be saying. He felt I was taking liberties; I could tell.

The happy position for England was that all their players were fit. Greaves was back in full training and pictured being tackled by Frank McLintock, the Arsenal captain, in a practice match arranged for the England squad at London Colney, Arsenal's training ground. McLintock was a tough tackler and Greaves rode his challenge well. He looked in good form, which was heartening. England's world-class striker was ready, just when he would be needed.

The general view was that Ramsey faced the most difficult decision of his career as a manager and, in fact, the toughest any England manager had yet to make. He might well decide that Greaves was the very type to nick a winning goal: a side-foot tap into the net from a couple of yards, having stolen up on a defender's blind side; a lightning volley like the one he executed for Spurs on his return from Italy; or a goal reminiscent of that he had scored against Czechoslovakia in May 1964 in Bratislava – a dink over the head of his marker and, as the ball fell, a calmly placed shot away from the keeper. That one had inspired England to a 4–2 victory and their first win under Ramsey.

The manager had said that there would always be a place for Greaves, and I and many others did not see how he could leave him out. What if he favoured Hurst and the West Ham man reverted to the standard of his early days at Upton Park, when he had been a reserve defender? Ramsey would not be able to correct his error. Substitutions during a game would not be part of football for another season.

There was a further option. Experts and fans alike wondered if Hunt should make way for Greaves. It felt the right idea to me. Hunt was a nice enough man and good with kids. At the stations, he had never let his head get too big when Liverpool came up from the second division with Orient and continued to far bigger things. But he rarely did anything that was out of the ordinary. Of course, he scored a goal or two and was fine for a tap in or a lucky header through the keeper's hands. But what would a player of Hunt's workaday character contribute to winning the final of a World Cup?

I went to bed with my transistor radio shortly before midnight and the reports that the BBC was to launch an 'all pop music' channel on the wireless, to be known as Radio 1. It would be about time but, what with the BBC's record on introducing colour TV, there was no telling when that time might be. The news had been full of the government wanting to close down pirate radio stations like Radio London and Radio Caroline, which were said to be blocking the air waves. Off the east coast, Radio London had beamed out of an old freighter, with Kenny Everett and other disc jockeys on board, moored beyond the three-mile limit by Frinton-on-Sea. Wedgwood had described the pirates as 'squalid', but then again he looked the classical music type.

The BBC only broadcast one hour a week of music that most people of my age wanted to listen to: *Pick of the Pops* on a Sunday afternoon with Alan Freeman, an Australian DJ who, at 39, was almost as old as Jimmy Savile. Some estimates said the pirates had a huge and largely young audience of 25 million. At school, I had taken up the matter with Pete Francis, our Labour supporter, saying it was just as well for the government that 18-year-olds did not have the vote. He agreed, with the qualification that it was a shame since there were more important things to concentrate on, like steel nationalisation and, he reminded me, taking control of the 'means of production'.

A little after midnight going into World Cup final day, Radio London played 'Out of Time' by Chris Farlowe, the number one in the charts. Mick Jagger and Keith Richards had written the song and it was also on the Rolling Stones' *Aftermath* long player, which I had bought when it came out in April. Jagger produced the one by Farlowe, whose voice was deeper and if anything more bluesy.

Farlowe was among a bunch of my uncle Keith's mates from the Caledonian Road in the late fifties and early sixties. One of them, Dave Duggan, formed a group. He ran a basement club in the lengthy road's more sordid reaches, near King's Cross (that said, it was a toss-up whether the Pentonville prison end was any smarter). Duggan made himself lead singer and my uncle's best friend, Dickie, played double bass. My uncle had been his best man. Dickie might also have been my uncle's but he did not talk much and would not have been up to giving a speech. My mum, who was apt to reach snappy conclusions, said he was 'on drugs'.

The group played at the club and other venues around the area. Whether looking for drugs or to make a nuisance of themselves, the police regularly raided the club. In the early fifties – before my uncle's and his mates' time – they had found a stash of IRA weapons there. On some nights, when the group was playing elsewhere, Duggan might have been preoccupied either by the raids or other events at his place, and Farlowe stepped in. The group gave him the job permanently when Dave failed to show once too often. Alas, Dickie was not destined for the charts either. As the fifties faded in memory and the sixties proper took hold, he did not make the conversion from double bass to bass guitar.

The lyrics that Farlowe sang were on the cruel side. They were about an old love, a former flame that was 'obsolete' and 'out of touch'. They spoke of 'my poor discarded baby' and someone – or something – that was being moved on from. Was it Jagger's girlfriend, Chrissie Shrimpton, Jean's sister? She was more likely to have figured in 'Under My Thumb', one of his other *Aftermath* songs and no less cruel. It may have been that it was about no one in particular, and that Jagger was writing about us all.

Farlowe would do well out of it. He soon set himself up in Camden Passage with a stall selling German war memorabilia: helmets, uniforms and things. Only 20 odd years on from the war, these were hardly antique but obviously had a market. He was eventually able to expand into far larger premises: the former amusement arcade next to the Screen on the Green, where the Mods had once hung out.

# Chapter 13

# NO DREAM

The newsagent was grumbling around in his sitting room at the back of the shop when I went to get the paper, so I had a few minutes to kill browsing some of the other headlines. Only one small article on *The Times*' front page referred to football, and that made no mention of it being World Cup final day. SIR S. MATTHEWS 'SATISFACTORY' said the bold type above five lines or so of information.

Sir Stanley had suffered three fractured ribs and head injuries in a car crash in Leek, Staffordshire. The Potteries was the area Matthews came from. He was the original 'wizard of the wing', who had played 54 times on the right flank for England and was the most famous footballer in Britain during my childhood. A decade ago, and at 41, Matthews had starred in that 4–2 win at Wembley in England's first international against Brazil. He carried on playing for another seven years. His regret, he said, was not continuing until he was 50, which he had been fit enough to do.

As a result of the accident, he had undergone an hour's surgery but would survive. Matthews was well ahead of his time in that he was supremely fit. Although he had lent his name to cigarette adverts, this had been in the days of football's maximum wage of £21 a week, and I could not imagine him smoking. He certainly wasn't on the occasions I had hung around him. In the *Charles Buchan's Football Monthly* magazines I bought in my early teens, Matthews had once written a column that instructed us sternly to treat our bodies like sensitive machines. He had bran for breakfast and drank orange juice. On match days, he walked to the stadium in heavy boots to make his football boots feel lighter. For most of his playing days, boots were clumpy with thick leather above the ankle and hard-capped toes. His routines made him sound quite miserable, and he was.

I had a colour picture of him from the *Football Monthly*, skinny legged in his baggy white shorts and orange Blackpool shirt. Most of his career he had spent at Blackpool, with spells before and after at Stoke City. My father spoke of Matthews' performance in the 1953 Cup final, when Blackpool beat Bolton 4–3, as one of his greatest sporting memories. Everything had seemed perfect that year, he said: my sister had been born, there had been the Coronation, and Matthews had won the Cup final, virtually on his own. Only Ferenc Puskás and the Hungarians had come along and spoiled the year a few months later.

At the age of ten I had sent the picture to Matthews, care of Blackpool FC, together with a letter saying he was mine and just about everyone else's favourite footballer, plus a stamped addressed envelope. It came back by return of post; it was a thrill to know he had been handling it only 24 hours earlier. But it was signed with a scrawl lost down amid the grass at his ankles, and with no 'Best Wishes'. I had gone through a similar routine with Brian Clough of Middlesbrough, who had just made his first appearance for England, and the small black and white newspaper cutting that I sent him came back with good wishes flowingly written across it.

Sir Stan had also nearly got me beaten up at Euston station. When he returned to Stoke near the end of his career, the club were modestly placed in the second division, and I had not expected any big kids on the platform. On the contrary, they were all there for him, and in a bad mood because he was, too. As I slipped off, one of their aspirant lieutenants was delegated to sort me out but was not able to manage more than a tap on the chin before I got away. I subsequently cornered Matthews myself. I saw him early one Saturday in Russell Square taking a walk in the park in front of the hotel. I was the only kid there and here was Matthews, star of my dad's generation. He scowled as he took my pen. He signed with what appeared to be a 'Best Wishes', just about decipherable if I looked at it hard enough. I eventually came to the conclusion that older people could be like that without meaning any harm.

In today's match, there would no longer be any place at England's table for wingers like Matthews. Their day had gone. That was not to say that the old world wasn't hanging on. The reports indicated that there was very little place for women either. After the game none of the players' wives were going to be at the main reception at the Royal Garden Hotel in Kensington. They would be allowed in the building, but only for a smaller party, upstairs where they were to dine with Pickles and David Corbett. No England or Fifa official seemed to think that mattered. Speaking for herself, Norma Charlton, Bobby's wife, also said she didn't care. She had been to these things before and they were full of boring speeches.

Thanks to her husband, however, football was acquiring a new charisma, a word that seemed to have come into use from the time of Jack Kennedy. With his comb-over hair and quiet manner, Bobby did little to foster the idea that he had it, but Donald Zec, *The Mirror*'s entertainment writer, pinpointed him as the star of today's show. Zec normally stuck to Hollywood. Four hundred million people from all over the world, he wrote, would be watching the game and mainly looking at 'Bobby Dazzler'. No Burton or Taylor, or any collection of Hollywood stars, could count on such a following.

When I went to get the paper I had wondered whether by the following morning we really would find ourselves on top of the world. It was unthinkable, surely, that we would let this chance slip: a World Cup final against the Germans?

No final decision from Ramsey on his team by morning was good news for Greaves, some correspondents said. The manager was weighing matters painstakingly and assessing how he would reshuffle the line-up to accommodate the Tottenham man. But at about midday, Ramsey revealed he had not been doing any shuffling. England teams in the old days chopped and changed. This one had settled into playing with each other and would stay. Greaves was to sit out the game in his collar and tie; the only sensible decision, said Ramsey. He would not change a winning team.

My parents were driving off for the day to Sandy to see my grandma Chapman. I went three doors down the street to watch the match with Ernie. In preparation, Mrs Michael had hoovered and emptied the ashtrays of the basement TV room at the back of the house for the convenience of the men and boys. Ernie's two older sisters had long since left home – June to get married to a scaffolder out by Silvertown, and Maureen to join the RAF. (June soon had several children and Maureen periodically came back to the street looking good in uniform.) Ernie did not smoke but his brother Barry, the one who had got us into trouble with the Mods, did. Mr Michael had his Woodbines. They watched television with the door closed and back curtains drawn. On a summer's afternoon, the room was pitch-dark but for the flickering images before us. Mrs Michael generally kept to the basement front room, with its relatively streaming light, or to her kitchen under the front doorstep.

As the teams came out, the England fans in the stadium were acting as if already celebrating victory. A football held at his left hip, Moore walked unperturbed at the head of the England line. It would be nearly a half-century before a biography of the England skipper revealed that his groin strain of a season earlier had in fact been testicular cancer. He had been operated on and had one of his testes removed. Always immaculately attired on or off the pitch, Moore had worried that this might affect how he appeared in his football shorts. We would not have known. As far as any of us could tell, England's captain was all there.

Banks jigged and looked the most keyed up of the players. In the minutes before the players emerged from the tunnel, a shower had dampened the pitch and the Leicester City keeper was annoyed that he was going to have to wear gloves. I would have been pleased. Keepers traditionally had hands like plates, but mine were never those of Pat Jennings, who could catch a ball one-handed. Putting gloves on meant a psychological boost, if only in the wet. Banks, though, was unsettled at not being able to use his bare hands and get a 'proper feel of the ball'.

It was no surprise when the Germans got off to their usual quick start. Its circumstances, on the other hand, were alarming. At 31, Ray Wilson was the oldest member of the England team, and not one to make an error. His style was to work with an economy of motion, solemnly respectful of the task at hand – at times, anyone watching could be forgiven for not realising he was there. After football, he would become an undertaker. For now, he misjudged a header and nodded it straight to the feet of Helmut Haller. My first instinct was to imagine that the German midfielder would be as surprised as I was at such an unlikely gift and fluff it. But he maintained his composure and swept the ball into Banks' right-hand corner.

In the shocked silence around most of Wembley stadium, England's fans had little to console them. In that of the Michaels' back room, we were fortunate as the soothing thoughts of Kenneth Wolstenholme intervened. The BBC commentator – an ex-RAF man, after all – might also have been anticipating an early strike by the Germans, and he had a message to reassure us. We were not to worry, he indicated; whichever team scored first in a World Cup final always lost. I had not realised this but, I informed the room, the Germans would blow themselves out. Resilience and our powers of moral endeavour would wear them down. I did not exactly put it like that but, through the billowing smoke cloud, I thought I detected Mr Michael give a brief nod back.

We hit back quickly, far faster than I thought we would. It would have been far better to have left the Germans in front for a good while and lulled them into a false sense of security. Under usual circumstances, that would be their undoing, whereupon we would devastatingly strike back late in the day. Only six minutes after the German goal, Hurst scored powerfully with his head. Greaves would not have done that. One–one was the tally registered by the two men who, on the high gantry, were in charge of the Wembley scoreboard; and it was one-up already to Ramsey for his team selection.

A further peculiar thing immediately happened. We, not they, mounted a furious aerial assault, and it was the Germans who resisted stubbornly. High balls rained down on Hans Tilkowski in the German goal. Hurst clattered him in mid-air and laid him out in a fashion that I was familiar with from my junior encounters with Spurs. England had decided before the game that they would adopt this tactic, continental keepers being historically dodgy on the cross. But as the spectators in the stadium, and indeed those around me, began to sense blood, Hurst and the other England players were surprised how well Tilkowski stood up to the onslaught. I began to feel sorry for him.

The West Germans carried the game into the second half, which could have gone either way, but neither I nor the crowd were dissuaded from the belief that only we could possibly win. Just 12 minutes from the end, Peters seemed to have sealed it. Expertly following the course of a ball bobbing around in the penalty area, he steered it firmly into the net. This was exactly the kind of time when our qualities emerged to leave the enemy floundering. England would surely see the game out to victory now. Against all history, however, it was the Germans who came back. After a scramble in the England goalmouth, Wolfgang

Weber forced the ball across the goal-line in the final seconds of normal time.

Left having to summon the Churchillian spirit, Ramsey picked up the team in the couple of minutes' break before the half-hour of extra-time. The Germans' equaliser had been a doubtful one. From a free-kick for a foul said to have been committed by Jack Charlton, it actually looked like a German had fouled him. Ramsey took this as his theme. His exhausted players had already and fairly won the Cup once, he told them. They had only to get up and win it again.

Whether it was Ramsey's words that galvanised the fates in England's favour over the next few minutes, no one has been certain since. What went on to happen, however, worked out perfectly, and took on the qualities of a dream. When, early in the first period of extra-time, the ball reached Hurst on the edge of the German six-yard area, in my mind he seemed to move into slow motion. Almost casually, he was strolling across the face of goal and away from any prospect of scoring, until suddenly he twisted back on himself and fired in a shot. Now too fast for the eye to follow, the ball smashed into the underside of the crossbar and down towards the goal-line. Tilkowski, diving backwards, helped obscure the view. Weber retreated fast to head the ball out of play, whereupon the action froze.

Good try but no goal. My thought returned to the moment we had hit the bar against Tottenham and their defender had slumped back to sit on the ball as it came down on or around the line. The referee had merely waved play on and the key issue became whether the full-back would lose his manhood as Ronnie Wigg and others attempted to hack the ball out from under him.

Yet, here there was no play to wave on. The game had stopped, allowing a brief time for deliberation. And, wait a moment: something had caught the referee's eye. Ernie saw it, too, and said he thought we'd scored. Mr Michael reached for his cigarettes, realised that he had finished his standard quota and, exasperated, would have to send out for a fourth packet of the day.

An arm had shot up signalling a goal. Another followed, possibly indicating the same. The first belonged to Roger Hunt, who was almost under the crossbar. To emphasise how certain he was that the ball had gone in, he wheeled away, as if heading back to the centre-circle for the normal kick-off after a goal had been scored.

Who would have thought it? Hunt might never have been playing if Ramsey had listened to some people. But here was the Liverpool man, as ever, right up with the action. As his hand shot up, so did that of the linesman with his flag on the right side of the field. Had both arms been raised together or did one precede the other? Wasn't Hunt's first and didn't the official's instinctively follow? The ref was now using the time to determine the facts of the matter and walking over to his linesman to talk to him, in one fashion or another.

I had not noticed the Russian official during the game, yet now he was thrust into its limelight. Had it not been for Wolstenholme saying so, we would not have known he was the 'Russian linesman'. To me, he did not look very Russian. He was not, for example, the blond steely-eyed assassin in *From Russia With Love* (as played by Robert Shaw, an Englishman). With a shock of grey hair falling over his forehead and in his long baggy shorts, he looked too jovial for someone that you would have seen standing on a tank in Budapest, or otherwise promoting the Soviet cause. Tofiq Bahramov was, of course, not a Russian name, and the linesman was not a Russian at all; although didn't his bushy moustache bring back memories of Joe Stalin?

'It's all right!' I shouted to Ernie, Barry and their dad, each of whom were little more than the width of a chair away, 'He'll remember Leningrad!' I had seen a BBC documentary on the siege of Leningrad. During the war the Russians had survived the months-long German blockade of their second city, which temporarily had lost its name of St Petersburg. Supplies shipped in from Britain had been transported by lorry across frozen Lake Ladoga. Mrs Michael was so alarmed by the noise that she came rushing in to see if someone had shouted for tea.

An hour later, I arrived at the Marquee. Saturday evenings were not normally a time that any of my mates went there, but I thought I'd see who might be hanging around. Paul Fuschillo, on the junior books at Arsenal, came by. Alex Gardner arrived soon after, who I had not seen at the club before. He had left Highbury early after O-levels and looked pleased with working life. He was a steward for Alitalia and he had his girlfriend with him. Neither had any interest in football; she was American. But he had wanted to show her the celebrations.

Wardour Street was full, and we spent a couple of hours in the Intrepid Fox on the corner of Peter Street. Such was the struggle to get through the crowd to the bar that it did not cost us much for the privilege. We stood at one side of the room on a staircase, which was jammed with people, and joined the mass chanting of 'England', 'Ramsey' and the names of the England players. That of Geoff Hurst featured the most.

Maybe ten thousand people crammed into Piccadilly Circus and the way to Leicester Square. Some reports compared the celebrations with VE Day after victory in Europe was declared in May 1945. Of course then there wouldn't have been many Germans in the London crowd; they were numerous now, and shaking hands with them on Shaftesbury Avenue made it feel like the war was truly over. They said, 'Well done,' and had the good grace not to mention the third goal.

We had all endured the seconds when Dienst, the Swiss ref, and his moustachioed linesman had come face to face on the touchline. As the linesman nodded vigorously, the grey hair across his forehead jumping about, the referee concluded that England had scored. The German players did not, and several gathered around the officials. Dienst brushed them away and marched off. When they turned their attentions to the linesman, one of them remembered their orders. Uwe Seeler came to usher his countrymen away and, deterred from further antics, the Germans returned to what they had been doing for the past 20 years. They took their medicine and got back to playing the game.

When he had long removed himself from the line of fire, I met Hans Tilkowski at Wembley. Years on from the final, some old England players were getting together to recall it, and the former goalkeeper came on behalf of the German team. I asked him about England's third goal and the dreamlike sequences we had seen so many times since: shots fired in, balls crashing down from crossbars, modern-day slow motion applied to see if the ball was in. For Tilkowski, it was no dream, or rather, as he told me, 'Es war kein Tor.' ('It was no goal.') I was inclined to agree, but when I looked again at the pictures of the German keeper diving backwards as Hurst's shot beat him, he was hardly at any better angle to judge than others.

Years later, too, when many of us came to know more about Soviet geography, it turned out that linesman Bahramov was from a part of the old Communist bloc called Azerbaijan, a virtually unheard of location. When I looked it up, it was not much nearer to Leningrad than I had been in Ernie's back room. The Azerbaijanis would later erect a statue of Bahramov and name their national stadium after him in Baku, their capital, grateful for what he had done to put them on the map.

Following the final, we quickly told ourselves that the third goal did not matter. England had scored a fourth and that had decided things. Hadn't it? With a few seconds left, as Moore released a perfect ball from his penalty area to Hurst far up field, our attention was distracted by the sight of the fans who came running on to the pitch. I wanted to scream at them that this was not the moment; the match was under the jurisdiction of a rule-oriented Swiss, and didn't the laws say referees could abandon games if spectators stormed the field? Kenneth Wolstenholme showed his alarm as he shouted that they thought the game had finished. Hurst charged on, intending, he said, to hit a shot so far into the stands that the referee would blow his whistle for time. Everything in that instant, however, came together for him – timing, technique and strength – as his left foot connected with the ball. The shock was such that I had no recollection of Wolstenholme's summarising words: the ones that have been repeated over the years regarding the fans on the pitch thinking it was all over . . . 'It is now!' The sight of the net bulging behind Tilkowski's right shoulder with the power of Hurst's shot obliterated them. I only felt a jolt at the realisation that the ball had flown under the bar and that we had won something at last.

With the victory, Ramsey began to let his Britishness slip. Stuck to his seat at the sidelines as the game ended, he did allow others to pull him out of it. Before long, he made to walk towards the tunnel and to the quiet of the dressing room, until he had second thoughts and turned to join the celebrations. Moore coaxed a laugh out of him as he made the manager hold the trophy aloft, after which Ramsey left the team to parade it around the pitch.

Harold Wilson also went through something of a transformation. He became a football convert. Within a year or so when Huddersfield were promoted to the first division, the prime minister was to be seen taking his seat proudly in the stands, as if a lifetime season ticket holder. For the World Cup final, he had returned from across the Atlantic to slip into the stadium at half-time to sit some way along from the royal family beyond Angus Ogilvy, the husband of Princess Alexandra. Much of the afterglow would come the prime minister's way. A crowd of thousands formed in the evening from Whitehall up to 10 Downing Street's door chanting, 'We want Harold!'

Wilson was not there. He was hosting the reception for the team at the Royal Garden Hotel. 'Well done, Bobby,' he told Moore. 'Thank you, sir,' replied the England captain. Wilson had alongside him his deputy leader George Brown. From just south of the river in Lambeth, Brown was more at one talking the language of football. The team had played 'a blinder', he told them. At some early stage, Jimmy Greaves quietly slipped away to go on holiday, saying he was both the proudest and saddest man in England. When the rest of the players appeared on a balcony to the crowd's roar, Ramsey initially refused to come out until Wilson persuaded him. It was a 'once in a lifetime thing', the prime minister said, and for a few minutes Ramsey appeared.

When I asked my mother some decades later how this compared with VE Day, she said, yes, there had been lots of crowds. In May 1945, nearly everyone was given two days off, and she had come down from Sandy with my grandma, aunt Olive and six-year-old Keith. They brought the meat ration with them from the butcher's on Sandy High Street, the coupons not being transferable to the one they would have used at the bottom of Gerrard Road.

My mum went to Buckingham Palace and stood to the left of the gates by the army barracks. 'We saw Churchill,' she said. The crowd were 'kicking up a fuss' and the King and Queen eventually came out, princesses Elizabeth and Margaret with them. A deferential Churchill stood to the side of the balcony until the Queen, the future Queen Mother, beckoned him forward, this similarly being a once in a lifetime thing. When my mother left, she walked up the Mall into Trafalgar Square. Progress was slow because of the huge crowds as she crossed into the Strand. A lot of buses were lined up there unable to move and by chance she met cousin Hilda, a conductress on one of them. 'Oh, I do feel funny,' Hilda said as they chatted. Some of the drivers and clippies had brought drink with them and, not given the day off like the rest of the population, they were enjoying themselves as much as they could. Members of the crowd plied them as well, anyone in uniform being a hero. Hilda did not drink normally but the revellers and her workmates would not take no for an answer.

On World Cup night, we went back to Hoxton. Alex had a rented flat there near the Waste, the Saturday street market on Kingsland Road. My granddad went there occasionally to pick up the odd chisel or second-hand hacksaw he might want for a bit of carpentry. Already away from his parents, Alex had a job abroad. How did you get one? No banks advertised openings other than behind a counter in your local high street. Hong Kong and Singapore were not on the map as financial centres attracting the youth of London. One kid from Hoxton three years older than me at school, had got a job in the civil service and been sent to Bahrain, another place of empire. It had sounded attractive, if only as a means of getting away from Islington, but, when you looked at it, it was only working in an office at some distant remove.

Alitalia were looking after him, Alex said. They would be sending him to classes soon to learn some of the language. I knew more than he did from listening to my dad. Being a steward was fine. Going by air was luxury travel and planes were rarely full. On your overnights away, the stewardesses were good fun. While the pilots had first pick, the stewards never went short. His girlfriend had just popped out to the kitchen. Apart from an English teacher we'd had in my Highbury second year, she was the first American I had spoken to. But how did you get to the US? And how did you get an American girlfriend? The cheap flights Alex was allowed at a tenth of the price meant he would be able to get across to visit her soon. The world was opening up.

We talked about the football here and there but not much. It would have been impolite to in front of a girl. Paul and I left at dawn, noted a kitchen light coming on in a tower block along Kingsland Road and went our ways at Dalston Junction. I turned left towards Essex Road at Denis Parsons' shop. The area was pretty rough, and the De Beauvoir estate still to be passed, but the few people around were fine. What it was to be 18 and out early on the morning after England had won the World Cup, even walking along the Balls Pond Road.

# After

# Chapter 14

# EMPIRE'S END

A friend of later years who had been serving with the British army on the Rhine told me he had gone to see the final with a group of his mates in a bar on the rough side of Münster. They sat one side of the room, the locals the other, and all had proceeded more or less well until at the end of the game an almighty fight broke out. But behind the upturned tables and beneath flying glass the squaddies had taken shelter and played no part in it. The trouble was strictly a row between resident Germans and Turkish guest workers, the latter of which had been cheering on England. When the excitement passed, the Turks left and the locals called over to the soldiers to come and join them. Together they drank out the night.

I slept for a couple of hours and saw my dad getting something from the car as I went for the papers. 'I never thought we'd do it,' he said, looking amazed that we had. No, we always beat the Germans, I told him. My uncle had picked up a copy of *The Telegraph* in Fleet Street the night before and put that through the door. The newsagent had no *Mirror*s left because the vans had left him short. The blokes in the print room must have been celebrating the result so much that they had not kept the machines running properly. 'Take this,' he said and gave me a *Sunday Times*, along with the other papers as normal.

London had celebrated 'Latin American style', a variation on the lunatics theme of a week before. Chants of 'England, England' had resounded throughout the West End to the accompaniment of bugles, bells and horns. Everyone agreed that it was amazing how suddenly the national mood had changed when less than three weeks ago our chances had been written off. Denis Howell, the sports minister, said on behalf of the government that it was the 'best £500,000 we ever spent'. He had been delighted to find flowers in the ladies lavatory at Goodison Park. Some grounds did not even have a ladies lavatory.

Suddenly, people who had not talked football before were doing so – professional types, accountants and publishers. On holiday in France, they had gathered in roadside groups to listen to the final on their car radios. In the resorts of the English southwest they came off the beaches, from Bude to Budleigh Salterton, to find out the score. John Freeman, High Commissioner to India, had declared that he was unavailable for calls during matches. Freeman had made himself well known for the interviews on TV he did with people like Evelyn Waugh, the novelist who had died in April. Freeman introduced the idea of asking quite personal questions. When it came to football, however, his privacy was sacred.

Some had not changed. A later reading of the diaries of Tony Benn – his name stripped to the bare essentials by the time he published them – revealed he returned to his constituency home in Bristol exhausted after a week's work and sat in his garden oblivious to the game. As for Wilson, his latter-day conversion failed to work any magic with the England team when he asked for a special photograph with them. The players refused, saying they did not want to be exploited for political reasons.

The Duke of Edinburgh, who had been at the World Cup final, was soon off to Argentina for a month to play polo. Following the Rattín incident there was clearly no enmity between the two nations there. Other sport carried on. Next to the pigeon racing results, the *News of the World* pictured Berkshire taking the strain in the county tug-of-war championships in Hastings. Essex beat them in the second round.

The police had made swoops in the 'London suburbs'. Ten men and a woman had been arrested in Camberwell. My uncle Keith had his flat in neighbouring Lewisham, but that was hardly a 'suburb'. Whoever wrote the article probably just meant 'south London'. No arrest warrants had been issued because to have applied for them would have tipped off the criminals, who must have had their contacts in the courts and the police. Charlie Richardson was among those arrested, and all were thought to be connected to his gang. The arrests related to the incident at the Catford nightclub but, when the matter came to trial, stories emerged of how the gang tortured its victims, especially those deemed to be involved with the Krays. Charlie Richardson lived in a big house off Denmark Hill, just round the corner, I imagined, from Mendelssohn's place.

An advert for Coutts, the posh person's bank in the Strand, caught my eye. 'Awaiting your GCE results?' Interesting and rewarding careers started at £550 per annum, rising to '£1,345 at 31'. An annual £550 was what I would be starting on at the town hall in a few days' time. In another 13 years would I be getting an extra £800? In Edinburgh, the British Linen Bank proposed a starting salary of not less than £2,500, but this was for a data-processing manager, which had something to do with computers.

The only paper to mention the end of the British Empire was the *Sunday Telegraph*. The Colonial Office was to close at midnight after two hundred years of administering the dependencies. Most of the fans at yesterday's final had walked to the stadium along Empire Way. What was it to be called now: Post-Imperial Passage?

As I initially understood it, we had taken control of such places as Bechuanaland, Basutoland and Barbados to civilise them. Vaguely, I had wondered about that when, eight years or so ago at Sunday school, a young grey-uniformed missionary in a hat gave us Bible readings on her way to West Africa. The Bible was 'the sword', she said, and commanded us to 'lift up your swords!' I had felt relieved she was moving on from us to the Africans, but the empire had provided us with the opportunity for a broad education: from Ian Smith to Tafawa Balewa. Without it we would not have known of the Rann of Kutch or Tristan da Cunha or seen Kip Keino run at the White City. In history classes at school we had learned of the island of Socotra, off Somaliland, the coasts and fertile valleys of which produced dates and gums. It belonged to us for no obvious reason than, presumably, it was better ours than someone else's. Seretse Khama was in charge in Bechuanaland, where a wicked uncle wanted him out. My mum often talked about how Khama, educated in Britain, had married a white woman, Ruth Williams from London. This had displeased his uncle, neighbouring South Africa and us. A British government report by Lord Salisbury – whose family had a long history in Rhodesia – referred to this 'unfortunate marriage'. The couple had held firm and Khama was about to become the president of Botswana.

With the empire gone, where was there to look to? On the day before the World Cup, Auberon Waugh – son of Evelyn – had written an article for *The Mirror* about Belgium. I knew Belgium. Ostend had wide and windy beaches, and we stayed in a hotel on the harbour front which served tomatoes stuffed with prawns. Why couldn't we do interesting things with tomatoes, except serve them with a tin of salmon on Sundays? Brussels had the Manneken Pis, which was also very un-English. Bruges had canals that no one shouted at you to keep away from, although on a barge trip my dad had had to push my head down just as one of its low bridges was about to remove it.

If you liked Belgians, Belgium was the place to go. It had a lot of them, Waugh wrote, and was more crowded than Hong Kong. Things were going well. Belgian workers zoomed away from the factory gates in their own cars. Ours pedalled or walked. More and more Belgians had their own homes, not that many of them had bathrooms, personal hygiene not being a local priority. But nor did a lot of families in Noel Road, where one bath and change of underpants a week was quite normal. British people needed to appreciate their neighbours across the Channel more, Waugh suggested, although it would take a while. Locals told him that they could always spot the British disembarking from ferries: they looked miserable and had vaccination plasters on their arms.

Wilson had given the job of closing the Colonial Office to Lord Longford, a peer with absent-minded professor glasses and hair, but had then sacked him in April. Longford's heart was not in it, and he moved on to campaign against the looser homosexuality and pornography laws, while attempting to persuade the public to forgive Myra Hindley. Wilson handed the task to Fred Lee, MP for Newton, the area around Manchester United's ground, and former head of the Amalgamated Engineering Union. A trade unionist on the Labour left was more at one with laying two centuries of history to rest.

With the empire's passing, I got my first kiss. Of the two East End girls that had started at the Tote, Sandra had dark hair cut in a Mary Quant-ish style, while Doreen was fair and had hers tied at the back like a piece of rope. She was the arty one of the two. I fancied Sandra. She stared at me a lot, which I mentioned to Doreen. She said Sandra was nearly blind and refused to wear glasses. Sandra was my age and had just finished her A-levels – she looked the type who would have passed. Doreen was still doing her Os and not that interested; she was more sketching and dressmaking. She designed her own clothes, and a retired dressmaker, a lady in Forest Gate, made them up for her. I was not sure about them. They were baggy and came in lots of colours, many featuring velvet.

One evening on a day that Doreen had off, I took the tube with Sandra from Blackfriars and, instead of getting off at the Monument, stayed on until Mile End. I chatted with her on the platform as numerous Stratford trains went by, and then she told me: she had a boyfriend. His name was Dave and she had known him for years. Not that he worked or did anything useful; he played the bongos and lived off Stratford's Angel Lane, just up and over the railway from the Theatre Royal. He was presently in Belgium, doing nothing in particular, holed up in a disused lighthouse.

I wangled my way into joining Sandra and Doreen on a trip to Southend. ('I'll come!' I'd said, when Sandra mentioned they were going. Doreen was not with us at the time and, when she found out, glared at me.) We wandered around the Kursaal looking at the rides, ambled along the muddy beach and spent most of the time by the pier. We took the train the mile and more to its end, came back and sat under it by the sea wall for the evening hours. Doreen had a small portable record player and between them they had brought a bagful of LPs.

We arrived back in London too late for the tube and I had to persuade a taxi driver on London Bridge to take us home. Islington was OK, he said, but Stratford was more than six miles and I'd have to pay for his journey back. I offered 30 bob, and from the shocked look on his face he would have accepted a pound. From the appearance of mine he knew I was desperate. In the taxi between London Bridge and Islington I got my kiss. It was as we passed the Bank of England. She was passionately interested, and the blokes in top hats should have dashed out with the rise it gave me. I ought to have been ashamed with Doreen sitting next to us but reached home elated, nonetheless.

I had handed in my notice a few days earlier. Tony knew I must have had the job lined up for some while and felt deceived that I had come to the Tote knowing I was moving on to somewhere else. I'd had the chance to learn everything he knew, so what now was I going to do instead? I said I wanted to be a chartered accountant and was going to Islington town hall. They'd train me. Not to be a chartered accountant, they wouldn't, he said. Councils had their own accountants and they were not chartered, but municipal, so I'd be stuck in town halls all my life. Peter, my art school friend, had said much the same.

From the marbled glory of the town hall's front entrance, I was led along dark corridors into a high-ceilinged office at the rear of the building. A dozen people occupied it but all that could be heard was the squeak of hole-punches and click of lever arch files. 'Hello, I'm Anita,' the person I was put nearest to said quietly, 'Anita Christmas.' She was about my age, had dark hair trimmed short, and a bust significantly bigger than the sixties norm. Anita showed me the kind of papers that I would be filing: costs for bollards destroyed in Holloway Road, ashes scattered at Trent Park crematorium, overtime by the dustmen of Ashburton Grove depot, and towels hired out to people having their weekly scrub at Ironmonger Row. Should I answer one of the few phone calls we received a week, I was to know we were the department of highways, cemeteries, cleansing and baths.

Sandra said yes, she would like to come out. Dave was still away and presumed missing near Blankenberge. For our first official date I took her to Hampstead Heath, where Islington boys fancied they could impress women. From the East End, she'd probably never seen Hampstead. She had, but not the night view of whatever area it was twinkling beyond Jack Straw's Castle. We sat kissing on a park bench near the three ponds, just off the footpath as you came on to the heath. Self-control was nonetheless enforced, and Sandra reprimanded me for my effort at what I later learned was called heavy petting. 'Don't! I've told you,' she snapped, more heavily, if anything, in her put-down.

On the Friday of my first week I was sent to the computer room. A small, ill-lit office containing, with me, seven people, it had a window looking through to a much brighter room, with its large space almost entirely occupied by the computer. In its specially air-conditioned area, its operator, Diana, wore a white coat and nursed the machine through the working day. It rarely managed a full one. At great expense, the borough had hired a portly, amiable character called Don to run the department. He might have done so had he been there more often. When he was present, it was to have lunch with Cathie, his friend in the compositing room. The national press spoke of an alarming 'brain drain' from Britain of technical people leaving for the US. Don was among those left behind.

My colleague sitting next to me I knew by sight from our street. He was an in-law of the Italian family who lived a few doors down from us and with whom my father, in particular, was friendly. 'I see your neighbour's on TV tonight,' said my colleague, after we had been talking a bit. Who was that? We were arranging the road sweepers' time-sheets in the orderly manner that Mrs Blackwell, in charge of the punch-card operators, might accept for her dozen or so girls to handle. 'Joe,' he said. 'He's got a new play out.' I knew no Joe. 'You know, the library books. Joe and Ken.' Joe was the younger one in the leather cap. Orton, his surname, meant nothing to me. The older one, Ken Halliwell, had been a writer himself, he told me, but had more recently fitted the role of housekeeper for the two of them. They lived in the top flat of the house next to his in-laws.

I watched Orton that night on a programme in the once empty slot that the BBC had filled between the end of kids TV and the start of grown-ups' stuff at about seven. Here was the bloke who we had held up our kick-abouts for at the top of the street, as he and his friend scurried past with their satchels of mutilated volumes. Among us, he had looked shy; in performance he was inspirational. He had written one play already, *Entertaining Mr Sloane*, which had gone completely outside my notice. The critics denounced it as rubbish, he said, which was fine. That had not stopped its success. His latest, *Loot!* was transferring to the West End. It dealt with things such as hypocrisy and police corruption. The reviewers wouldn't like that either, but what did they know?

Sandra came round on Saturday evening, my parents having gone to Bedford. I cooked her spaghetti, a dish she was unlikely to have had with Dave along Angel Lane, Stratford, I figured, though more common these days around the Angel, Islington. We played the Beatles' *Revolver* and the Stones' *Aftermath*. The Beatles wanted you to listen: 'Eleanor Rigby', even 'Taxman', which though not so great was George Harrison's protest against the 90% tax charged big earners. The Beatles were getting fed up with girls screaming through their concerts and – in San Francisco's Candlestick Park – were about to do their last one. Whatever the Stones wanted, it was not only for you to pay attention to the lyrics. The 11 minutes of 'Goin' Home' at the end of *Aftermath*'s first side could only have been written to writhe around to on the floor, with the help of a few cushions. Under such conditions, Sandra and I made love. Not that the verb to 'make love' meant having sex.

At work, nearly everyone was back from holiday. My immediate boss, Lionel Bellman, had greying brushed-back hair and wore a baggy but well-pressed blue suit. Previously he had worked for the Tote on the night racing at Harringay dogs, but the town hall offered more of a career structure and a pension. Just across the desk, he sat with his head down, steel-rimmed glasses on the end of his nose, fussing through some papers until Anita introduced us. Behind his back she called him 'Urinal Lionel', and he referred me to a box of index cards, which he had compiled. They contained the names of the urinals in the borough, of which there were many. These were distinct from conveniences, Lionel advised. Conveniences had attendants stationed by day, and during many hours of the night. The unattended urinals, I learned in the course of time, were famous for something called 'cottaging'.

My job was to extract details of the charges for each establishment from the bills of the London Electricity and Metropolitan Water Boards and insert these on the cards. Someone, however, was taking the Mickey at a couple of them. Mostly the expenditure on each pissoir was a few pounds and shillings each quarter. Holloway Road's urinal, under the railway bridge, and that of Astey's Row, next to Essex Road library, however, used next to no electricity. From Orton's diaries in later years, I learned that such locations were among those frequented by him and passing friends, who unscrewed the light bulbs to protect the sensitivities of more unsuspecting users. Thanks to the forensic accounting inspired by Lionel and practised by the likes of me, Islington eventually bricked up its facilities to guard the borough's morals and save spending a few pence on the rates.

I was to see Sandra again on a Thursday evening. The plan was to go to Stratford to meet her. She lived in a small terraced house in Station Street with her parents and a cat called Stanley (Dave's second name, as Doreen told me). You could see the Central Line platform from her house. Her family did not have a phone and, if ever she called me, she did so from the red telephone box by the station entrance. She had rung a couple of nights before to say her parents were being rehoused. A lot of building was going to be done around Stratford and the council were giving her family a flat high up in one of the East End's new tower blocks. After twenty years waiting on the housing list, they were really excited. But before I went to work that Thursday morning she called to say her boyfriend had returned late the previous night and would be coming round that evening. She would not be able to see me and said she was really upset. I was, too, but, this being expected, that was the end of it. Then, next morning she called again. They had talked and she had told him she had met someone else. That was fine by him, he had said, and after his lighthouse experience he needed to 'find his feet'. So, they had broken up: 'You've won,' she told me. And we agreed to meet that night.

The walk to work took me along Colebrooke Row to Essex Road, and up the alley at the back of St Mary's church, where my grandparents had been married. Via a right turn into Upper Street opposite the big post office and King's Head pub, there remained a few hundred yards along to the town hall. Overall, it usually took just over ten minutes; today I may have bounded it in five. It was computer-room day and Diane the operator's birthday. A group of us went for lengthy lunchtime drinks in a pub on Islington Park Street. I starred in the conversation, *Round the Horne* featuring large. Back at work, the computer hummed through the afternoon as I internally sang. At five o'clock, as I was leaving by the town hall front steps – it did not feel like a day for the staff side entrance – it occurred to me that Sandra and I had not talked about when or where we would meet.

At home I waited and nothing happened. Unable to call, after two or three hours of gathering despair, I thought I might as well go to Stratford. I stared from the platform at Sandra's house, and saw Stanley circle it a few times. At about 11.30, her boyfriend's blond hair emerged from the house and they kissed goodnight. When he had loped past the station on his way home, I walked towards her house but we met as she was on the way to the telephone box. They had been together for so long that he had asked for reconsideration. So she had opted for her bongo rather than borough council boyfriend. It left me bereft.

We had the Highbury old boy's dinner a little into September, the venue a private dining room towards the Trafalgar Square end of Charing Cross Road. Peter, allowing himself time off from the evening pleasures of Chelsea art school, suggested we go together. I assumed he would come straight from his easel but he let me down, went home, changed and came in a suit. I had gone for a pair of dark-green jumbo cords from Carnaby Street and a red crew-neck sweater. Everyone else was formally attired. I spent some of the evening telling Ray Wood, the Mekon, of the lucrative career before me in municipal computers. What he had told me about reading *The Mirror* was at the front of my mind, while he had probably forgotten it. For a while I was in the company of Alan Foster and Denis Parsons. Would-be graduates of the school of Hoxtonian hardnuts, they said they were only there to decide who they were going to beat up afterwards. I was on the list of possibles. Attention was soon distracted, however, by the guest of honour, the new headmaster. With his bald head, Dickensian sideburns and large cigar, he spoke loudly in a northern accent. His name was Rhodes Boyson but he had just finished a PhD on the broad subject of education and, in his introductory remarks, the Mekon made it clear that we were to call him Dr Boyson.

His speech was short and his approach similar to that of Reggie King, if without the five o'clock-scraping. Boyson would whip malcontents but offer them a post-thrash game of table tennis. For a while he was to become the best-known headmaster in the land, which won him a seat for the Conservatives in Parliament and an eventual place in Margaret Thatcher's government. But as he moved on, Highbury became another local school to which cabinet ministers – now housed in upscale Barnsbury – shunned sending their children. Thatcher herself tired of Boyson. Always receptive to calls from Highbury old boys, not least if they were contacting him from the media, he had rather imagined that he would become her Minister of Education. She did not like his cosy assumptions and exiled him into a junior post to deal with the Troubles in Northern Ireland.

After one of my Friday nights at the Marquee, my mum had waited up for me with the news that three policemen had been shot dead in the West End and that three gunmen were on the loose. She was worried that by chance I might have crossed their path of flight. The murders turned out to have happened in Shepherd's Bush, in west London, far from Soho, and two of the men were quickly caught. The third, the one who had done the killing, went on the run for more than three months. A veteran of the Malayan emergency, he used his army skills, learned while fighting Chinese guerrillas, to evade the combined forces of the police across the Home Counties until eventually caught in a hay barn in Bishop's Stortford. He was named Harry Roberts, the coincidence prompting considerable family interest. We had had a Harry Roberts, the late and main rival to my granddad in the billposting business, and who spent his wartime black market years evading the police until he too was caught in Bishop's Stortford. The police allowed the killer Harry Roberts a few hours out of jail to show them where he had hidden his gun. He took them to where he had buried it under the trees and just off the road near the ponds on Hampstead Heath.

Roberts was sentenced to a minimum of 30 years; one of the consequences of the murders was to revive the debate on hanging. My view was one of amazement that it had gone, if only for a five-year trial. The hangman – who we knew as Albert Pierrepoint, although he had been retired for some years – was a feature of life. I thought of him every time I went through Camden Passage and past the antique stalls of Pierrepoint Row. We remembered the executions and the names of the executed: from my teens and earlier, there were Podola, Marwood, Hanratty, all of them part of the grey memory of the fifties and early sixties. MPs, in a free vote, had abolished hanging but with the Moors Murders, and now Roberts, the majority of people that I knew would have had it back tomorrow.

In mid-October, and with Roberts still on the run, a decision was quietly taken that may have settled the capital punishment issue for ever. The Queen, advised by Roy Jenkins, pardoned Timothy Evans, hanged in 1950 for murdering his wife and daughter. Evans had lived in the same house in Notting Hill as John Christie, who was executed in 1953 for a series of murders, among which Christie was found belatedly to have killed Evans' wife and child. The police and prosecution service had pinned the charge on Evans, who was of limited education and an easy target. But still some people retained the view that the rope was worth keeping in spite of the occasional mistake.

I was in the computer room when news of the Aberfan disaster came through. A slag heap in the South Wales mining community had slipped and inundated a primary school. We were used to the ritual of pit disasters – reports of an explosion; women gathering at the pithead; men trapped underground; some dead, some caught in an air pocket and still alive. Could they be rescued? But this one could not be rationalised as an occupational hazard. Welsh coal had fuelled British imperial ambitions and the old industrial empire had struck back, not to kill members of the workforce but to consume its own children. First figures said more than one hundred had died. Harold Wilson visited the site and walked through the slurry to the remains of the school. He could not find the words to describe what he saw. The government ordered an inquiry, but doubts existed about the role of government itself. Merthyr Tydfil council had rejected requests for the tip's condition to be examined. The Coal Board, state-run like the Tote, was accused of ignoring warnings that the school was in danger. The very role of coal was called into question. The North Sea had oil, and BP was soon to announce that it had discovered the best gas-producing areas yet, just east of the Humber. Some breakthrough thinking was required, more efficiency, more technology – and, for that matter, computers that worked.

Ramsey's England returned to action next day. With the same team that had secured the World Cup, they won 2–0 against Northern Ireland. The result was more significant than in the past because the Home International Championship had been elevated into a qualifying competition for the European

Nations Cup. The match was in Belfast, divided again along religious lines. Pat Jennings (Catholic) and George Best (Protestant) were the big names of the home team, in front of a Windsor Park crowd of 48,600. An efficient England won at a jog, Peters and Hunt the scorers.

Banks had little to do but nonetheless commanded attention. You could see something different about his jersey when he rose to take the ball off the head of Derek Dougan, the Leicester and Northern Irish centre-forward. Dougan was both a great bloke with kids and, as the Troubles worsened, argued that Ireland, north and south, should play as one international team. A yet wider unity was also in the air, however, as Banks took the cross. His England jumper had a number one on its back, which had not happened before. I never did mention it to my dad, but we had gone continental.

# Chapter 15

# AFTERMATH

Sandra had let it slip in one of our conversations that Doreen fancied me, so I gave her a call and we started going out. This was less to spite Sandra than to remain near to her. Doreen suspected this and drew a hard bargain. Despite all the permissiveness floating around elsewhere, she insisted that she was an old-fashioned East End girl and there would be no sex; not now, nor for any foreseeable period into the future. I would have to serve my time.

We went on chaste nights out to the Plough and Harrow in Leytonstone High Road. As a gathering point for anyone of our age from Maryland Point to Whipps Cross, the pub was packed every evening and, while above the hubbub it was difficult to speak, a consistent theme concerned the latest rumours about the Krays. The police had pulled them in for questioning again, so what were they asking them? Which part of the Bow flyover was Ginger Marks buried under? Who killed Freddie Mills, shot in the face and found in his car outside his West End nightclub?

Nothing stuck. Despite everyone knowing that Ronnie and Reg were involved in many a crime, they were escaping serving any time at all.

Doreen was perfectly at one with the fact that I got along well with her father, John, and two brothers, Tony and little John. Her mum, Nell, red-haired, was very sweet and sat smiling and staring at me. Sandra had stared. Nell stared. Were all East End people like this?

'She just does that,' said Doreen. 'I'll tell her.' Nell's early hours office cleaning and running the family left her very tired, but I also felt she looked to see whether things I did from my bit of London were different from the way they did them. I had bought a beige corduroy and button-down shirt from Carnaby Street which, for no obvious reason, I left unbuttoned at the cuffs and collar points. She asked Doreen, 'Why does he do that?'

Nell and John invited us on a coach trip to the West End to see *The Sound of Music* one evening. We had both seen it before, but I met them outside the Two Puddings in Stratford Broadway. Once the coach reached the lights of Oxford Street, by Tottenham Court Road, others on the trip ooh-ed and ah-ed. Doreen and me looked at each other; we went twice a week to the West End. Her parents and other people on the coach may have gone once a year.

Both the Johns and Tony were West Ham fans, and fond of pointing out that their club had not only left Orient behind in the ranks of the football league but also – with Moore, Hurst and Peters – had won the World Cup. If there happened to be a game on television that the men of the household were watching, Doreen was quietly tolerant but otherwise she did not want me talking football in her company. From her school, she knew two of the kids I had played with at Brisbane Road and, although one of them she had quite fancied, she did not expect me to be like them. She did not want a 'football boy' as a boyfriend. She had art books around, and talked of paintings having 'depth' and 'textures'. For want of knowing where else to start, I began reading up about the Impressionists and others of their time. My dad had drawn very well and sketched his way up from Syracuse in Sicily to the Rialto Bridge in Venice. The latter he had sat by for hours, at some post-VE point of 1945, and captured with pencil on paper. He told me how much he liked Toulouse-Lautrec and the early fifties version of *Moulin Rouge*, with José Ferrer as the artist sketching and painting the Paris *demi-monde*.

*Loot!* was a hit in the West End, on at the Criterion Theatre by Piccadilly Circus. I took Doreen to see it. Its literary merit went above my head, but I hoped she would be impressed by what was coming out of Islington these days, not least my street. With an eye on the censor, there was only one swear word: a 'fuck!' from the chief character, the police officer, right at the end. This hardly rated with the tirade I had received from the Canonbury policemen on my walk home from school.

As for police corruption, and as an East Ender, Doreen said she had heard it all before. The new Islington classes and many others like them were fascinated. As Orton had come out of prison so he had started to write in his upstairs garret and read of the case of Detective Chief Inspector Challoner. He had based *Loot!*'s main character on the policeman who had stitched up the Greek-Cypriot kid a couple of years above me at Highbury school. It helped prompt a new questioning attitude towards the police and authority, and for our neighbour down the road brought considerable fame.

A kid from Tottenham, Gerry Harniman, had started work at the same time as I had at the town hall and, having quickly abandoned any thought of a council career, began turning up in jumbo cords and mauve corduroy jacket. He was keen on art and told me Athena Reproductions in Oxford Street printed copies of Lautrec posters. I tried but had no grasp of how to draw, and contented myself with having Jane Avril on my bedroom wall. Also there, I had an old street sign – Helmet Row, EC1 – which the dustmen's depot in the same street in Finsbury, by St Luke's church, had let me have when I had gone there to pay wages. This stood above a table on which there was one of the lamps that the North Thames Gas Board left at night by its holes in the road, and that I had painted gold.

Doreen indicated that I would need to improve myself further, if I was to improve my chances with her. When she saw one of my sketch efforts, she shook her head and, in effect, said to leave the art to her. There were other things I could concentrate on. She was on her way to a place at Goldsmith's, the sole problem being that she had to do the occasional piece of writing for liberal studies. She would welcome a sharpening of my compositional skills. Why not help with her college essays?

In late October, the first funeral took place in Aberfan. One hundred and sixteen children had died, as well as 28 adults. An underground spring, long since forgotten, was thought to have loosened the bottom of the slag heap and set off the avalanche. There were slag heaps like this all over South Wales and other coal-mining areas of Britain. In the coal towns, most of the mines would eventually be shut and the slag heaps removed or 'remodelled'. Near the end of the Thatcher period, when I visited Silksworth, the mining village near Sunderland where my aunt Joan came from, the slag heap there had been turned into an artificial ski slope.

In football, three weeks later, in mid-November, England unsentimentally disposed of Wales 5–1 at Wembley. Hurst scored two, the Charlton brothers one each and the other was a Welsh own goal. This felt like a new clinical England. Former England star Brian Clough, meanwhile, said he would work for nothing. Forced by injury to retire early as a player, he now managed Hartlepool at the bottom of the fourth division, and they had minimal funds. Orient were struggling, too, their crowds at Brisbane Road having slumped to 4,000. Bernard Delfont and Lew Grade announced that they were resigning from the Orient board. Their attentions had always been directed, anyway, towards *Sunday Night at the London Palladium.*

Mick Jagger looked sad but, in part thanks to Grade and Delfont, was doing well. He'd broken up with Chrissie Shrimpton and was pictured in collar and tie, eating alone at a Soho trattoria. The Stones were soon to top the bill at the Palladium, the occasion to coincide with their New Year's single 'Let's Spend the Night Together'. Designed to shock, the title set off a row at the town hall between Gerry and Derek, a young manager whose dad was on the board of Gordon's Gin in Goswell Road. It was 'disgusting', said Derek, whose long-term girlfriend he planned to marry soon and with whom, unbeknown to his and her parents, he had been having sex for some time. 'We think the Palladium is ready for the Stones and the Stones are ready for the Palladium,' said Jagger. I made a mental note not to be watching with my parents.

The £50 limit on what anyone taking a foreign holiday could spend abroad each year had just come into effect, but the spirits of the tour operators – very low when Callaghan had announced the measure in July – had surprisingly revived. While the government had hoped that vast numbers might be deterred from travelling, when the operators looked hard at their costs, they saw they could do a fortnight in Spain for £20. This, plus extra mileage out of encouraging people to beat a government restriction, led many who might not have thought of taking a foreign holiday to decide otherwise. Tony, Doreen's older brother, said he would be going to Spain in June.

Harold Wilson decided to join this let's-go-to-Europe movement. The Europeans, with the exception of President de Gaulle in France, wanted Britain to join the Common Market. Wilson was out to rally support and change a few French minds. He took George Brown with him, which was logical given that he was not only number two in the government but also foreign secretary. It was not necessarily helpful that Brown could get very drunk at embassy parties, though he was pro-Europe, while Wilson was coming around to it. Other Labour people needed persuading. Willie Hamilton, the Scottish MP who had long campaigned to abolish the monarchy, told his fellow party members in the Commons to stop being so parochial. They were all for international socialism, so should get used to the idea of mixing more with people 20 miles away across a stretch of water.

The prime minister plunged in on the last day of November. He appeared at a dinner to mark Winston Churchill's birthday at the English Speaking Union, a body created to promote the advancement of English speakers around the world. The way he saw things going, he told his audience, was that Britain's role was to help Europe build its economy to avoid US domination. In his recent meetings with President Johnson, Wilson could have accepted lots of dollars to relieve whatever economic problems Britain had in return for dispatching troops to Vietnam, but he had avoided, as I heard on *Radio Newsreel* at seven o'clock one evening, sending so much as a 'ceremonial goat'. The Tories had decided that Europe was the target in 1963. The Labour party had joined them, and kept us from going to war again at the same time.

In matters of law and order, a number of embarrassing breakouts were happening from British prisons, some reports of which had the Plough and Harrow's rumour mill slipping into fifth gear. Ronnie Biggs, the great train-robber from Stockwell in south London, had climbed the wall of Wandsworth jail last year and had been on the run since. A few weeks ago in October, George Blake, the spy, had escaped by way of a rope ladder from Wormwood Scrubs. The authorities blamed criminal gangs connected to Moscow. But were Soviet spymasters in the habit of leaving potted chrysanthemums by the walls of prisons they arranged to have their people escape from? Characters more likely to have sympathised with the anti-war 'flower power' movement getting under way in the US were eventually found to be responsible.

The latest fugitive was Frank Mitchell, an East End criminal styled the 'Mad Axeman', who was on the run from Dartmoor. His escape caused such panic that a detachment of the Argyll and Sutherland Highlanders regiment was sent to search for him. Pictured prowling the moor with axe handles they were led by a Scots' piper.

The Plough and Harrow's attention was caught by the description of the people thought to have helped Mitchell get away. He had walked free from a detail working outside the prison walls, which rather belied his reputation of being the most dangerous man in Britain. Two men in flashy suits and speaking in Cockney accents had visited a local inn, saying they had come to see a prisoner who was mentally disturbed. The front page story of *The Mirror* on 13 December that announced Mitchell's escape might also have had some connection with a smaller report on page 10. Ronnie Kray had failed to appear in court, as a witness in a case against an alleged corrupt detective. Was it possible that Kray had had other business to deal with, conceivably out of town?

In times past, Ronnie Kray had been in prison with Mitchell, who was serving a life sentence but had been given no idea how many years that might entail. Kray may have felt sorry for him or, as was said, fancied him. Mitchell, the son of a fishmonger from Old Ford Road, Bow, was educationally backward but described as having a bodybuilder's physique. Letters from Mitchell saying his apparently open-ended sentence was inhuman were received by the *Daily Mirror* and *The Times*. *The Mirror* published one in return. Mitchell had drawn attention to his plight, wrote L. A. Lee Howard, the editor, and it was time to give himself up: 'Call me personally at Fleet Street 0246.' Every available Flying Squad officer in London was put on the job of finding Mitchell, who was never seen again by anyone hoping to find him.

At the town hall party at Christmas, Anita made the occasion appropriately hers. Too embarrassed to dance, I spent the first half-hour slumped on a chair pretending to be drunk. Anita lurched me to my feet and on to the dance floor, whereupon we were snogging. After wondering for years how you went about this kind of thing, I was taken aback at how easy it could be. She moved on after a couple of dances and Joan Pierce replaced her in my arms. With tightly curled blonde hair, and in her fifties, Joan was unhappily married to a civil servant. He occasionally appeared in the office to tell us how good apartheid was and that Basil D'Oliveira merited no place in the England cricket team. With her Marje Proops glasses and red-painted lips, Joan snogged me as well.

Figures for the Christmas period of Friday to Tuesday showed that 158 people died on the roads, more than double the toll of last year. West Bromwich Albion appealed to their players to use safety belts, after the team's wing-half Graham Lovett crashed on the M1 and broke his back. The AA and the RAC cited bad weather conditions. Barbara Castle spoke of 'drink happy' drivers and that the breathalyser was due to become law.

For New Year, Doreen and I ended up in Shoreditch. With the last day of the year a Saturday, we went with Gerry to a party in Tottenham. We spent the early hours driving around with a friend of his who had a car, and the idea came up of catching the opening of Petticoat Lane market, where the bakeries operated overnight. We parked in a street by a railway bridge near a sign for Shoreditch Underground station. I hadn't realised the tube came down here, in such a remote place. Dossers and meths drinkers called out 'Happy New

Year' to each other. In future times, we might think of them as homeless people. I thought of what kind of year it would be for them yet, after not sleeping, I was far less cheery than they were. It amazed me that such areas existed. Even the poorest areas of Naples did not match this, and this was no more than a brisk walk from where I was brought up. During this year's election, when Oswald Mosley had run for the Shoreditch constituency, the old fascist leader had imagined that he might capitalise on its awfulness. As it was, he was beaten easily and thus ended his final effort to regain a place in British politics.

*The Mirror*'s Felicity Green said dress tops were going to plunge this year to areas that had not seen 'the light of day – or night' for years. Women were also being urged to step into the future 'without your bra'. Doreen and I next met in Bunjies, in Litchfield Street, near Cambridge Circus. You entered by a normal street front door and down a flight of stairs to a coffee bar. Guitar and folk music played behind a curtain. We sat at a table in a hole in the wall at the other end of the place, about midway under the street, with a candle stuck in a wax-encrusted bottle for light. Doreen told me she also might go to Spain this year.

Early on my granddad's birthday, 4 January, Donald Campbell killed himself on Coniston Water. He was trying to beat the world water speed record in *Bluebird*. 'She's tramping!' he cried, his term for being buffeted by the wind and water as *Bluebird* took off, stayed airborne for several seconds and somersaulted backwards. 'I'm going . . .' Campbell had shouted. With him went one of the last of the mad heroes whose reputation we had been brought up with. Jokes circulated at the Tote (now my Saturday job): Campbell had been found and 'his Timex watch was still working'. The money was not found to mount a successful search for his body until the millennium.

At the town hall, Derek took me to task for the way I spoke. He corrected my assumption that 'we was' and 'I done' were acceptable Islingtonian forms. Some of my day was spent writing letters to pensioners who had failed to pay for having their drains unblocked. They had called in the council imagining it was part of the service. It wasn't, and many of them were referred to Sid Porrett, the chief legal clerk upstairs who had organised the prosecution of Orton and Halliwell. My options closed in the computer room, when a full-time job came up as a programmer and Anita got it. Gerry declared that he was off to art school. Everyone who was anyone was going there.

Two alternatives were popular: being depressed or dropping out. Some opted for both. I favoured the latter but, by family tradition, would always need to have a job. Being a dustman, I thought, offered possibilities. One of the best parts of my town hall job was, each Thursday or Friday, handing out the wage packets of the workers in the various refuse depots. From Sussex Way in the north of the borough to Wharf Road in the south, theirs seemed to be the life. Cheery characters, they spent their days on the open road. Paul McCartney had said once that – apart from black being the only colour he wore his socks in – if he had not been a Beatle, he would have wanted to be a tramp. Dustmen enjoyed that sense of freedom, plus a living wage supplemented by the scrap metal they scavenged on the side and sold to Joey Pattman's dad.

To work as a dustman in Islington would have been too much indignity to heap on the family, so I put on some old clothes and went to the City depot in Upper Thames Street by Southwark Bridge: 'Chance of a start, mate?' I mumbled. I had heard from my dad that that was how you did it on building sites. The bloke by the time-clock must have recognised that I had only worked in an office; either that, or as I knew, dustmen were like the hangman and tended to keep the job in the family. I thought of Soho. Dustmen did the night shift there, chatting to prostitutes, partners all in the Lautrec-ian *demi-monde*. I practised one night tilting a bin with my left hand and swinging it up on to my right shoulder. As my father said (about the right way to push a wheelbarrow), it was all in the knees. I noticed one of the women watching me from a doorway and stopped. I was testing out a potential vocation but she saw someone in a PVC mac picking up filthy bins for no reason but to put them down.

With the East End not delivering on the physical front, I was going to have to look to the West End to lose my virginity. I did not have the nerve to ask the woman in the doorway: what of VD? Didn't they lie back leaving you to get on with it? What was it that you got on with? I struck lucky in the Macabre, the coffee bar in Meard Street, which had next to no lighting and Ortonesque tables shaped like coffins. Its jukebox played Saint-Saëns' 'Danse Macabre' and an orchestral version of *Slaughter on Tenth Avenue*. Pretending to read my life of Cézanne in the dark, I fell into conversation with two girls in their final year at Saint Martin's art school. One of them said her name was Linda but she liked to be called Elle. She came from the county part of Sussex and spoke like Eleanor Bron, or a presenter of cultural programmes on the BBC.

'Oh, you come from there?' she said, when I mentioned Islington. When we said goodnight, I was too shy to ask for her address but, since we had swapped names, I manfully told her to 'look me up' should she ever be around Noel Road. She as good as took me at my word; she called directory enquiries and, possibly, one of my operator colleagues from the Tote. She gave him a name and a street and he gave her the family number.

We met up at the Macabre again and moved on to her flat. She lived in Turnham Green, on a crescent near the tube line. Matters took a reasonably straightforward course, quickly reaching the stage, once again, of heavy petting. Only there was no protest this time, at which point events went out of control.

So they would during the next couple of years over the increasingly heated subject of Vietnam. Thanks to Wilson we had not gone in, but the Americans would not get out and, at the height of the demonstrations, activists stormed the steps of the US embassy in Grosvenor Square. Tariq Ali, a student leader, was at their head as they broke through a police cordon around the embassy and made for its front doors. As he clambered up the steps, Ali's principal thought, he later said, was, what on earth would he do if he was let in? Salvation was at hand, in his case, in the shape of US Marines barring his way.

In Turnham Green, and in a wild skirmish that might have only lasted a few seconds, at each succeeding stage it became clear to me that I had no idea what was meant to happen should I reach my eventual goal. Largely as a result, sensations from below told me that nothing would happen, and it didn't. But that didn't matter, Elle insisted sweetly, lighting a Gauloise while we lay reviewing the situation. We would get back to it at another time.

Both my girlfriends slipped me books seeking to improve my mind. Elle passed me her collection of Jean-Paul Sartre. I learned what 'existentialist' meant but found him difficult. *Nausea* and the self-educated man who kept rewriting his first paragraph were not encouraging. Doreen got it right with Albert Camus, the former Algerian goalkeeper, and his *L'Etranger*, as she called it – *The Outsider* – which I felt I could make more sense of. She was not bothered to read it but had heard about it from some former Mod friends.

Elle expressed herself fascinated by my football background and roots in the 'working class'. This was not a term my parents or grandparents would have agreed with, let alone used. She had me visit her studio in Saint Martin's and her fine arts friends gathered round, quietly content to have me on parade as her bit of rough. Over the next couple of months, she invited me to her succession of flats; from Turnham Green she moved to Earl's Court, from there to the Pavement at Clapham Common. All her flats were student-slummy. She had a long-term boyfriend who was at Chelsea doing sculpture and who we always managed to avoid running into.

Bunking off from the town hall, I often went round to see Peter as he weighed up whether he was going to make it to the King's Road by the afternoon. He would rise to work on a sketch or lithograph or, as on one day, meticulously pin William Morris cloth wallpaper to the chimney breast of his bedsit. He lived in a basement off the Essex Road and was that area's sole exponent of its pre-gentrified Bohemian phase. He had a grant from the government, his second-hand Triumph Herald, and his mum sent him marks to help with the rent.

The talk in Britain about 'devaluation' of the pound that had gone on for a while after the July collapse had died down. George Cohen, England's full-back, said that in a chat with the team Harold Wilson had confided that the World Cup's boost to public morale had staved off a cut in value of the currency. Now a kind of contrary concept was being aired, which I struggled to understand: 'revaluation'. This was for the Germans to do, not us. If they would only make the required adjustments to the deutschmark, such that their exports became more expensive to buy than ours, it would do wonders to right the British trade imbalance. The West Germans obliged and, in this, Britain pioneered the movement which would progressively see Germany asked by other economies in Europe to bail them out.

Peter's suggestion one day was that we drive down to Brighton to visit Bobby Blake. Bobby had made it to Sussex University to study English and developed an ambition to join Jamaica's diplomatic service. He later served in its embassy in Addis Ababa and became a Rastafarian. On the early spring day we visited him, his was the only black face we saw on campus. From some good way across it, he sprinted to us. He had told everyone about us, he said, and his new friends had been impressed by his background. The Jay twins had gone but, as he indicated and we could see, the girls were stunning. There was a party that night, so why didn't we stay? Peter said he would, but I couldn't, it being my obligation to serve the ratepayers of Islington. He dropped me off at Patcham on the outskirts of town. Just stick your thumb out, he said. I had not hitched before but within two minutes a Rover 2000 was taking me all the way to Tooting Bec station on the Northern

Line. Ticketless and by use of the emergency stairs at the Angel, I reached home for nothing. Friends said you could hitchhike your way around the Continent. One kid had hitched to Sitges with people putting him up on the way. I did not need to travel with my parents any more.

Doreen suddenly loosened up and shockingly (to me) started smoking marijuana. She and Sandra had been listening to Jimi Hendrix. Sandra still had her boyfriend but had been seeing another one on the side. He was a bit older and – from just the other side of Wanstead Flats – wealthier, with access to illicit substances. Hendrix, said Doreen, went especially well with them and she would bring some 'hash' round to Islington on a Saturday night when my parents were away. I imagined that it had already taken hold on the canal side of the street, leaving ours a little behind. We smoked it in the garden, the people at the back on Gerrard Road – yet more backward – watching us from their kitchen window. They probably thought we were too poor to afford a cigarette each. I could not see what the fuss was about and, for the next hour or so, said so.

When I was outside the Marquee a couple of weeks later seeking pass-outs, a taxi braked abruptly at the kerb a few yards along from the door. The driver seemed uncertain where his passenger wanted to be. The Cream – Ginger Baker, Jack Bruce, Eric Clapton – were on. Clapton we had seen before with John Mayall's Bluesbreakers. Lurching out of the cab, Hendrix came towards us. In a navy-blue cape, he carried a silver-topped cane, and was beaming in a distracted way. Three of us were there and we chatted with him for the next five minutes, in so far as Hendrix was fit to. Yes, he was really looking forward to seeing Eric. Clapton, that was. Eric Burdon of the Animals might also be here. We had not seen him tonight, we told him, but you could often find him just along the street at the Ship.

The taxi driver had stayed looking at us and beckoned me over: 'Who was *that*?' 'Jimi Hendrix,' I told him. '"Hey Joe" and "The Wind Cries Mary"?' 'I don't know about that,' he said, shifting his vehicle into gear. 'I only picked him up because he looked like he fell out of a fucking tree.'

With money in my pocket, I saw my first international at Wembley. Spain came for the return match to the one played in freezing Madrid. London was contrastingly warm. Banks was stood down for the occasion and Peter Bonetti of Chelsea given an international run-out. Greaves was back. Ramsey said how 'intriguing' it would be to stay on and defend England's World Cup title in 1970 in Mexico. We need fear no one – Brazil, West Germany – there was no telling what we could move on to now.

As the game kicked off, it took me a few seconds to realise that an England crowd around me were chanting, 'We are the champions.' Greaves scored one and Hunt, inevitably, the other, as England beat the Spaniards 2–0 again.

Shortly before Doreen went to Spain she told me that she had looked into it and would start taking the pill. We made love, therefore, in the more modern sense, and near disastrously so. We doubled up on preventive measures by my wearing a Durex. Unfortunately neither of us knew how to fit one and it fell off. By the time she had recovered it, it looked conspicuously empty. We worried for the first week or more that she was away, but midway through the second she wrote to say that all was well. When she returned from holiday, Doreen was far more relaxed. Love-making on the pill was fine. Working-class girls did this now. Spain had been great and she had taken to learning the language. She spent time practising and writing letters to people she had met. One Saturday when I dropped round to her desk at the Tote to see what she wanted to do that night, she shielded the letter she was writing from my view. She did not discuss it with me. I did not ask.

Like football, this was something we were not going to talk about.

# Acknowledgments

My many thanks to Sally (Holloway) for the idea and encouragement and to Felicity and all at Felicity Bryan for their support and for being such a lovely group of people.

Thank you to Charlotte (Atyeo) at Bloomsbury for taking this on and for her calm and friendly guidance and to Ian Preece for his superb editing.

My special thanks to my colleagues at the *Financial Times* for their comradeship – not a traditional FT word – and for being such a great bunch to work with. That goes particularly for all on the committee of the National Union of Journalists FT chapel.

# Index

Aberfan disaster, the   240, 245–6
abortion   181–3
Abse, Leo   135, 139, 202
AC Milan   116–17
Albert, Flórián   161
Ali, Tariq   254
amateur football clubs   53–4
Andrews, Eamonn   162
Argentina   169, 176–81, 183–7, 227
Armfield, Jimmy   115
Arsenal FC   10, 11, 25, 137
Ashington   117
Astle, Jeff   13
Attlee, Clement   26
Australia   60

Bahramov, Tofiq   200, 215–16, 218
Bailey, David   106, 162
Bailey, Roy   42
Baily, Eddie   57, 58–9, 62–3, 72
Banks, Gordon   21–2, 48, 168, 190,
   211–12, 241, 258
Barker, Tony   147, 203, 231
Barnsbury Secondary Modern   16, 83
Baxter, Jim   78, 80
BBC   24–5, 135–6, 182, 204–5
Beatles, the   40, 86, 95, 234
Beckenbauer, Franz   197
Bedford Town FC   95–7, 111–12, 152
Belgium   ix, 229
Bellman, Lionel   234–5

Bellotti, Derek   112, 152–3
Benfica   189, 190
Best, George   190, 241
Biddlecombe, Terry   18
Biggs, Ronnie   248
Birmingham   xviii, 42–3
Blackpool FC   208
Blake, Bobby   68, 108, 132, 157–8,
   248, 256
Blond, Anthony   201
Bloxham, Terry   102
Blumson, Dave   41
Bonetti, Peter   19, 258
Bonham Carter, Mark   185
Boothby, Lord   63
Botley, Johnny   114
Bowie, David   103
Boy Scouts   32–3
Boyson, Rhodes   237–8
Brady, Ian   103–4, 118
Brazil   37–9, 77, 157, 161, 166, 188
Breasley, Scobie   129
Brighton   128–9, 157
Brightwell, Robbie   108
Bristol Rovers FC   14
British Empire   67–8, 228–9
British Guiana   xiv
Brocket, Lord   21
Brocket Hall   21
Brown, George   219, 247
Bulgaria   161

Burgess, Ron 97, 152–3
Burton, Richard 163
Busby, Matt 98

Calais ix, xii
Callaghan, James 187, 247
Campbell, Donald 251–2
Campbell, Joe 95–7, 111
capital punishment 103–4, 239–40
car industry 154–5
Carey, Johnny 72
Carnaby Street 95, 102
Castle, Barbara 66–7, 155, 178, 250
censorship 164
Chaplin, Charlie 101
Chapman (Mother) xii, xv–xvi, 6–10,
    20, 144, 182–3
Chapman, Bim xviii, 4, 6, 23,
    61, 91
Chapman, Cecil 4, 5–6
Chapman, Grandma 5, 8–9, 172, 210
Chapman, Hilda 4
Chapman, Jim
    bricklaying 6–7, 145–6
    family background 4–6
    holidays xii–xiii, xiv–xvi, 137,
        138, 178–9
    Hungary match, 1953 23
    infantile paralysis 27
    and *The Mirror* 26–7
    New Year's Day 1966 8–10
    reaction to victory 225
    school football 11–12
    war service xii, 8, 27–8, 46, 61–2,
        112, 113–14, 195–6
Chapman, Joan 4–5
Chapman, Joyce 4
Chapman, Peter
    18th birthday ix–xix
    autograph collecting 42, 47, 48–52,
        79, 98–9, 115, 120, 208–9
    birth 21
    bricklaying 6–7
    council job 131–2, 231–2, 234–5,
        236, 250, 252
    dustman practice 252–3

education 12–13, 14–16, 43–4,
    87–9, 129–30, 194–5
exams 133–4
family background xi–xii, 3–11,
    18, 33–4
family politics 26
first day at work 143, 146–50
football career xvi–xvii, 13–14,
    19–20, 53–60, 62–3, 72, 96–7,
    111–12, 152–3
gambling 104–7, 129, 130–1, 191–2
Highbury old boy's dinner 237–8
loss of virginity 258–9
New Year's Day 1966 14–19
relations with the opposite
    sex xvii, 138, 148, 230–1, 232,
    234, 235–7, 242–5, 250–1, 253–5,
    257, 258–9
World Cup final victory
    celebrations 216–17, 221–2
Chapman, Reg 4, 5–6, 26–7
Chapman, Sam 6
Chapman, Zachariah 9, 27
Charlie (family friend) 87
Charlottown (racehorse) 105, 129
Charlton, Bobby 44, 46, 98, 117, 138
    Munich air crash 116
    vs. Mexico 159, 162
    vs. Portugal 190
    vs. Uruguay 154
    vs. Wales 246
    vs. Yugoslavia 115
    World Cup final 210
Charlton, Jack 47, 116, 167, 190,
    214, 246
Charlton, Norma 209–10
Chelsea FC 55–6
Chile 39–40
China 198–9
Christie, John 239
Christmas, Anita 232, 235, 250
Churchill, Winston 6–7, 8, 26, 58, 220
City of London 109
Clark, Teddy 34
Clay, Cassius 132–3
Clough, Brian 51, 209, 246

Cohen, George   22, 47, 256
Cole, Mike   147–8
Coleman, David   24
Coleman, Tommy   19, 56, 58
Colonial Office, closure of   228, 229–30
Commonwealth, the   91–2
comprehensive schools   16, 202
Connelly, John   154, 158
Connie (family friend)   87
Connor, William   28
Cooper, Henry   132–3
Corbett, David   81, 209
Cornell, George   72–3, 132
*Coronation Street*   xviii
corporal punishment   87–8
Cottle, Miss (teacher)   12–13
Cousins, Frank   68, 158
Crawford, Ray   42
Crowley, John   65–6, 130
Cuban missile crisis   95
Cyprus civil war   124

*Daily Mirror*   43
Dash, Jack   137–8, 166
Davies, Len   17
Davies, Reg   13
Davis, Spencer   103
de Gaulle, Charles   xiv, 247
decolonisation   xiv, 44–5, 67–8, 133,
   228–9
Delfont, Bernard   20
'devaluation' of the pound   256
Dick, Johnny   42, 51
Dick, Peter   130
Dienst, Gottfried   199–200, 217
Dimbleby, Richard, memorial
   service   36
Dimmock, Peter   24
divorce   108–9, 163–4, 202
*Dixon of Dock Green*   122–3
Docherty, Tommy   80
Doreen (girlfriend)   230–1, 242–5,
   250, 257, 258–9
Dougan, Derek   241
Douglas Home, Sir Alec   86
Drew, Freddie   131

Duggan, Dave   205–6
Duke, Reggie   49–51
Dunkirk   ix–xix
Dunkley, Jimmy   47, 51, 93, 109
Dunnett, Jack   157
Dwight, Roy   171
Dylan, Bob   156–7

economic crisis   93–4, 155, 169–74, 187
Eden, Sir Anthony   23–4
Edmonds, Peter   102, 108–9, 132, 255–6
Edwards, Duncan   116
Elle (girlfriend)   253–5
Empire Games, 1958   192
England
   players' wives   209–10
   qualifying stage   xvii
   summer tour   136, 138, 139
   team   46–8
   vs. Argentina   169, 176, 178–81,
      183–7
   vs. France   166, 167, 167–8, 180
   vs. Hungary   22–3
   vs. Mexico   158–9, 161, 162
   vs. Northern Ireland   240–1
   vs. Poland   26, 35–6, 44–6, 139
   vs. Portugal   187, 188–90
   vs. Scotland   78–9, 80–1, 99
   vs. Spain   22, 26, 258
   vs. Uruguay   xiii, 152–4, 161–2
   vs. Wales   246
   vs. West Germany,
      February 1966   68–9
   win bonus   200
   World Cup, 1958   38–9
   World Cup, 1962   39–40
   World Cup build-up   25–6
   World Cup expectations   xvii–xviii,
      179, 192–3
   World Cup final   200
   World Cup final entry   211–12
   World Cup final extra time   214–16
   World Cup final extra-time
      third goal   214–16, 217–18
   World Cup final fourth goal   218–19
   World Cup final second half   213–14

World Cup final, team    203–4, 210
  vs. Yugoslavia    112–13, 115
English Speaking Union, the    248
Eton Manor sports club    59–60
European Common Market    xiv, 91–2,
  247–8
European Cup    189
Eusébio    166, 188–9, 189–90, 190
Evans, Bobby    12
Evans, Dennis    131
Evans, Timothy    239–40
Eve, Johnny    63
Everton FC    96, 119, 122–3, 125

family planning clinics    135
Farlowe, Chris    205–6
Farr, Garry    102–3
Finney, Tom    38
First World War    34
Flanagan, Bud    40
Foster, Alan    92, 237
Foyles bookshop    193
France    25, 64–5, 166, 167, 167–8, 180
Francis, Peter    54, 90, 205
Freeman, Alan    205
Freeman, John    226
Fuschillo, Paul    102, 216, 222

Galba, Dr Karol    200
gambling    104–6, 119–22, 129, 130–1,
  146–50, 191–2
Gardner, Alex    216, 221–2
Garrincha    39, 157
Gauld, Jimmy    119–21
General Election    69, 85–6, 89, 90–5, 97
Geoff, Uncle    9–11, 95–7, 112, 198
Germany    194–6
Ghana    xiv
Gifford, Josh    18
Glasgow Rangers FC    49
goalkeepers    61–2, 168, 211–12
Gott, Richard    65, 66
Grade, Lew    20
Graham, Billy    134–5
Graham, George    19
Grand National    95

Grandstand    24
Greaves, Jimmy    46, 78–9, 84, 97,
  117–18, 138, 152, 190, 258
  at AC Milan    116–17
  vs. France    169
  vs. Mexico    162
  vs. Uruguay    154
  World Cup final    203–4, 210, 219–20
  vs. Yugoslavia    115
Green, Felicity    251
Greene, Graham    28–9
Gregg, Harry    98, 99
Gregory, Paul    110
Grimsby FC    66
Grossman, Martin    90–1
The Guardian    65–6
Guttmann, Béla    189
Guyana    133

Haffey, Frank    79
Haller, Helmut    212
Halliwell, Ken    233
Hamilton, Willie    247
Hanover primary school    6–7, 12–13
Harbinson, Robin    157–8
Hargitay, Mickey    30
Harniman, Gerry    245
Harris, Mr (teacher)    15
Harvey, Laurence    162
Hateley, Tony    13
Heath, Eddie    14, 56
Heath, Edward    85–6, 164
Held, Siggi    197
Hendrix, Jimi    257–8
Highbury grammar school    11, 13, 16,
  43–4, 87–8, 237–8
Hindley, Myra    103–4, 118
Ho Chi Minh    64, 160
Home International
  Championship    240–1
homosexuality    71–2, 135, 139, 235
Hodgkinson, Alan    112
Hopkinson, Eddie    112
Horne, Kenneth    70
house prices, Islington    35
Howell, Denis    226

Hoxton   92, 132, 221
Hull City FC   66
Hull North by-election   65–6
Hungary   22–3, 38, 40, 161, 208
Hunt, Roger   47, 99, 139, 161, 167,
   188, 190, 215, 241, 258
Hurst, Geoff   52, 68–9, 97
   vs. Argentina   183, 185, 186–7
   vs. Wales   246
   World Cup final   204, 213, 218
   World Cup final extra-time goal
   214–16, 217–18

illegitimate births   104
Ipswich Town FC   24–5, 41–2
Ireland, Republic of   23
Isaacs, Ernie   132
Islington   4, 29–36, 100–1
Italy   60, 136–8, 166–7
ITV   35

Jagger, Mick   106, 246–7
Japan   31
Jenkins, Roy   182, 239
Jennings, Pat   97, 211, 241
Joan, Aunt   xviii, 246
Jockey Club, the   202–3
Johanneson, Albert   189
John Mayall's Bluesbreakers   102
Jones, Cliff   11, 22
Jones, Ken   28, 81, 138, 180
Jones, Paul   156
Jones, Tom   118

Kagan, Joseph   84–5
Kay, Tony   119–22
Keith, Uncle   3, 7–8, 70, 85, 100,
   128, 227
Kelsey, Jack   38
Kenya   67
Khama, Seretse   228–9
Khrushchev, Nikita   39
King, Cecil   172–3
King, Reginald   16–17, 87–8, 238
Kitchener, Barry   55
Knight, Jill   182

Kosygin, Alexei   161
Kray, Ron and Reg   50, 63, 73,
   242–3, 249
Kreitlein, Rudolf   183, 184–5, 186

Lane, Tim   68
Laura, Aunt   8, 9–10, 27, 91, 95–7, 198
Law, Denis   78, 79–80
Layne, David   119–22
Leadbetter, Jimmy   42
Lee, Fred   230
Lee Kuan Yew   44–5
Lehane, Johnny   95
Leicester City FC   48
Levin, Bernard   160
Leyton Orient FC   xvi–xvii, 11–12,
   13–14, 18–20, 22, 54–60, 62–3, 72,
   109, 246
Liberal Party   90–1
lightermen   81–2
Little Highbury (gang)   83, 86–7
Liverpool   xi, xix
Loach, Ken   182
London, Swinging   106
Longford, Lord   229–30
Lord's Day Observance Society   70
Lorenzo, Juan Carlos   178
Loxley, Bert   13
Luton Town FC   11

McGillvray, Archie   102
McGowan, Cathy   133
Mackay, Dave   11, 78
McLintock, Frank   203
Maier, Sepp   168
Manchester United   79, 98–9, 116
Mansfield, Jayne   30
Marquee Club   102–3, 134, 216, 257–8
match fixing   119–22
*Match of the Day*   24–5
Matthews, Stanley   28, 38, 117, 207–9
Maxwell, Robert   85
Mazurkiewicz, Ladislao   154
Mears, Joe   77, 82
Medical Termination of
   Pregnancy Bill   181–3

Medwin, Michael   30
Mehew, Granddad   3, 4, 18, 33–5, 127–8, 251
Mehew, Grandma   3, 4, 7–8, 33–5
Mellor, Stan   18
Mercer, Joe   176, 184
Metcalfe, Adrian   108
Mexico   158–9, 161, 162
Michael, Barry   211, 216
Michael, Ernie   25, 104, 144–5, 210–11, 216
Michael, June   211
Michael, Maureen   211
Middlesbrough   60, 166–7
Mills, Freddie   27
Mills, William   129
Millwall FC   13, 54–5
*The Mirror*   26–8, 32, 64, 74, 86, 91–5, 103, 104, 132–3, 146, 151, 170, 188, 210, 249
Mitchell, Frank   248–9
Mitchell, Warren   135
Mods   100–2, 106–7, 133
Moore, Bobby   19, 46–7, 115, 117
   vs. Poland   36, 44, 46
   World Cup final   211, 218, 219
Moors murder trial   103–4, 118
Mosley, Oswald   11–12, 21, 92, 251
*Mrs Dale's Diary*   202
Muhammad Ali-Cassius Clay   132–3
Murder (Abolition of Death Penalty) Act   103–4

Nabarro, Sir Gerald   165, 172
Nagle, Florence   202–3
Naples   178–9
National Health Service   21
National Service   9, 147
Newby, Tom   92–3, 132
*News of the World*   67–8, 128, 162, 164, 165, 166, 227
Nicholson, Viv   172
Nigeria   68
Norman, Maurice   39
North Korea   60, 166–7, 188

Northern Ireland   199, 238, 240–1
Notts County FC   13

O'Sullevan, Peter   24
Orton, Joe   71–2, 233–4, 235, 244–5
Osborne, Sir Cyril   139
Osgood, Peter   55, 80

Paine, Terry   158
Parnell, Jack   163
Parsons, Denis   71, 110, 237
Pattman, Joey   76
Pelé   38, 157, 161, 166, 188
Perfumo, Roberto   178
permissive society   103, 104–7
Perón, Eva   178
Perón, Juan Domingo   178
Peru   25
Peters, Martin   81, 183, 185, 186–7, 189, 213, 241
petrol prices   170
Philip, Prince, Duke of Edinburgh   227
Pickles the dog   81–3, 209
Pierce, Joan   250
Pierrepoint, Albert   239
pill, the   258–9
Poland   26, 35–6, 44–6, 60, 139
police and policing   122–5, 238
Portsmouth   88
Portugal   166, 187, 188–90
prostitution   201, 253
Puskás, Ferenc   208

Queens Park Rangers FC   12, 55

Race Relations Board   185
Radio 1   204–5
Radio Caroline   204
Radio London   204, 205
Ramsey, Alf   xvii, 22–3, 25, 40–2, 192–3, 258
   Argentina match   179–80, 181, 183, 186–7
   France match   166
   as Ipswich manager   24–5, 41–2

Mexico match   158–9
Poland match   44
Portugal match   190
tactics   22, 24, 168–9
team selection   48, 80–1, 203–4, 210
Uruguay match   153–4
on West Germany   60–1
West Germany match,
   February 1966   68–9
World Cup build-up   25–6
World Cup final   214
World Cup final victory
   celebrations   219
Rattín, Antonio   176, 178, 184, 186, 196
Regent's Canal   32–3
Rhodesia   67–8, 172
Richard, Cliff   135
Richardson, Charlie   227
Rimet, Jules   78
Roache, William   30
Roberts, Harry (family member)   34
Roberts, Harry (police murderer)   238–9
Rockers   100–1, 133
Roma, Antonio   178
Round the Horne   70–1
Rous, Sir Stanley   37, 40, 77, 136,
   161, 189

St James's Park (Newcastle)   60
St John-Stevas, Norman   181–2
Sandra (girlfriend)   230–1, 232, 234,
   235–7, 242, 257
Sandy   4, 5, 7–8, 9, 61
Savile, Jimmy   118–19, 205
Schön, Helmut   196, 197
Scotland   78–9, 80–1, 99
Searchers, the   95
Second World War   x, xi, xiii, 4,
   5–8, 10, 26–7, 27–8, 34, 46, 61, 112,
   113–14, 194, 195–6, 216
Seeler, Uwe   197
Sexton, Dave   19–20, 22, 54, 168–9
Sharman, John   102, 125
Sheffield   xviii–xix
Sheffield Wednesday FC   119, 120,
   122, 122–3

Shilton, Peter   60
Shrimpton, Jean   156, 162
Silksworth (village near
   Sunderland)   xviii, 246
Singapore   44–5
Sistiana (Italy)   137, 137–8
Smith, Ian   67–8, 172
Smithson, Tom   50–1
smog   145, 177
smoking   84, 118
Southend   231
Spain   22, 25, 64, 258, 258–9
Spinner, Harry   54–5, 56, 57, 58, 72
Sportsview   24
Springett, Ron   39
stamp collecting   75–7
Steel, David   182
Stiles, Nobby   44, 68–9, 97–9, 180–1,
   189–90, 190
strikes (seamen)   ix–xix, 126–8, 137
Suez Crisis   23–4
Sunday People   121, 122
Sunderland   xviii, 4, 51, 60
Swan, Peter   39, 119–21
Sweden   37–9
Switzerland   x–xi, 197

Tafawa Balewa, Sir Abubakar   68
Tambling, Bobby   19
Taylor, E. G.   17
Taylor, Elizabeth   163
television coverage of the
   World Cup   xviii, 37, 135–6, 200–1
Thatcher, Margaret   238, 246
Thorpe, Jeremy   91
Tilkowski, Hans   213, 214–16, 217–18
Till Death Us Do Part   135, 164
The Times   44–6
Tito, Marshal   113, 115
Tonbridge, Henry   109
Tottenham Hotspur FC   55, 56–7
trade unions   126–8
Trautmann, Bert   195
Trieste   112, 115
Turpin, Randolph   133
Twiggy   106, 156

unemployment 143–4, 187
universities 129–30
urban redevelopment 29–36
Uruguay xiii, 77, 152–4, 161–2
USSR 38–9

VE Day 220–1
Vietnam War 64, 65, 66, 160–1, 172, 199, 248, 254
Viollet, Paul 50–1

wages 146, 170, 187–8, 227–8
Wakeman, Mr (headmaster) 12–13
Walden, Brian 94
Wales 38, 246
Waugh, Auberon 229
Webb, David 22
Weber, Wolfgang 213–14
Wedgwood Benn, Anthony 31–2, 84, 158, 226–7
Welton, Pat 13, 136
Wesley, John 75
   West Germany x–xi, 60–2, 197–8, 212–13, 256
   football statistics 193–4
   vs. England, February 1966 68–9
   World Cup final 200
   World Cup final extra time 214–16
   World Cup final extra-time goal 217
   World Cup final first half 212–13
   World Cup final second half 213–14
   World Cup performance 196–7
West Ham FC 14, 19
White, Fred 110
White, John 11, 79–80
Who, the 102
Wigg, Ronnie 55–6, 214
Williams, Kenneth 70–2
Willis, Lord 69–70, 72
Wilson, Harold xi, xiii, xiv, xvii, 26, 44–5, 66–8, 69, 83–4, 85–6, 89, 93–5, 97, 106, 127, 137, 157, 158, 160–1, 164–5, 167, 169–74, 187–8, 197–8, 199, 219–20, 227, 240, 247–8, 254

Wilson, Peter 28, 167–8, 180, 186
Wilson, Ray 47, 139, 212
Winwood, Stevie 103
Wolstenholme, Kenneth 99, 185, 190, 215
women, football fans 175
Wood, Raymond 43–4, 237
World Cup, 1958 37–9
World Cup, 1962 39, 119–21
World Cup, 1966
   first day 151–4
   opening game xiii
   qualifying groups x, xvii
   semi-final 187, 188–90
   television coverage xviii
   ticket sales 60
   venues 12
   women's issues 135–6
World Cup, 1966, final
   England team 203–4, 210
   England's fourth goal 218–19
   extra time, third goal 214–16, 217–19
   first half 212–13
   linesmen 200, 215–16, 217
   reactions to 225–7
   referee 199–200
   second half 213–14
   teams come out 211–12
   television coverage 200–1
   victory celebrations 216–17, 219–22
World Cup, 1970 258
World Cup, 1974 60
World Cup (Jules Rimet) trophy 74–6, 77–8, 81–3
Worsthorne, Peregrine 31–2
Wright, Billy 137, 175–6, 184

Yashin, Lev 38–9
youth World Cup 136
Yugoslavia 25, 112–14, 115

Zec, Donald 210